Understanding
Care Homes

A Research and Development Perspective

Edited by
Katherine Froggatt,
Sue Davies
and Julienne Meyer

Jessica Kingsley Publishers
London and Philadelphia

First published in 2009
by Jessica Kingsley Publishers
116 Pentonville Road
London N1 9JB, UK
and
400 Market Street, Suite 400
Philadelphia, PA 19106, USA

www.jkp.com

Library of Congress Cataloging in Publication Data
Understanding care homes : a research and development perspective / edited by Katherine Froggatt, Sue Davies and Julienne Meyer
    p. ; cm.
Includes bibliographical references.
    ISBN 978-1-84310-553-4 (pb : alk. paper) 1. Old age homes--Great Britain--Administration. 2. Older people--Institutional care--Great Britain. I. Froggatt, Katherine. II. Davies, Sue, 1958- III. Meyer, Julienne.
    [DNLM: 1. Homes for the Aged--organization & administration--Great Britain. 2. Aged--psychology--Great Britain. 3. Health Services for the Aged--organization & administration--Great Britain. 4. Housing for the Elderly--organization & administration--Great Britain. 5. Long-Term Care--organization & administration--Great Britain. 6. Models, Organizational--Great Britain.]
    HV1454.2.G7U63 2009
    362.61--dc22
                                                                        2008029083

British Library Cataloguing in Publication Data
A CIP catalogue record for this book is available from the British Library

ISBN 978 1 84310 553 4

Printed and bound in Great Britain by
MGP Books Group, Cornwall

Contents

Part 2 The Organisation

Part 3 Beyond Care: The Wider Perspective

List of tables and figures

Tables

Figures

Acknowledgements

We would like to thank all the older people, their families and the staff of the care homes who took part in the research reported in this book, without whom we would not be able to make this contribution to better understanding care homes.

We would also like to thank the members of the National Care Homes Research and Development Forum for all the stimulating and insightful discussions that have informed the reflections reported here.

CHAPTER 1

Research and Development in Care Homes: Setting the Scene

Katherine Froggatt, Sue Davies and Julienne Meyer

Introduction

As people age they may face situations when they require further support and care as a consequence of ongoing disabilities, adverse health events, or increasing frailty. In the United Kingdom (UK), government health and social policy promotes the provision of support to enable people to live in their own homes. However, there will always be some individuals who require extra support and care that cannot be provided anywhere but in an institutional context, such as a care home. Given that this is the case for some older people, this book seeks to address the following question: how do we ensure that care homes for older people are experienced as positive and beneficial for those who live, work and visit in them? Whilst this question is raised and addressed in this book in the context of the UK, many countries worldwide are addressing similar issues of how to provide appropriate support and care for ageing populations.

This chapter has three main objectives: to describe the current context of the provision of long-term institutional care within the UK; to present the methodological context for research and development activities in and about care homes; and to outline the key values that underpin the book's conception and structure.

Current UK care home context

The context within which older people reside in care homes is complex: care home organisations engage with diverse populations, operate with different models of care and support and are located in a mixed care economy. Underlying this complexity is both confusion and ambivalence about the position of care homes within the UK health and social care sector (Reed and Stanley 1999). This reflects the historical origins of the institutions that we now call care homes (Davies and Seymour 2002; Townsend 1962), and a succession of policy directives that have left institutional forms of long-term care for older people marginalised and even mistrusted. Further details of these perspectives can be found in Dudman (2007).

In the UK (and throughout this book) the term 'care homes' is used to describe 'institutional' settings that provide long-term care for people with ongoing health or social care needs (DoH 2003). This encompasses two formerly distinct types of home: those that provide on-site nursing and personal care (formerly called nursing homes) and homes that provide personal care only and rely on primary care nursing services to meet nursing needs (formerly called residential care homes).

In the UK there are an estimated 15,700 care homes providing nursing care and/or personal care, to more than 400,000 older people with a range of different needs (OFT 2005). Care homes (personal care) greatly outnumber care homes (nursing). For example, the proportion of place, rather than homes, is 39% of places in care homes (nursing) and 61% of places in care homes providing personal care (OFT 2005). Since the 1990s, in the UK, there has been a steady decline in the numbers of all types of care home through closures arising from changes in the commissioning and funding of these services, along with new regulation and inspection processes and the introduction of national minimum standards (DoH; Netten, Darton and Williams 2002).

Diverse populations

In the UK, the proportion of the population that resides in care homes increases with age. Only 0.8 per cent of people aged 65–74 years live in care homes, whilst 4.1 per cent of 75–84-year-olds and 16.9 per cent of people aged 85 years and over do so (Laing and Buisson 2007). The population living in care homes is ageing, and in 2001 63 per cent of the population were women aged 75 and over (Banks *et al.* 2006). With respect to ethnicity, older adults from ethnic minorities are under-represented in the care home population compared to the general population, even taking into account the different demographic profiles of the two populations (Banks *et al.* 2006).

The population of older people who reside in care homes is an increasingly frail and dependent one. Many older people living in care homes live with multiple diseases and there are high levels of cognitive impairment and other communication issues. In a survey of 244 UK care homes, and 15,483 residents (Bowman, Whistler and Ellerby 2004), 41 per cent of residents had two or more diagnoses and dementia, stroke and other neurodegenerative conditions with mental impairment dominate. High levels of dependency with respect to mobility, mental state and continence were identified, with 27 per cent of the population being confused, incontinent and immobile.

Range of services

In order to meet these diverse and fluctuating needs, which vary within any one care home, but also over time for any individual resident, the care provided needs to be responsive and flexible. The services provided by, and in, care homes encompass health and/or personal care, and are shaped by structural elements such as size of the home and the nature of, and access to, internal and external health and social care staff.

The size and design of individual care homes varies, influencing the amenities, services and activities available within any one facility. Small homes of four beds or fewer do exist, but the average size is 30 beds, with the largest comprising over 100 beds (OFT 2005). Personal care homes are usually smaller in size than care homes providing nursing care (OFT 2005). Care homes may be purpose built, but a significant proportion of all care homes are in converted premises (Darton, Netten and Forder 2003).

In order to provide high-quality care and support to individuals residing in care homes, such organisations need to be able to draw upon a wide range of resources. The most important resource available to a care home is its staff. Historically, there have been ongoing difficulties in recruitment and retention of staff (Redfern et al. 2002) and much care is provided by untrained carers. Whilst the National Minimum Standards stipulated that 50 per cent of the workforce must have a vocational qualification in care by 2005 (DoH 2003), this is not always the case. In the UK, a high proportion of the workforce are non-nationals, raising challenges with respect to communication skills and mutual cultural awareness (Burton-Jones and Mosley 2004). There are also known difficulties in care home staff accessing education in a range of areas (Dalley and Denniss 2001).

Care homes also have varied relationships with wider healthcare providers. The differentiation between care homes (nursing) and care homes (personal care) can create confusion. Whilst care homes (nursing) can provide general nursing care with their on-site nurses, access to specialist nursing services is not always straightforward. This may be because specialist nurses are not always clear about their remit in such settings, as illustrated in the work of specialist palliative care nurses (Froggatt, Poole and Hoult 2002). This may reflect workload pressures, or contractual issues reflecting the location of care homes predominantly within the independent sector.

All care homes rely on external services for medical advice and support. Currently, in the UK, all residents of care homes are entitled to receive free individual direct patient services from a general practitioner (GP). However, medical services to the care home beyond this, such as proactive screening or medications management, can be charged for. In such situations, GPs may receive a retainer payment from the care home, or may establish what are termed Personal Medical Services through a private contract. Concerns have been raised that older people residing in care homes receive an inequitable service (Glendinning *et al.* 2002). A more proactive system of medical care for older people residing in care home settings is seen in the Netherlands, where since 1990, the medical speciality of a nursing home physician has allowed the development of integrated medicine that considers the synergy between discrete diseases and illnesses (Ribbe 1993).

Mixed economy of care

Care homes sit within a mixed economy of care in two ways: in the funding sources utilised to support an individual's residency and care in a care home, and in the financial basis of the service provider organisations that own and manage care homes. Funding for an individual's care in a care home can come from a number of sources. For example, health monies can be accessed if a person is assessed to have a nursing need, and social care funding is available for personal care. Individuals and their family members may also be asked to contribute towards personal care using a means tested system (Dudman 2007).[1] Fees can also vary between care homes, and local statutory funding bodies set the maximum rate they will support, so an individual choosing to reside in a care home that charges above this rate will be expected to make up the difference. The process of assessment underpins the decisions made about placements and the funding provided, unless an individual funds his or her own care.

The mixed economy of care is also apparent in the range of service providers who operate and run care homes, being situated in the private, not-for-profit and public sector (Table 1.1), with the vast majority of providers being located in the private sector.

Table 1.1 Mixed economy of UK service providers

Type of provider	Number of places	Percentage
Private	344,900	73.7
Not for profit	66,300	14.2
Public (NHS and Local Authority)	56,600	12.1
Total	467,800	100

(Laing and Buisson 2007)

Even within the three categories identified in Table 1.1 there is still heterogeneity, as the private sector encompasses a great range of provider types, from the single owned and managed care home, through small limited companies that own and run a number of care homes in one locality, to large chains, which encompass hundreds of care homes across the UK, sometimes with an international focus too. Within the private sector, 48 per cent of provision is from the major providers and 52 per cent from small independent businesses (Laing and Buisson 2007). The relationship between different ownership types and the quality of care provision is not clearly understood. In the US it is suggested that for-profit providers, particularly where profits are sought above a certain threshold, are associated with more adverse events and deficiencies in care (O'Neill et al. 2003).

In summary, the care sector that provides for the most vulnerable and

---

1   This is not the case in Scotland, where personal care, as well as nursing care is funded by the state, with financial implications for the Scottish government (Audit Scotland 2008).

frail members of society operates amidst sometimes confused and blurred clinical, financial and provider boundaries. Its status is often questioned and the sector's societal marginalisation impacts upon the people who live and work there.

Research and development in the care home context

The circumstances described above raise particular challenges for care homes as organisations, for care home staff and for researchers with respect to the place and nature of research and development work in this sector. For care home organisations and staff, research and development work can be seen as yet another pressure in an already burdened sector. It can be difficult to see the relevance of research and development in a care sector struggling to resource quality care provision, let alone activities beyond this. Similarly, for researchers, the heterogeneity of the sector in terms of the population residing in care homes, the nature of the different organisations involved and their location in the wider health and social care economy all raise particular challenges in terms of how research is funded, the way in which it is conducted, and how research findings can be used to inform care delivery. In this section we outline the role of research and development activities in improving the quality of care provided in care homes through the generation of new knowledge relevant for care home managers, staff, residents and relatives.

Researchers in health and social care aim to generate new knowledge (often referred to as evidence) that can be used ultimately to inform the care received by clients, patients and service users. We define research and development activities as being a systematic approach to the generation of new knowledge (research), which is then used in the care home context to improve the way care is provided and enrich the lives of people who live, work and visit there (development activities). Research is a broad term that encompasses different approaches and ways to produce this new knowledge.

Research is often classified into two broad approaches: quantitative and qualitative. Quantitative studies often aim to test hypotheses or establish the impact of clinical interventions on an individual's condition. Qualitative studies, meanwhile, seek to understand people's experiences through a consideration of the way they make sense of and understand what happens to them. This can happen at a cultural, organisational or individual level. However, these ways to do research can be criticised for their lack of attention to how the knowledge produced is actually used in practice to improve care delivery and people's experiences. Similarities can be seen between research, practice development and quality assurance methods, as all seek to improve the care received by people in any particular care setting. However, how they do this differs (Froggatt and Turner 2008). In contrast, more participatory approaches to research, such as action research, do specifically address the generation and utilisation of new knowledge (often practical knowledge) within specific situations and settings (McCormack et al. 2007). As we describe next, these participatory values are a common thread within the work presented here.

The extent to which care homes, as organisations, have been passive or active participants in the research undertaken to date varies. It could be argued that care homes have been neglected within the research and development agenda because of their marginalisation at a number of other levels. Nonetheless, there are some bodies of work that are of both direct and indirect relevance to the care home sector.

Within the medical disciplines, the various medical conditions that older people live with in care homes have been extensively studied. However, such research is often undertaken in isolation, with specialists focusing on their own area of interest, with minimal, if any, attention to other conditions and their impact upon the older person. While some work focuses upon individuals and their experiences of care, another strand of work in the US utilises large data sets to describe the particular medical conditions that older people living in care homes experience (for example diabetes (Travis, Buchanan and Wang et al. 2005) and multiple sclerosis (Buchanan 2001)). These types of studies are limited to health economies where uniform routine data is collected on admission and at regular time periods, which is not the case in the UK. Research with a wider focus also concerns care homes as organisations and businesses. This body of research considers the place of care homes in the wider health and social care economy (see the work of the Personal Social Services Research Unit (PSSRU), for example, at www.pssru.ac.uk).

Another strand of activity concerns in-depth case studies of nursing homes, for example Gubrium (1975), Gubrium (1993), Henderson and Vesperi (1995), Kayser-Jones (1981), Savishinsky (1991) and Stafford (2003). The majority of the studies described in these books have been undertaken in the US in the last 30 years, with some exceptions (e.g. Kayser-Jones' comparative work between the US and Scotland). Many of the studies have utilised ethnographic research methods, involving participant observation in the care setting. This has resulted in the culture of long-term care being explicated. The picture often painted of these settings is of poor care and desperate circumstances faced by residents (see Kayser-Jones 1981). However, the different health and social care system in the US limits the direct applicability of this knowledge within other Western countries and their long-term care settings.

While this research activity is clearly important and influential in its respective spheres, the relationship between the research undertaken and the lived experience of the daily lives of residents, staff and visitors is not always explicitly addressed. Within the UK, large-scale epidemiological studies and in-depth ethnographies have largely been absent, to date. A number of centres for research are being developed within the UK, and a growing body of knowledge about older people's experiences of care homes now exists, for example Reed, Payton and Bond (1998). Other areas addressed include relatives' experiences (Davies and Nolan 2004), and models of care (Nolan *et al.* 2004). A new generation of researchers is coming to the fore in this area and we present some of their work here.

Values and perspectives

Researchers undertaking research concerning care homes in the UK have until recently, been working in relative isolation. The establishment in the UK of the National Care Homes Research and Development Forum (NCHRDF) in 2003 (Cook 2005) sought to address this. The forum was initiated in order to provide a network for academics and practitioners who undertake research and practice development work in care homes, primarily for older people. A key issue that brought people together in this network concerned questions of process – how do we undertake high-quality research of relevance to the care home sector? More particularly, how do we undertake research that does not distance the researchers from either the care homes or the people living in, working in and visiting them; to move from an approach that is about doing research 'on' people to researching 'with' and 'by' them (Reason and Bradbury 2001)? Members of the forum were also seeking to address the ethical and governance issues relating to undertaking research in a UK sector that sits largely outside the mainstream research governance structures (Reed, Cook and Cook 2004). As part of this exploration, we identified the need for a text to draw together some of the exciting and innovative work being undertaken in this field.

In 2005 members of NCHRDF were commissioned by the UK charity Help the Aged to prepare a review of the literature (NCHRDF 2007) and short report on quality of life in care homes (Owen and NCHRDF 2006). The *My Home Life* literature review identified a series of key themes and messages about best practice aimed at promoting quality of life for the older residents of care homes (see Table 1.2).

Table 1.2 *My Home Life* themes

Theme	Message
Managing transitions	Easing the transition into a care home by recognising the effects of the transition and ensuring that care homes are seen as a positive option
Maintaining identity	Working to help residents maintain their identity; the need for creative approaches to person-centred care
Creating community	Recognising the importance of relationships, creating positive environments and maintaining links to the local community
Sharing decision-making	Involving residents, families and staff in ongoing decision-making through negotiation
Improving health and healthcare	Ensuring adequate healthcare services including health promotion
Supporting a good end of life	Valuing living and dying, ensuring a 'good death', providing support for staff
Keeping the workforce fit for purpose	Identifying the need for education and training and promoting care homes as learning environments
Promoting a positive culture	Recognising the multidimensional nature of culture within care homes and the importance of leadership

These key themes encompass the various dimensions of a person's life in a care home, from entry to his or her eventual death.

In this book we build upon the work undertaken for the *My Home Life* review that now underpins a UK-wide vision for best practice, uniquely owned by the care home sector (see www.myhomelife.org.uk). The vision is evidence-based and relationship-centred and, by focusing on positive messages, challenges the negative image so often portrayed by the media when reporting on care homes. We aim to highlight the breadth and diversity of care provided in care homes; to further raise the profile of innovative and creative work being undertaken in this sector; to consider the challenges of undertaking research and development work in care homes; and to offer strategies for engaging with these issues. This edited book focuses upon exemplars of good research and development practice in care homes. The initiatives presented here have been selected for inclusion because they place particular emphasis on informing and supporting practice development through partnership working. In particular, we are concerned with partnership working where this involves residents, their families and staff within care homes, and health and social care professionals external to the care home.

A fundamental premise of the book is an emphasis on participatory engagement and collaborative working, both within care homes, and between care homes and external agencies. Within such participatory engagement we propose that the following values and principles are important:

- equity – the assumption that all people (older people living and dying in care homes, their visiting families, staff working in care homes) have equal worth and should be valued

- engagement – ensuring that all people involved have the opportunity to participate as they would like

- mutual learning – the recognition that in any situation all participants have the opportunity to learn from each other

- honesty – the importance of being explicit about processes and recognising the learning that can happen in any situation, even when things do not work out as planned.

The research and development examples presented in each chapter illustrate many of these principles and key messages and demonstrate practical ways in which the quality of life for residents, relatives and staff can be addressed in care homes.

This book considers research and development in care homes from three perspectives: care for individuals living in care homes and their families; a broader organisational focus that considers staff and the care home environment; and a wider community and development focus. Although the chapters are divided into three discrete sections there are overlaps between the specific foci. In many of the studies it is not always possible to focus solely on one element; for example, research that considers individuals also often addresses organisational and wider community issues.

The majority of contributing authors describe research and development activities involving care homes providing care for older people, usually nursing care. However, other types of care home and institutional long-term care settings are also included. Specifically, research with care homes (personal care) (Chapter 10: Goodman *et al.*; Chapter 9: Fear) and NHS continuing care settings (Chapter 2: Wilkinson *et al.*; Chapter 8: Holman and Crowhurst) is described. Research engaging with care homes supporting people with learning disabilities (Chapter 5: Jenkins) is also presented.

The first section of the book, with its focus on the individual, encompasses initiatives that address ways to improve the care received by older adults (Chapter 2: Wilkinson *et al.*), older adults with dementia (Chapter 3: Stanley) and people with learning disabilities (Chapter 5: Jenkins) in three different long-term care settings. The role of narrative as a means to establish relationships between residents and staff, and relatives and staff (Chapter 4: Brown Wilson *et al.*) illustrates the way a person-focused approach can facilitate relationship-building in this setting.

The next section focuses on the wider organisation, and broadens the focus to consider the role of the environment, family and friends, and staff. The nature of the relationship between individuals and their environment, particularly the natural environment, is addressed (Chapter 6: Chalfont). The role of family and friends in care homes can add an extra dynamic to the life and living that occurs there and an account of establishing Friends Groups in care homes is presented (Chapter 7: Furness and Torry). Staff are the focus of the next chapter (Chapter 8: Holman and Crowhurst), mirroring the research presented in Chapter 2, where a psychodynamic approach is again used to inform participatory working.

The final section goes beyond the care home as an organisation to consider its place in wider health and social care systems. Fear (Chapter 9) considers partnership working on a larger scale as she describes the development of a Care Home Learning Network in one locality, demonstrating partnership working between the care homes in the area and a higher education institution. In an intervention-based research study Goodman *et al.* (Chapter 10) also consider partnership working between the care home staff and district nurses in improving bowel care for residents. We conclude this section by considering the role of the researcher within care homes and how they can approach research with care homes in a constructive and sensitive way (Chapter 11: Dewing).

The final chapter (Chapter 12: Davies *et al.*) draws together the threads that have emerged from the contributions to this book, with a view to highlighting some of the insights gained from undertaking research and development in this field. The links between this work and the themes of the *My Home Life* programme are specified, followed by a summary of pointers for practice that should be helpful to others engaged in research and development work in care homes. This book is offered as a contribution towards this important UK-wide initiative that seeks to share best practice and promote quality of life for those living, dying, visiting and working in care homes for older people.

Acknowledgement

Thanks to Claire Goodman for her insightful reading of an earlier draft of this chapter.

References

Audit Scotland (2008) *A Review of Free and Personal Care.* Edinburgh: Audit Scotland.

Banks, L., Haynes, P., Balloch, S. and Hill, M. (2006) *Changes in Communal Provision for Adult Social Care 1991–2001.* York: Joseph Rowntree Foundation.

Bowman, C., Whistler, J. and Ellerby, M. (2004) 'A national census of care home residents.' *Age and Ageing 33,* 561–566.

Buchanan, R.J. (2001) 'Profiles of nursing home residents with multiple sclerosis using the minimum data set.' *Multiple Sclerosis 7,* 3, 189–200.

Burton-Jones, J. and Mosley, P. (2004) *'One World' Working with Racism: A Report of a Partnership Project between Anchor Trust and the Relatives and Residents Association.* London: Anchor Trust.

Cook, G. (2005) 'National Care Homes Research and Development Forum.' *Generations Review 5,* 4, 48–49.

Dalley, G. and Denniss, M. (2001) *Trained to Care? Investigating the Skills and Competencies of Care Assistants in Homes for Older People.* London: Centre for Policy on Ageing.

Darton, R., Netten, A. and Forder, J. (2003) 'The cost implications of the changing population and characteristics of care homes.' *International Journal of Geriatric Psychiatry 18,* 236–243.

Davies, S. and Nolan, M.R. (2004) 'Making the move: Relatives' experiences of the transition to a care home.' *Health and Social Care in the Community 12,* 6, 517–526.

Davies, S. and Seymour, J. (2002) 'Historical and Policy Contexts.' In J. Hockley and D. Clark (eds) *Palliative Care for Older People in Care Homes.* Buckingham: Open University Press. pp.4–33.

Department of Health (DoH) (2001) *Community Care Statistics 2001. Bulletin 2001/29.* London: Department of Health.

Department of Health (DoH) (2003) *Care Homes for Older People. National Minimum Standards and the Care Homes Regulations 2001.* London: TSO.

Dudman, J. (2007) 'Context.' In T. Owen and NCHRDF (eds) *My Home Life: Quality of Life in Care Homes – Review of the Literature.* London: Help the Aged.

Froggatt, K.A., Poole, K. and Hoult, L. (2002) 'The provision of palliative care in nursing homes and residential care homes: A survey of clinical nurse specialist work.' *Palliative Medicine 16*, 481–487.

Froggatt, K.A. and Turner, M. (2008) 'Practice Development in Palliative Care.' In S. Payne, J. Seymour and C. Ingleton (eds) *Palliative Care Nursing. Principles and Evidence for Practice.* 2nd edn. Maidenhead: McGraw Hill.

Glendinning, C., Jacobs, S., Alborz, A. and Hann, M. (2002) 'A survey of access to medical services in nursing and residential homes in England.' *British Journal of General Practice 52*, 480, 545–548.

Gubrium, J.F. (1975) *Living and Dying at Murray Manor.* New York: St Martin's Press.

Gubrium, J.F. (1993) *Speaking of Life: Horizons of Meaning for Nursing Home Residents.* Hawthorne, NY: Aldine de Grutyer.

Henderson, J.N. and Vesperi, M. (eds) (1995) *The Culture of Long Term Care. Nursing Home Ethnography.* Westport, CT: Bergin and Garvey.

Kayser-Jones, J. (1981) *Old, Alone and Neglected.* Berkeley, CA: University of California Press.

Laing and Buisson (2007) *Care of Elderly People.* UK Market Survey 2007 (20th edn). London: Laing and Buisson.

McCormack, B., Wright, J., Dewar, B., Harvey, G. and Ballantine, K. (2007) 'A realist synthesis of evidence relating to practice development: Findings from the literature analysis.' *Practice Development in Health Care 6*, 1, 25–55.

NCHRDF (2007) *My Home Life: Quality of Life in Care Homes. A Review of the Literature.* London: Help the Aged (also available from www.myhomelife.org.uk).

Netten, A., Darton, R. and Williams, J. (2002) *Closure of Care Homes for Older People. Summary of Findings 1.* Canterbury: PSSRU, University of Kent.

Nolan, M.R., Davies, S., Brown, J., Keady, J. and Nolan, J. (2004) 'Beyond "person-centred" care: A new vision for gerontological nursing.' *International Journal of Older People Nursing* in *Journal of Clinical Nursing, 13*, 3a, 45–53.

Office of Fair Trading (OFT) (2005) *Care Homes for Older People: A Market Study.* London: Office of Fair Trading.

O'Neill, C., Harrington, C., Kitchener, M. and Saliba, D. (2003) 'Quality of care in nursing homes: An analysis of relationships among profit, quality, and ownership.' *Medical Care 41*, 12, 1318–1330.

Owen, T. and NCHRDF (eds) (2006) *My Home Life: Quality of Life in Care Homes.* London: Help the Aged (also available from www.myhomelife.org.uk).

Reason, P. and Bradbury, H. (2001) *Handbook of Action Research: Participative Inquiry and Practice.* London: Sage.

Redfern, S., Hannan, S., Norman, I. and Martin, F. (2002) 'Work satisfaction, stress, quality of care and morale of older people in a nursing home.' *Health and Social Care in the Community 10*, 6, 512–517.

Reed, J., Cook, G. and Cook, M. (2004) 'Research governance issues in the care home sector.' *Nursing Times Research 9*, 6, 430–439.

Reed, J., Payton, V.R. and Bond, S. (1998) 'The importance of place for older people moving into care homes.' *Social Science and Medicine 46*, 859–867.

Reed, J. and Stanley, D. (1999) *Opening Up Care: Achieving Principled Practice in Institutions.* London: Hodder Arnold.

Ribbe, M.W. (1993) 'Care for the elderly: The role of the Dutch nursing home in the Dutch health care system.' *International Psychogeriatrics 5*, 2, 213–222.

Savishinsky, J.S. (1991) *The Ends of Time: Life and Work in a Nursing Home.* New York: Bergin and Garvey.

Stafford, P.B. (ed.) (2003) *Gray Areas. Ethnographic Encounters with Nursing Home Culture.* Oxford: James Currey Ltd.

Townsend, P. (1962) *The Last Refuge.* London: Routledge & Kegan Paul.

Travis, S., Buchanan, S. and Wang, M.K. (2005) 'Analyses of nursing home residents with diabetes at admission.' *Journal of the American Medical Directors Association 5*, 5, 320–327.

PART 1

The Individual Resident

CHAPTER 2

Developing Person-centred Care in an NHS Continuing Care Setting

Charlotte Wilkinson, Julienne Meyer and Angela Cotter

Introduction

This chapter describes a three-year action research project that aimed to support staff in the development of person-centred care, in a continuing care facility for up to 50 older people, located within an acute general hospital NHS Trust. The project commenced in January 2000, when the lead author (Charlotte) took up the post of Research and Development Nurse: Care for Older People within the trust. Julienne, with Angela, academically supervised Charlotte's work in part fulfilment of her professional doctorate.

For the purpose of this project 'person-centred care' was seen as an interpersonal process, taking place within a system of relationships, which affords dignity and respect to others. There were six main interventions (or action cycles) used in the project to foster person-centred care: the collection and sharing of residents' life histories; weekly team supervision meetings for staff; an action learning set for managers; the establishment of a user and carer group; audit activities on person-centred care; and building networks with other organisations.

At the close of the project both staff and residents reported higher levels of satisfaction, and repeat baseline audit findings showed improvements. Given that current policy requires that care should be person-centred and emphasises the need to foster dignity (for example, DoH, 2006a), this project provides a possible mechanism for putting person-centred care into practice (Ashburner *et al.* 2004b).

This chapter includes the following sections:

1. background contextual information to the project to help readers familiarise themselves with, and better understand, the key issues

2. methodological information on the research approach (action research) used in the project

3. the main activities and findings of the three phases of the project: exploration phase, intervention phase and evaluation phase.

Background to the project: Policy and other key issues in working with older people as an action researcher in the NHS context

At the time of the study older people were (and have continued to represent) a significant proportion of direct and potential users of health and social services in the statutory, voluntary and private sectors, with those over 65 years occupying two-thirds of all hospital beds (DoH 2001b). Furthermore, there was evidence that older people experienced considerable social and economic inequality compared with the rest of the population, particularly in London where the project took place (Howse and Prophet 2000). There were also concerns about the quality of health and social care received by older people (for example, SNMAC 2001). The National Service Framework for Older People (NSF) was established to drive up standards and reduce unacceptable variations in health and social care (DoH 2001a) and focused on rooting out age discrimination, providing person-centred care, promoting older people's health and independence and fitting services around people's needs. The NSF has subsequently been complemented by more recent policy that focuses upon patient choice and the promotion of dignity and respect (for example, DoH 2006b). The project described within this chapter was initiated to assist the trust in taking forward the NSF for Older People, but the agenda was left open for the post-holder to decide how best to do this in consultation with staff.

The milieu of care for older people now demanded represents a very significant change from the passive, task-focused, depersonalised, mundane and 'heavy' images and stereotypes that are accorded to traditional gerontological care (Nolan and Tolson 2000). However, the person-centred care advocated in policy, for example the NSF for Older People (DoH 2001a) with its emphasis on independence and choice, is very different to the person-centred care advocated in the gerontological literature which places more emphasis on humanistic psychology (see for example, Kitwood's 1997 work in relation to people with dementia). Kitwood (1997) describes personhood as a sense of self-identity which is based upon the unique biographies, personalities and life circumstances of the individual, maintained through relationships with others. In dementia, the maintenance of personhood resides with those who are cognitively intact through effective interaction with the person living with cognitive impairment. This humanistic approach to dementia care, drawing on Rogerian ideas (Rogers 1967), set precedents for valuing the quality of the psychosocial environment and the conditions necessary to support personhood, not only in relation to dementia, but also care for older people more generally.

From an organisational perspective, the depersonalisation frequently associated with more traditional approaches to care for older people in institutional settings can also transcend the patient/professional divide. The individual contribution of the professional may also be negated and depersonalised (Menzies Lyth 1988). Hirschhorn (1997) suggests that staff cannot be expected to provide care based upon dignity and respect if these are not part of the overall culture of work life and endemic in how teams work. Positive cultures of care for older people are associated with staff members who feel well supported and appreciated, along with effective leadership (Nolan et al. 2002). However, it is not always clear how to achieve such a culture, particularly when staff are feeling undervalued and demoralised.

The first task of the project therefore was to decide on the exact focus, in consultation with staff, residents and family members. It was agreed that person-centred care would be better developed through working towards an improved quality of relationships and psychosocial care rather than through developing more consumerist approaches, such as enabling 'choice' as emphasised in the NSF for Older People (DoH 2001a).

In some qualitative methods of inquiry, and in much action research, the researcher not only collects data but serves as 'the instrument' through which the data are collected. Rew, Bechtel and Sapp (1993) in their description of the 'self as instrument' advocate that the researcher needs to include details about the self in any presentation of their research in order to ensure a rigorous research process. This enables the reader to begin to evaluate how any resultant research was influenced by the personality and experience of the researcher. In line with that approach, some details about the lead author are included here (see Box 2.1).

Box 2.1 Background details about the lead author (Charlotte Wilkinson)

I qualified as a nurse in 1987 and learnt as a student that care for older people could be improved through change and effective leadership. I was fortunate to win a scholarship to study overseas and went to the USA to undertake a Masters in Nursing where I researched the incidence of post-operative restraint practices on older people in hospital. On my return to the UK in 1991 I worked in coronary care and became increasingly interested in the support and development of nurses in this speciality. I moved into an education and practice development role in 1997 in a local general hospital and worked on developing clinical supervision. During this time I wanted to understand organisational change and undertook the Masters programme at the Tavistock Clinic in London, developing my learning around psychodynamics and systems theory of organisational behaviour. In 2000, I took up the full-time post as lead nurse for research development in the care for older people, which was the starting point for this project.

The attributes of the researcher as instrument are described by Rew *et al.* (1993) as being authenticity, credibility, intuitiveness, receptivity, reciprocity and sensitivity. The lead researcher recognised that keeping true to these attributes was challenging and sought out a number of support systems to help her be 'good enough' throughout the research process. These systems included not only regular academic supervision with a leading international action researcher (Julienne Meyer) and an analytical psychotherapist/nurse researcher (Angela Cotter), but also active membership in a monthly action learning set, bi-monthly supervision with a psychotherapist working on group facilitation skills and personal bi-weekly psychotherapy. She also had peer support from other action researchers doing similar work in other trusts as part of a larger project (Meyer *et al.* 2003). All these systems of support helped foster personal growth, self-reflection and development for the lead researcher throughout the period of this project from 2000 to 2003. It is argued here that working on such challenging projects as an action researcher demands careful thought about the nature of supervision and support required. For Charlotte, this involved several different dimensions: academic, peer and therapeutic.

Local context

The nursing home that provided the focus for the project was a purpose-built facility, which opened in 1995 in an ethnically diverse and economically deprived area of London. Both staff and residents had been relocated there from long-stay 'geriatric' wards. Residents living in the home were aged 65 years and older, and highly dependent with chronic and enduring ill-nesses. Immobility, incontinence, feeding and swallowing difficulties and cognitive impairment were the main determinants of admission into the home. From a curative biomedical perspective these people can represent 'the worst' that modern medicine has to cope with – surviving, but far from cured. Nearly all people permanently living in nursing homes die in residence. The home in essence provided long-term palliative care.

There were 46 nursing staff in post, including 17 (37%) registered nurses. Staff turnover was low, particularly for registered nurses (12% as compared with 22% for non-registered nurses). The study took place at a time when most acute inner NHS Trusts and teaching trusts, particularly in London, were reporting turnover rates from 11 per cent to 38 per cent (Finlayson et al. 2002).

Sixteen staff members had worked within the NHS for more than 20 years and 45 per cent were close to retirement. The staff group was ethni-cally diverse (43% black Caribbean, 30% black African, 20% Indian and Asian and 5% white European), caring for a predominantly white client group (61% white European, 29% black Caribbean, 5% black African, 5% Indian and Asian).

At the beginning of the project staff members were informed that a research and development nurse undertaking an action research project would be part of a new organisational structure. In essence, there was no choice for staff about having the researcher in the nursing home. This saw the coming together of a keen and enthusiastic white researcher with a largely black, sceptical and suspicious staff group, who had not been con-sulted or given a choice over the researcher's arrival. This was a complex and paradoxical start to a project espousing the values of person-centred care.

Senior managers within the organisation had a number of financial and managerial concerns including issues of over-staffing, inflexibility of service provision, poor cleanliness within the home, environmental prob-lems (such as call bell systems not working properly), security issues, and isolation. The staff felt misjudged, victimised and undermined by outsiders.

They identified their own strengths as being a stable nursing workforce 'who know the ropes', with time to talk to residents and get to know them. In contrast, they suggested their weakness lay in the monotonous routine, which caused difficulties in motivation and a feeling of apathy about making things happen. They reported tensions between registered and unregistered staff and a sense of vulnerability over nursing homes being generally 'sold off' to the private sector. Staff were in the invidious position of recognising the need for change but feeling resentful that it had been thrust upon them through the arrival of an outside researcher.

Methodological approach and data collection methods

Although action research is not necessarily the most suitable choice in all settings, Hart and Bond (1995) consider it particularly appropriate when problem-solving and improvement are on the agenda. In particular, action research can be useful in the face of scepticism on the part of participants (Pasmore 2001).

Coghlan and Brannick (2001) identify three common attributes of action research. First, the approach is participatory whereby research subjects are themselves researchers, or in a democratic partnership with the researcher. Second, the research itself is a force for change, and, third, the actions make a difference to those directly involved and to the wider community. Although such attributes can be defined, the spectrum of approaches to action research is diverse (Hart and Bond 1995). The approach taken in this study attempted to integrate group relations theory, psychoanalysis and open systems theory with learning from experience and understanding organisational life (Gould 2001). There were two main tenets:

- The structural systems in which people work impact on their behaviour. This includes the division of labour, levels of authority, the nature of the work, the task and mission of the organisation, and transactions across boundaries. These systems affect individuals in significant psychological ways. Exploring and understanding these influences can positively support organisational understanding and learning (Gould 2001).

- Psychodynamics describes a range of mental processes (e.g. transference, resistance, projection and social defence systems) in which the emotional life of groups and individuals can be understood. The process of working through issues integral to a 'classic' therapeutic relationship is applied to the collective social defences of organisations (Menzies Lyth 1988). This may create opportunities for learning and development. Awareness and insight through acknowledging and understanding difficult feelings is seen to be a hallmark of good professional practice (Hawkins and Shohet 1994).

These tenets of systems and psychodynamic theory were integrated into the diagnosing, planning action, taking action and evaluating spirals of action research (Coghlan and Brannick 2001), through the various systems of clinical supervision and action learning that promoted active reflection on organisational and emotional constraints to changing practice. The lead researcher's training at Masters level in organisational consultancy using systems and psychoanalytic approaches meant that she was ideally placed to support this way of working.

Findings of the the three phases of the project (exploration, intervention and evaluation)

For clarity and simplicity, the story of the process, learning and outcomes of the project will be told in relation to the three phases (exploration, intervention and evaluation). Throughout these phases, a mixed method approach to data collection was taken, including participant observation, in-depth and focus group interviews, use of structured instruments to measure change over time (audits) and analysis of documents.

Exploration phase

During the exploration phase, in addition to establishing baseline data to measure change over time (see evaluation phase), Charlotte worked with a healthcare assistant one nursing shift per week, as a participant observer, to 'get a feel' for the home and meet staff and residents. During this time she experienced the unrelenting routine of the work, the depersonalised physical focus of nursing care, the overwhelming heat in the home, the smell of incontinence, the shabby and dirty environment (e.g. chipped and mismatching plates and dirty wheelchairs), the lack of visitors and strained relations between staff and family members. In addition she became aware of her own fears of working with highly dependent and vulnerable residents.

During this phase, regular supervised monthly meetings were established with the lead nurse for services for older people. The purpose of these meetings was to explore organisational and emotional constraints to changing practice in line with the systems and psychodynamically informed process of action research being undertaken. The manager gave the researcher freedom to work with all grades of staff. Staff members were asked by the researcher in one-to-one interviews and focus group meetings to identify what they wanted from the project and the strengths and weaknesses of working in the home. A number of areas for development were identified (see Box 2.2).

Box 2.2 Areas for improvement in the nursing home identified by staff

- better equipment e.g. more hoists
- more recreational activities for patients
- healthcare assistant education – 'responsibility issues'
- working with relatives – how to cope with angry relatives
- bereavement – better understanding
- closure of life – improved palliative care
- infection control – better hand-washing
- lots of pressures – feel like being in two or three places at once
- team working – more open and honest relationships
- clinical supervision – never had it
- performance management – current systems not working

The focus of this staff consultation was on what staff wanted to change. This was not necessarily problematic, but rather missed the pressing issue of how staff felt about the presence of the researcher and their concerns and misgivings about the project. With hindsight, it is possible to see the lack of attention to these important issues as an oversight. One staff member reflecting on this phase said:

> The staff needed to tell you what they had been through. The staff should have had an opportunity to tell their story, to get a feel for what the past five years had been like. (Interview 1.3, p.2)

It needs to be remembered that the researcher was a white, relatively young researcher entering into an environment of experienced and mature black staff. Resentment and misgivings were high and evoked comments like:

> I thought you would be spying and looking at how we worked... I was very wary and I had my doubts... Was this about to meddle in our business or stir up trouble? I thought it would go back to the higher people and would have nothing to do with patient care. (Interview 2.4, p.1)

Nonetheless, this phase brought issues out into the open that could not be ignored. In particular, it became apparent that staff were working in a highly routinised way and struggling to value residents' personhood. Furthermore, there were difficulties with relatives, who were not actively encouraged to be involved in care at the home. In addition, staff felt marginalised and isolated within the organisation and had lost the motivation to initiate change. A staff member described how she felt at the beginning of the project:

> [I felt] knocked left to right... We were sold badly from the outside... The staff were very demoralised... The bosses from outside had trashed the place... It was bad. There was a lack of trust. (Interview 1.3, p.1)

Building relationships during this period was not easy. Charlotte's presence appeared to be tolerated by staff but she was treated with a great deal of suspicion and was largely met by silent resistance. It would be unrealistic to expect no suspicion and indeed a degree of healthy cynicism is to be expected at the start of a project of this nature. Charlotte's impression was that anxieties were not effectively contained resulting in a defensive and resentful mentality held by the staff group who felt maligned by 'the outside' and persecuted by some family members. Residents and family members raised concerns over smells of incontinence, the dirty environment, unfriendly staff and poor management. Equally, staff reported low morale, conflicts between registered and unregistered staff, unfriendly and difficult visitors and family members, poor equipment and a dirty environment. There was certainly scope for improvement.

Intervention phase

Within the intervention phase, there were six main cycles of research activity:

- cycle 1: sharing biographical information about residents

- cycle 2: staff team clinical supervision
- cycle 3: action learning for managers
- cycle 4: promoting user and carer involvement
- cycle 5: dementia care mapping
- cycle 6: building networks with other organisations.

ACTION CYCLE ONE: SHARING BIOGRAPHICAL INFORMATION

Having established that residents were not being recognised in a person-centred way, this action cycle focused on assisting staff to get to know the residents better as individuals. Staff were invited to identify a resident whom they wished to know better. The resident was then approached and permission sought to interview him or her as part of the project. Family members were involved at the resident's suggestion or in the face of communication or cognitive difficulties. Interviews took place in private and lasted between 1.5 and 3.5 hours (with breaks as determined by the resident) and were undertaken by staff with support and role modelling from Charlotte. Whenever possible photographs were shared and discussed. A total of 21 residents' life stories were collected over two years. With permission a biographical booklet was written up concerning the story told for each resident.

The staff member involved shared the story and experience with other staff in weekly, facilitated team supervision meetings. The purpose was to engage the team in learning more about the resident and to consider how this may relate to nursing issues. Attempts to foster person-centred care and engage with residents produced strong emotional reactions in staff, which seemed to support the need for a psychodynamically informed approach. This level and type of engagement felt very different from an 'activities of daily living' nursing culture (Roper, Logan and Tierney 2000), which tends to focus more on physical losses and rarely considers what these mean in the context of a person's life. Trying to establish this approach to care proved extremely demanding for all the participants.

The collection and sharing of biographical information changed relationships and attitudes within the care home, as illustrated by one healthcare assistant:

> The biography is another thing and now we know our residents and relatives as well. They can relate to us. Now, when I first came I was frightened of him, and now he is much better: with the biography I got to know him better. (Interview 2.4, p.3)

Staff described a deepening of relationships, and residents and family members described feeling more comfortable and less antagonistic towards staff and management. However, collecting biographical information was time-consuming and required the provision of extensive support and encouragement by the lead author. For example, the staff had not been trained in interviewing skills, such as the importance of asking open-ended questions. Nonetheless, sharing biographical information proved to be a powerful intervention in developing the quality of relationships.

ACTION CYCLE TWO: STAFF TEAM CLINICAL SUPERVISION

During this action cycle, Charlotte facilitated 104 small clinical supervision group meetings which were attended by between 4 and 12 staff members. There was an open agenda in which staff could raise issues relating to their experiences at work. This built on Charlotte's earlier work in developing psychodynamically informed group supervision for hospital nurses (Ashburner et al. 2004a). Each meeting opened with a brief review of the previous week's discussion and then staff raised issues and challenges encountered in their practice. Before leaving they were encouraged to identify actions that might be needed to resolve issues and were invited to report back on developments at the next meeting. Attendance at these supervision meetings was generally good, although not always consistent due to the irregular shift patterns worked by staff.

A content analysis of the main focus of discussion at each team supervision session is shown in Table 2.1.

These sessions formed the backbone of the project and supported successful changes across a wide range of initiatives, for example the cleanliness of the nursing home. The clinical supervision sessions provided a forum for difficult, often 'unsaid' emotions to surface. Interestingly, talking about a resident's life in supervision led to a surfacing of issues around loss and death. Data from staff interviews (n = 22) identified four key outcomes of clinical supervision:

- learning in practice about 'real' issues
- support and building morale
- 'letting off steam'
- better team working.

Table 2.1 Content analysis of team supervision sessions

Focus of discussion	Frequency	%
Presentation of a life history	21	20
Working with relatives	19	18
Team working	17	16
Death	13	12
Behavioural difficulties of residents	7	7
Environmental issues, e.g. cleaning	5	5
Clinical care	5	5
Psychosocial activities, e.g. parties	5	5
Food quality	3	3
Professional accountability	3	3
Review meetings, e.g. ground rules	3	3
Changes in care for older people over time	2	2
Child care issues	1	1
Total	104	100

Collecting and sharing residents' life histories was supported by the clinical supervision taking place in these sessions, which also led to the additional benefits described above.

ACTION CYCLE THREE: ACTION LEARNING FOR MANAGERS

An action learning set was established for managers working in elderly services across the acute Trust to come together and develop their leadership skills. The manager of the nursing home was now familiar with this reflective style of working and was able to make a valuable contribution to the group. Group meetings were well attended over two years. The action learning set met for a day every month, and members presented for approximately one hour on a work issue of their choice. After each hour, action points were agreed and reflected upon in subsequent meetings. Leadership development was seen as key to supporting changes in the service. The researcher co-facilitated this group with another colleague and both were members of their own action learning set. Again, there was a focus on exploring the emotional and organisational constraints to change, supporting the psychodynamically informed action research approach.

The action learning sets fostered a growth in managerial confidence. In particular, through this process, set members recognised and valued their own strengths and felt more able to change practice. One member stated:

> I have presented out of my comfort zone but it has offered a different perspective on life, and the challenge has been very positive. Professionally, I feel as if I have grown up. (Interview 1.2, p.4)

Revans (1983) argued that for people and organisations to flourish the rate of learning has to be greater than, or equal to, the rate of change. McGill and Beaty (1992) advocate action learning as a way for managers to achieve this. The support of leadership development was seen as a crucial component in securing the success of this project.

ACTION CYCLE FOUR: PROMOTING USER AND CARER INVOLVEMENT

The focus of this action cycle was the successful re-establishment of a family and resident's forum in which residents and family members could raise issues and influence the running of the home. A group was established, called 'Friends of the Nursing Home', and this met on five occasions during the project. A total of 56 residents and relatives attended the meetings with from 6 to 12 participants at each meeting. A representative of the staff and management team was always present. Table 2.2 shows the topics raised at the meetings together with actions and achievements.

The group was successful in supporting and directing change and development in the nursing home.

ACTION CYCLE FIVE: DEMENTIA CARE MAPPING AND OUTCOMES

Funding was available to support the training at Bradford University of three staff members to undertake Dementia Care Mapping (DCM) (Bradford Dementia Group 1997). This tool is validated to measure person centred practice in residential environments. Using this tool, a baseline audit was conducted within the nursing home. A repeat audit was undertaken at the close of the project and will be reported on later in this chapter (see the evaluation phase). DCM revealed that the most prevalent observed behaviour of residents observed in lounge areas was of passive involvement or withdrawal from surroundings. This was a cause for concern and led to the establishment of an activities and social care group. This group met in

Table 2.2 Issues raised and outcomes through the 'Friends of the Nursing Home' group

Issues raised	Outcomes
Clinical care: chiropody and therapy services	• A new chiropody referral system with regular chiropody sessions and satisfaction with new arrangements • Surgery sessions with the physiotherapist established and new wheelchair referral systems • Quarterly visits from speech and language therapists
Environmental concerns	• A new notice board for better communication with visitors • Relocation of the activities room • A new designated smoking area • Fish tank cleaned and new fish supplied • Replacement of unreliable washing machines and dishwashers
Food quality	• Change of meal times • More varied menu planning • Introduction of 'cooked breakfasts' • More snacks available
Social activities	• Increased social events, e.g. a barbecue and Queen's Jubilee celebration • Involvement in planning of events and increased participation
Direction of the action research project	• Guiding the researcher in the collection of data, e.g. developing interview schedule and acting on findings

November 2001 for the first time and there were three subsequent meetings during the project. The group was instrumental in getting a range of activities off the ground. These included:

- a visit by the group to a local dementia unit to share good practice on person-centred care

- the purchase of a range of equipment including radios, CD players, games, etc.

- art therapy input for one day per week

- organisation of a range of social activities including parties, a trip to a local park and museum

- introduction of pet therapy

- contact with a local charity and access to a befriending scheme

- monthly input from an entertainer/singer
- contact with local church groups to provide Sunday services
- staff sharing activities and good practice in social care with other nursing homes
- aromatherapy taster sessions for staff and residents
- access to an aromatherapy service for staff and residents.

Prior to the project, there was no input from a qualified occupational therapist (OT) and, in the light of the DCM findings, recruitment of a qualified occupational therapist (0.5 whole time equivalent) was considered necessary. The DCM findings were a useful lever for change and helped to secure new funding from the occupational health budgets within the acute NHS Trust. The OT took up post in January 2003. This post was to support the development of person-centred care and was important in terms of continuity and sustaining change at the close of the project.

ACTION CYCLE SIX: BUILDING NETWORKS WITH OTHERS IN THE ORGANISATION AND WITH OTHER ORGANISATIONS

As time progressed, the nursing home staff began to feel proud of the changes they were making and wanted to share their experiences with others in the Trust. Staff in the nursing home began to feel less isolated from their peers in the hospital. This was captured by a staff member who said:

> Before the hospital took over, we were in the shadows. We are part of an organisation and we never had this before. (Interview 2.2, p.3)

The launch of the National Service Framework for Older People (DoH 2001a) raised the profile of older people services within the Trust and staff members were encouraged to change their practice in light of the new standards and to share their experiences with each other. With this in mind, a local steering group was established for the project. Valuing the efforts to change and raising the profile of the nursing home within the organisation were seen by staff as contributing to the eventual success of the project. This culminated in a presentation to the Hospital Trust Board concerning the achievements made in the nursing home over the three-year period. Staff reported feeling more respected within the organisation and as one staff member said:

> We are doing well, we have a different model, but we address the nitty gritty. (Interview 2.6, p.2)

The manager felt the nursing home was 'more on the map' in terms of networks with the local hospital. However, there was a concern that the nursing home needed to develop better links with other nursing homes in the borough. Networks and collaboration in this sector appear underdeveloped and with no obvious systems easy to access (Meehan, Meyer and Winter 2002). The findings reported by Meehan *et al.* (2002) acted as a trigger for local developments and a borough wide nursing home project was launched in 2004 to address this networking gap.

Evaluation phase

While it would never be possible to attribute change directly to the project, the final phase involved a repeat of the baseline audits using the shortened quality interaction schedule (QUIS) (Dean, Proudfoot and Lindesay 1993), Nursing Home Monitor II (Morton *et al.* 1991) and DCM (Bradford Dementia Group 1997).

The QUIS audit was undertaken in December 2000 (exploration phase) and repeated in January 2003 (evaluation phase), and included eight observations of 15 minutes' duration, undertaken in communal areas, over a period of 48 hours. Communication between staff members, residents and visitors was rated according to four categories: positive social, basic care, neutral and negative (see Box 2.3 for a brief description of each category).

Box 2.3 Brief description of the four QUIS categories

Positive social interactions – care over and beyond the basic physical care task demonstrating patient-centred empathy, support, explanation, socialisation, etc.

Basic care interactions – basic physical care with task carried out adequately but without the elements of social or psychological support as above

Neutral interactions – brief indifferent interactions not meeting the definitions of other categories

Negative interactions – care provided which is disregarding of the residents' dignity and respect

Significant improvements in the quality of interactions were found between the two phases. Table 2.3 summarises these changes.

Table 2.3 Changes in QUIS scores (December 2000 and January 2003)

Coded interaction	Frequency December 2000	Frequency January 2003	% change
Positive social interactions	9 (10%)	31 (18%)	+8
Basic care interactions	46 (51%)	126 (74%)	+23
Neutral interaction	25 (27%)	13 (8%)	−19
Negative interactions	11 (12%)	0 (0%)	−12
Total interactions	91	170	

Between the two audits, positive social interactions increased by 8 per cent. A higher percentage of communication (74%, as opposed to 51%) was focused around caring activities. No negative social interactions were recorded (a comparative reduction of 12%). In addition, the proportion of neutral comments was reduced from 27 per cent to 8 per cent. Interestingly, substantially more interactions were coded in the second audit (170 interactions, compared with 91). The results indicated a strong improvement in the quality of psychosocial interactions in the home.

Audit findings from Nursing Home Monitor II undertaken in December 2000 and repeated in March 2003 showed positive changes in scores. Table 2.4 shows the changes in home management scores. The top score achievable in each category is 100. Each score represents the percentage of eligible audit questions scored positively.

Table 2.4 Nursing Home Monitor II management scores (December 2000 and March 2003)

	Audit in 2000	Audit in 2003	% change
Ground floor management score	72	84	+12
First floor management score	61	83	+22
Total home management score	67	84	+17

The following are examples of improvements made over the study period: new carpets/flooring and redecoration of the home, new nursing office facilities on the first floor, a new security system, an improved call bell system, better supplies for hand-washing, improved cleanliness, better storage of equipment, and better management of domestic and clinical waste.

Table 2.5 shows improvement in all areas with the exception of information collected on admission, although these improvements were more pronounced on the first floor compared with the ground floor. This could have been due to differences in leadership between the two floors as there was an unfilled senior staff nurse vacancy on the ground floor. However, overall there were positive improvements in all other areas. The most substantial improvement was in the range and frequency of activities and social care for residents, for example aromatherapy, live entertainment and pet therapy. Use of the Nursing Home Monitor tool indicates that there were quality improvements in management and nursing care over the study period.

Table 2.5 Nursing Home Monitor II nursing care scores (December 2000 and March 2003)

	Ground floor: 2000	First floor: 2000	Home scores in 2000	Ground floor: 2003	First floor: 2003	Home scores in 2003	% change
Admission information	72	68	70	59	63	61	−9
Care delivered: currently applicable	52	41	45	65	63	64	+19
Medication	88	66	75	91	93	91	+16
Practical nursing	72	66	68	78	72	75	+7
Nutrition	84	56	65	94	76	84	+19
Activities and social care	33	38	35	65	73	69	+34

A repeat DCM audit was undertaken at the close of the project. Below is a summary of improvements shown in DCM results in 2003:

- The ratio of ill-being to well-being in 2001 was approximately 1:3, whilst in 2003 this ratio had changed to 1:4.

- The profile of behaviours observed in the second audit reflected greater interaction by residents with others.

- There was a 5 per cent reduction in socially withdrawn behaviours in 2003.

- Residents spent increased time eating and drinking during the second audit.

In addition, 22 interviews were conducted with staff reflecting on their experiences of the project. In general, staff valued the role of the researcher, as expressed below:

> It has been a breath of fresh air, a lifeline. It has brought a bit of life to the home and it has made me see that they are interested in us here and also the carers and relatives. (Interview 2.6, p.6)

Overall, staff felt that there had been improvements and the majority stated that they were feeling happier at work:

> Skills have come to the surface and I mean my communication skills and my confidence... It has been about really understanding my work. I am happier in my work – this last three years I have been a lot happier. (Interview 3.4, p.4)

Staff reported knowing residents better, but this was not without an emotional cost. As one member reported:

> Relationships have grown during the project... They [residents] become part of your family. This makes the death hard...then it hits you like part of your family...it hits you. Colleagues need to understand the loss... Over the years she was not just a resident. It is no good saying you must not get attached, when they are ill, the love you feel for them is there and you want to protect them more. Seeing the deterioration [pause] watching it is heart breaking. (Interview 2.1, p.2)

Over time, death was more openly discussed, particularly through clinical supervision sessions. Through discussing and thinking about death, paradoxically staff appeared more able to think about life and personhood. Holman, Meyer and Cotter (2004) discuss the importance of understanding the impact on continuing care staff of constantly dealing with loss and bereavement. It is suggested that psychodynamically informed clinical supervision can help staff deal with their own anxieties about death and, through this process, form healthier relationships with residents (Holman, Meyer and Davenhill 2006). However, the difficult and painful emotions of getting to know a resident and then watching him or her slowly deterio-rate and die may cause an unconscious emotional 'backlash'. For instance, in this study the staff spoke positively of the process of getting to know residents in their care, but they also perceived difficulties with regard to relationships with colleagues and residents' relatives. Strong angry feelings were evoked and surfaced during this project and were frequently focused towards Charlotte. Psychodynamic understanding offers the theoretical concept of projective identification in which difficult emotions such as anger and frustration over death and deterioration are unconsciously transposed to others (Moylan 1994). This theoretical perspective allowed Charlotte to work with the dynamics within the organisation and to consider difficulties not as a personal psychological attack, but more as a constructive feature of the change process. However, to work in such a way requires robust sys-tems of support for all participants, particularly the change agent.

Conclusion

While the person-centred standard in the NSF for Older People (DoH 2001a) challenges negative stereotypes, it presents a limited vision (Nolan et al. 2002). For instance, it does not acknowledge the need for staff to feel valued as individuals in order to deliver person-centred care. Kitwood and Benson (1995, p.10) suggest that: 'staff can only give person-centred care to others in the long term, if their own personhood is acknowledged and nurtured'.

In preference to patient-centred care, Nolan et al. (2002, 2004) advocate 'relationship-centred care' (Tresolini and Pew-Fetzer Task Force 1994), in which the focus is upon the relationships that form in the context of care. Findings generated from this study support Nolan et al.'s (2004) thesis. It is argued that utilising more psychologically informed processes, such as clinical supervision and action learning, allows practitioners to address some of the emotional and organisational constraints that get in the way of changing practice. These approaches are seen as key to developing person-centred care in the future.

References

Ashburner, C., Meyer, J., Cotter, A., Young, G. and Ansell, R. (2004a) 'Seeing things differently: Evaluating psychodynamically informed group clinical supervision for general hospital nurses.' *NT Research 9*, 1, 38–48.

Ashburner, C., Meyer, J., Johnson, B. and Smith, C. (2004b) 'Using action research to address loss of personhood in a continuing care setting.' *Illness, Crisis and Loss 12*, 1, 23–37.

Bradford Dementia Group (1997) *Evaluating Dementia Care. The DCM method* (7th edn). Bradford: Bradford Dementia Group, University of Bradford.

Coghlan, D. and Brannick, T. (2001) *Doing Action Research in Your Own Organization.* London: Sage Publications.

Dean, R., Proudfoot, R. and Lindesay, J. (1993) 'The quality of interactions schedule (QUIS): Development, reliability, and use in the evaluation of two domus units.' *International Journal of Geriatric Psychiatry 10*, 819–826.

Department of Health (DoH) (2001a) *National Service Framework for Older People.* London: Department of Health.

Department of Health (DoH) (2001b) *The National Beds Inquiry.* London: Department of Health.

Department of Health (DoH) (2006a) *A New Ambition for Old Age: Next Steps in Implementing the National Service Framework for Older People.* London: Department of Health.

Department of Health (DoH) (2006b) *Our Health, Our Care, Our Say: A New Direction for Community Services.* London: The Stationery Office.

Finlayson, B., Dixon, J., Meadows, S. and Blair, G. (2002) 'Mind the gap: The extent of the NHS nursing shortage.' *British Medical Journal 325*, 538–541.

Gould, L. (2001) 'Introduction.' In L. Gould, F. Stapley and M. Stein (eds) *The Systems Psychodynamics of Organisations. Integrating the Group Relations, Psychoanalytic, and Open Systems Perspectives.* London: Karnac.

Hart, E. and Bond, M. (1995) *Action Research for Health and Social Care.* Buckingham: Open University Press.

Hawkins, P. and Shohet, R. (1994) *Supervision in the Helping Professions.* Buckingham: Open University Press.

Help the Aged (2006) *My Home Life: Quality of Life in Care Homes. A Review of the Literature.* London: Help the Aged.

Hirschhorn, L. (1997) *The Workplace Within Psychodynamics of Organizational Life.* Cambridge, MA: MIT Press.

Holman, C., Meyer, J. and Cotter, A. (2004) 'The complexity of loss in continuing care institutions for older people: A review of the literature.' *Illness, Crisis and Loss 12*, 4, 38–51.

Holman, C., Meyer, J. and Davenhill, R. (2006) 'Psychoanalytical informed research in an NHS continuing care unit for older people: Exploring and developing staff's work with complex loss and grief.' *Journal of Social Work and Practice 20*, 3, 315–328.

Howse, K. and Prophet, H. (2000) *Improving the Health of Older Londoners: Reviewing the Evidence.* London: Centre for Policy on Ageing.

Kitwood, T. (1997) *Dementia Reconsidered: The Person Comes First.* Buckingham: Open University Press.

Kitwood, T. and Benson, S. (1995) *The New Culture of Dementia Care.* London: Hawker Publications.

McGill, I. and Beaty, L. (1992) *Action Learning: A Guide for Professional, Management and Educational Development.* London: Kogan Page.

Meehan, L., Meyer, J. and Winter, J. (2002) 'Partnerships with care homes: A new approach to collaborative working.' *NT Research 7*, 5, 348–359.

Menzies Lyth, I. (1988) *Containing Anxiety in Institutions: Selected Essays*. London: Free Association Books.

Meyer, J., Johnson, B., Bryar, R. and Procter, S. (2003) 'Practitioner research: Exploring issues in relation to research-capacity building.' *NT Research 8*, 6, 407–417.

Morton, J., Goldstone, L.A., Turner, A., Harrison, S. and Morgan, R. (1991) *Nursing Home Monitor II* (2nd edn). Loughton: Gale Centre Publications.

Moylan, D. (1994) 'The dangers of contagion: Projective identification processes in institutions.' In A. Obholzer and V. Zagier Roberts (eds) *The Unconscious at Work: Individual and Organisational Stress in the Human Services*. London: Routledge. pp.51–59.

Nolan, M., Davies, S., Brown, J., Keady, J. and Nolan, J. (2002) *Longitudinal Study of the Effectiveness of Educational Preparation to Meet the Needs of Older People: The AGEIN (Advancing Gerontological Education In Nursing) Project*. London: English National Board.

Nolan, M., Davies, S., Brown, J., Keady, J. and Nolan, J. (2004) 'Beyond "person-centred" care: A new vision for gerontological nursing.' *International Journal of Older People Nursing* in association with *Journal of Clinical Nursing 13*, 3a, 45–53.

Nolan, M. and Tolson, D. (2000) 'Gerontological nursing 1: Challenges nursing older people in acute care.' *British Journal of Nursing 9*, 1, 39–42.

Pasmore, W. (2001) 'Action research in the workplace: The socio-technical perspective.' In P. Reason and H. Bradbury (eds) *Handbook of Action Research: Participative Inquiry and Practice*. London: Sage Publications, pp.38–47

Revans, R.W. (1983) *The ABC of Action Learning*. Kent: Chartwell Bratt.

Rew, L., Bechtel, D. and Sapp, A. (1993) 'Self-as-instrument in qualitative research.' *Nursing Research 42*, 5, 300–301.

Rogers, C. (1967) *On Becoming a Person: A Therapist's View of Psychotherapy*. London: Constable and Company Ltd.

Roper, N., Logan, W. and Tierney, A. (2000) *The Roper–Logan–Tierney Model of Nursing*. London: Elsevier.

Standing Nursing and Midwifery Committee (SNMAC) (2001) *Caring for Older People: A Nursing Priority*. London: Department of Health.

Tresolini, C.P. and Pew-Fetzer Task Force (1994) *Health Professions Education and Relationships-Centred Care: A Report of the Pew-Fetzer Task Force on Advancing Psychosocial Education*. San Francisco, CA: Pew Health Professions Commission.

CHAPTER 3

Action Research in Care Homes to Improve Care-Planning for People with Dementia

David Stanley

Introduction

This chapter describes and discusses selected aspects of the use of an action research approach in developing care-planning for people with dementia in two residential care homes, focusing on social and emotional needs. It describes how the research team worked with staff and managers to explore the use of a variety of techniques, including observational work, group discussions, diaries and life stories. The project aimed to help staff to understand the wishes and needs of people with dementia as a basis for planning and implementing changes in care practice to improve the quality of residents' lives. It also aimed to assist staff to enhance their skills in communicating with, and relating to, people with dementia and responding more effectively to their needs. A range of factors challenged the achievement of the service development goals, including the broader organisational and policy context, resource issues, social relations within the staff and resident groups, and occupational structures and assumptions. We discuss these challenges and give examples of staff and management participation in developing approaches that enabled some people with dementia to become more meaningfully engaged in shaping their care.

The principal objectives of this chapter are to:

- explore selected aspects of care practice in relation to people with dementia

- present the application of action research methodology as a means of developing good practice, using internal care-planning processes as an exemplar

- suggest ways in which staff can contribute to developing good practice

- identify broader organisational factors which can impact upon our understanding of care homes.

Context

Long-term care is very much a trans-national issue (OECD 2005) and the overall proportion of older people in need of long-term care is roughly the same in the European Union as it is in the USA: approximately 17 per cent of the over-65 population (Vreven 2006). The proportion of older people who have dementia rises as the population ages and it is estimated that a third of people with dementia in the UK live in care homes (National Audit Office 2007). This poses a challenge to care providers who recognise that a steadily increasing proportion of older people living in care homes have some form of dementia. Their needs are complex and ever-changing, but meeting those needs in a planned and consistent way is essential to their well-being. Caring for people with dementia places high demands on both the care staff and the managers of a home. There is increasing recognition that, whilst people with dementia need the same high-quality care as all other residents, they have additional needs that are often not recognised or met in non-specialist care settings. The research project upon which this chapter draws was commissioned by a public sector provider in the north of England. The research proposal was developed as part of the provider's overall commitment both to ensure development of the best possible quality of care in its homes and to meet the development needs of care staff. The action research approach was adopted in order to facilitate a high level of participation from staff throughout the research and development process.

Care-planning is a complex and multidimensional activity. There were existing arrangements for care-planning and quality management within the homes, but little work had been undertaken to tailor these arrangements to meet the specific needs of people with dementia. The action research project will be described, focusing on the practice development approach adopted; then the range of factors that need to be taken into account in developing care-planning will be summarised. In order to maintain anonymity for participants, limited specific details are given concerning the research sites and some identifying features have been changed or omitted.

Project aims

The project aimed to improve the care received by people with dementia in care homes by helping staff better understand the wishes and needs of people with dementia, as a basis for planning and implementing changes in care practice that would improve the quality of residents' lives. The objectives of the project were to:

- review the current care-planning process, including assessment, planning, monitoring and review, in relation to the needs of people with dementia and to identify the issues involved in identifying and meeting the needs of people with dementia in non-specialist care settings

- review current knowledge about 'best practice' as described in the literature, and by investigating innovative developments in other areas

- make recommendations to the commissioning authority and jointly to develop and implement action, including staff development, to improve care-planning for people with dementia

- evaluate the impact of the action taken to improve care-planning for people with dementia

- identify the general lessons of the work and produce a strategy for rolling out developments within the provider's residential homes and potentially other sectors

- disseminate the work more widely as appropriate.

Research approach

Service managers identified the area for the research and the sites for inquiry, and the study was conducted within the local governance procedures of the provider authority. It was confined to two pilot homes selected on the pragmatic grounds of geographical proximity to each other and the theoretical grounds of each being of a similar size in terms of resident population and sub-unit structure. An action research approach was adopted. Action research (Hart and Bond 1995; Patton 2002) uses a cycle of inquiry, intervention and evaluation which involves collaboration between the research team and service providers in working towards shared goals, the details of which will only become apparent as the work progresses. This approach is generally regarded as empowering (Wortley 2000) and context specific. It is particularly appropriate where the aim of the project is to solve problems and promote improvement in service delivery. A particular strength is that the collaborative team of researchers and staff 'own' the process, which should be re-educative and reflective. Therefore, in this project the researcher functioned as an integral member of the development team rather than as an external manager of a pre-determined process. As a result, it was necessary for the research team not only to establish good working relationships with the staff, but also to enable them to contribute creatively as the project developed. This interactive and dynamic approach is appropriate where the nature of a proposed intervention is both initially unclear and dependent for its success on the service providers.

The research team took the lead in:

- reviewing literature and other sources of information about best practice

- collecting and managing data on current practice

- developing methods of monitoring new care-planning arrangements and managing the data collected

- collecting and managing data for the evaluation of the project

- coordinating the project, particularly the facilitation and administration of the steering group and care-planning development group

- facilitating the development stage of the work, in conjunction with the staff of the homes and the staff development section of the local authority

- providing academic and management support for the project worker

- producing an evaluation report on the project.

The care-planning practice, procedures and philosophies recognised in the homes provided the framework for the project. Case studies of residents with dementia, their living environments and the arrangements for planning their care provided the vehicle for inquiry. In order to support the action research a steering group and a care-planning development group were convened. The steering group included service managers. The care-planning development group comprised the researchers together with the managers of the two homes, their immediate line manager and a training officer. The research team comprised one part-time research associate, supported by the director of Dementia North, and an academic member of the Dementia North Trust.

The full participation of the staff and management of the homes and other key departmental staff was central to the project's success. Representatives of the homes participated in both the steering group and the care-planning development group. They had a major role in identifying the practice issues to be addressed, in 'problem-solving' ways of improving practice and devising action plans. The members of these groups had lead responsibility for implementing and monitoring the action plans in the homes. This also required the participation of the whole staff of the homes and input from the service provider's staff development section.

Good care-planning for people with dementia is characterised by an approach that is person-centred. In trying to establish the baseline of care-planning in the homes it was necessary to examine the extent to which the characteristics of best practice were being met. Accordingly a number of questions were posed:

- To what extent was care planned and delivered taking into account the perspectives of the person with dementia? What efforts were made to uncover that person's perspective?

- To what extent did staff think positively or negatively of daily achievements of people with dementia and, in the verbal culture in which they operated, how, if at all, were these recorded?

- Did staff attempt to identify the physical, emotional, occupational and health needs of each person and try, inventively, to meet them?

- Were staff with specific skills, personalities or interests matched to individual residents in order to maximise their quality of life?

- Were families involved?

- How did staff share information with each other? How freely and in what format was key information about residents shared with care staff by senior staff, care managers and other care providers such as GPs and district nurses?

The project followed the cyclical three-stage pattern of inquiry, intervention (including assessment and planning) and review. The cycle was continuous as new ideas were developed and the project incorporated more residents.

For the purposes of this chapter the processes and data sources are reported in outline rather than detail and included the following:

- Ten residents, five in each home (two males and three females from one home, five females from the other), with ages ranging from 77 to 92 years were recruited as case study residents on a sequential basis in two cohorts of five each. The inclusion criteria included: the stage of dementia (to ensure a range of issues could be addressed); the interest of the family (to ensure they would be prepared to participate in the research work); and the interest of the key worker (to ensure staff were fully participative). These ten cases provided the core data sources. These comprised: a selective activity/triggers/events diary maintained over a three-to-four-week period together with a 24-hour diary of what happened to and around each resident (both recorded by their key workers); life stories (using a questionnaire in one home and a topic guide in the other); four group discussions of key workers; two meetings of staff groups in each home; and a mid-point workshop for participating staff which included 13 key worker care assistants, four senior homes managers and two senior residential service managers.

- The researcher visited the homes at various times of day in order to capture the cycle of care and observe and work with key staff on different shifts. The frequency of visits depended on the stage of activity, but data collection was ongoing throughout the project.

- Data about the organisation and processes of care and perceptions of those involved were gathered using qualitative methods. These comprised semi-structured interviews with four senior staff and three relatives, four focus groups and ten individual interviews with care staff, and numerous ongoing individual discussions with residents. Representative interviews and focus groups were tape-recorded for later transcription.

- Data were also collected through formal and informal observation and a review of care-planning documents. A small group of staff undertook development of the assessment section of the existing care plan. A research fieldwork diary was maintained for 15 months during the development period. This documented observations of daily life within the homes and the collaborative work of staff in developing care-planning tools.

In addition to these data sources there were eight meetings of the steering group over the two-year life of the project. All data were analysed through a recognised method of qualitative data analysis (Patton 2002; Silverman 2006) that involved identification, charting, matching and comparison of themes.

The research environment

Unless the wider system of the context in which care is delivered is understood then it is not possible to make sense of the sub-systems within it. It was therefore recognised that little progress could be made in talking about the importance of the individual, or for that matter the minutiae of the documents, without first understanding the work environments. These environments included key characteristics of the homes and their residents and general perceptions of, and approaches to, the care of residents.

The homes

The two homes, accommodating 60 and 50 older people respectively, including respite care residents, were subdivided into a number of units, each with an average of 15 residents. Each home had a manager who was supported by assistant managers and senior care assistants. The staff–resident ratio on any shift was approximately one to ten.

It was observed that routines dominated the delivery of care. Dressing, bathing, toileting, meal times and putting away the laundry dominated each day with afternoon diversions of television and dominoes for some. The people who had dementia spent a lot of time just sitting, with little diversion, activity or personal attention: 'just waiting' as one man described it.

The residents

The managers of the homes estimated that as many as a third of residents were experiencing dementia at its different stages: staff identified up to 20 per cent of their residents whom they considered to have mild or moderate dementia, in that they were disorientated, had poor short-term memory, had difficulty word-finding, or were losing their ability to care for themselves. However, only one person had a confirmed diagnosis of dementia. Some were incontinent. Some had been resident in the homes for a number of years. They lived alongside other residents who were mentally alert, could tend to much of their personal care and made independent trips out of their homes. As staff were critical to care-planning it was important for the researchers to understand the views of staff about people with dementia and their role in their care.

Staff perceptions of residents with dementia and approaches to care

Discussions and observation provided a picture of how staff saw the residents within the homes. The staff who participated most closely in these discussions were those who either were directly involved in caring for residents with dementia or had expressed an interest in that part of their work. Here we describe briefly their perceptions about the people they cared for and their practice. The broad and inevitably overlapping areas that emerged were as follows:

IDENTIFICATION AND DIAGNOSIS

Staff reported that they took a cautious approach to identifying signs of dementia. One care assistant said that the initial response to unusual behaviour was to eliminate medical problems and to avoid assuming 'confusion'. When residents became known to them, staff were likely to pick up progressive memory loss and observe changes in interactions and behaviours.

UNDERSTANDING OF THE DISEASE

Staff were able to differentiate between the stages of dementia and the impact each stage had on the person. However, their understanding of the experience of dementia varied and this was likely to have consequences for their approach to caring for residents with dementia.

RESIDENTS' INVOLVEMENT IN PLANS

Helping people with dementia to identify the goals of care that they wished to achieve was difficult for staff because of barriers to communication. Staff resorted to the family as informants, partly in order to check on the veracity of the older persons' statements, but principally as a source of information about wishes and experiences.

APPROACHES TO CARE PRACTICES

Informants shared the view that careful observation and flexibility were the key to good care practices for people with dementia. However, flexibility by staff needed to be placed in the context of providing stability for residents and the importance of routine. Coping with anti-social behaviour posed particular challenges for staff, and the language the staff used was often problem-oriented. Observations of care practices revealed a gap between how staff presented their work and the actual way it was carried out. For example, we observed staff being so focused on the task at hand, such as trying to wash someone, that they overlooked the basic needs for dignity and comfort. We saw people with dementia left alone for periods with no stimulation or direct interaction from anyone else. Similarly, attention to detail at meal times was often overlooked, for example we saw people struggling with cutlery they were unable to use or food that they could not chew.

THE INTEGRATION OF PEOPLE WITH DEMENTIA

Staff described a peace-keeping role in relation to supporting the integration of people with dementia within the home and this demanded skill and patience. The intolerance of older people who disliked any form of disturbance to their routines was a trigger for staff intervention. Tactics ranged from reasoning and trying to persuade residents to put themselves in the place of the person with dementia, to removing the person who was causing disruption for his or her own safety.

PLACEMENT

Reflecting the policy of the commissioning organisation, staff said that they aimed to provide a 'home for life' for the residents. However, they clearly felt that fulfilment of that aim was constrained by how well they could manage the person, how disruptive the person became and how well staff could meet the needs of someone who became very dependent. The physical environment was a frequently mentioned constraint on staff ability to provide for people with dementia.

Staff repeatedly pointed out that because of the staff–resident ratio they were unable to provide the level of care they wished, or that people with dementia needed. The needs of ten or more people had to be met throughout a shift and they said that there were not the staffing resources to provide individualised care. Senior staff in the homes endorsed this view.

Relatives' views

The small group of ten relatives who were actively involved in the study were generally satisfied with the care given to their family member. They saw the benefits of the placement in terms of securing better care than they were able to provide for their relative and believed that they were happy and felt safe in the care home environment. Significantly, all relatives pointed out the kindness of staff and thought that they cared about the residents. Paradoxically, they also thought that staff seemed very busy and so were unable to give residents one-to-one care. They used this to explain the lack of attention to detail in some aspects of care, for example, people who were dressed in clothes that were not their own and the time their residents spent unoccupied. Several felt residents should be involved in more activities. A few attended care management reviews and had intermittent contact with care managers but none seemed to be aware of the detail of care plans for their relative.

The care-planning documents

The existing care-planning documents, which were distinguished from the personal files containing confidential information, included sections with a life history, a personal assessment, a summary highlighting goals and priorities, and individual action plans and their review. The personal assessment included: background to the admission; social interests; contacts; beliefs; general health and mobility; and self-care. A sample of the care plans were examined and found to be incomplete, with generalised and vague goals, and with reviews not always up to date.

There were different perspectives on what should be recorded within the care plans and the stage at which certain sections should be completed or reviewed. Many staff found it hard to record achievements and instead reported the failings of residents to attain goals which were unrealistic. Where they did record the progress towards identified goals, they did not necessarily record the way they worked with people, for example how to facilitate someone to drink from a cup. Whilst the importance of life history information (e.g. past occupations, experiences, interests, likes, dislikes and fears) was recognised as crucial for relevant day-to-day care for each person, the assessment and personal details sections of the document presented problems for some care assistants. They felt uncomfortable intruding into people's affairs and suspected that their intentions could be misconstrued.

Furthermore, many care assistants found the process of writing very difficult. Although they fully recognised the value of recording, particularly the daily records, to enable staff to check back on what has happened, to monitor change and to learn the current care needs of an individual, some had understandable reservations about committing pen to paper for fear of exposing their limited literacy skills.

Lack of time, especially for the morning shift, was identified as a major reason for getting behind with updating care plans, particularly the demands of responding to residents calling staff on their buzzers. Staff could delay routine tasks such as the laundry to the following shift in favour of completing updates of plans. However, it was noticeable that they claimed it was feasible to work on plans only at the weekends because there was no laundry to be sorted.

A battery of photocopied pages from daily records, district nurse visits, weight charts, sight checks, hospital appointments and lists of personal possessions filled the files, all of which were ordered differently. In one home the daily record systems and the format of goal plans varied between the units, reflecting the particular preferences of senior staff.

Two perspectives seemed to prevail among care assistants in relation to the purpose of the written care plans. First, they were seen as a tool for communicating with colleagues about residents' progress and change, and the consequent care they required defined in terms of care goals. Second, documents were seen as a policy requirement, necessitated by expectations of the inspection and regulatory authorities and organisational policy. Some staff expressed anxiety about the need for accountability taking precedence over hands-on care. However, although senior staff acknowledged that keeping records 'covered their own backs' the predominant view was that care plans were working documents and 'not just there to show that the paperwork has been done'.

A few established staff were sceptical about the value of written records as a tool for care. The predominant view, however, was that care plans encouraged staff to sit down and think about the people with whom they were working and the goals they would work out with residents. In turn, this could lead to greater interest in the residents as individuals and motivate them to do more for and with their residents. There was evidence of uncertainty, however, amongst care staff about how to use the documents and there was considerable variability in practice. Care assistants' input into determining care plans and reviewing and updating them had not been uniformly developed. It appeared that in their role as supervisors some senior staff had taken sole responsibility for identifying and reviewing goals and updating written plans. Furthermore it was evident from interviews with relatives that they had no clear idea of the care plan approach followed in the homes.

Whilst most staff recognised the importance of written information transfer in care-planning and practice, many were clearly much more comfortable with verbal information exchange on a day-to-day basis. Verbal exchange, however, is dependent upon opportunity. It is therefore ineffective when people on different shifts do not overlap, and vulnerable to misinterpretation when conveyed second hand. A great deal of information was exchanged informally as staff arrived for, and departed from, shifts, with the handover briefing providing a forum for verbally reporting recorded information of immediate relevance to staff on the next shift.

The handover was recognised generally as an important opportunity for people to clarify problems and ask questions. However, several informants felt frustrated with the content of the information and the manner of its presentation. It was variously seen as irrelevant to their immediate needs for carrying out the next shift, or too long. The conduct of the handover and the level of interaction reflected the style of the senior member of staff conveying the information, some facilitating questions and encouraging discussion more than others.

There had been an expectation on the part of many staff, including managers, that the project team would arrive complete with a set of new documents for them to try out, with an aspiration that practice would be improved simply through the expedient of using a different tool. This was not the case, however, and staff generally seemed to like the format of the existing care-planning document, even though it was often poorly completed. It therefore seemed more constructive to work towards improving the way the existing document was used rather than to replace it.

Identifying the issues

Establishing an understanding of the issues was the prime purpose of the initial inquiry phase of the project. The review of practice drew on the perspectives of staff, relatives and care managers, and the observations of the researchers. The issues that emerged were both practice and policy related. They were set in an established structural context of care-planning within the homes that applied to most residents. These structures included the methods of assessment, goal identification and review, the role of the key worker and the care plans and associated documentation. Members of the research steering group, the care-planning development group and the researchers all agreed that care-planning encompasses both process and structure issues and, in particular, is as much about the delivery of care as about the ways in which it is documented. Issues that in essence encompassed both the individual and organisational journeys relate to both policy and practice perspectives.

The dementia-specific policy-related issues are shown in Box 3.1.

Box 3.1 Dementia-specific policy-related issues

- A home for life – to what extent was it viable to provide end-of-life care in these homes?
- Case mix – to what extent was it practicable to integrate residents with dementia with residents who did not suffer from the condition?
- Skills mix – to what extent did the staff group contain the necessary skills to manage dementia-related behaviours?

These policy issues have far-reaching implications for practice. They were highlighted by all levels of staff and throughout the study. The commissioning authority had a policy of offering people, wherever possible, a home until the end of their life. The caveats: were so long as they are not a danger to themselves or others; and for as long as the staff were able to provide the necessary level of care. How this policy was enacted at the level of the individual became clear in the study as service users became increasingly dependent. The mix of residents with differing needs was a consequence of a home-for-life policy and an increase in the dependence of newly admitted residents. The staff skills reflected the recruitment and training policies over many years.

The dementia-specific practice-related issues are shown in Box 3.2.

Box 3.2 Dementia-specific practice-related issues

- identification of people with dementia
- person-centred care practices
  - identification of needs
  - planning and delivery of care
- the roles and responsibilities of staff (key workers)
  - supervision and leadership
  - communication and continuity of care
- documentation

The practice-related issues were both process and structure related. They were underpinned by the values of person-centred care that form the benchmark of good-quality care and we used this benchmark as our goal.

Action research in practice

Multiple methods of data collection were used at each stage of the project, including diaries, interviews, focus groups and observation. After a period of observation and with staff members', relatives' and residents' consent, ten residents were identified as 'cases' to follow. These people with dementia, their key workers and their relatives provided the focus for the development work. The detailed process of data collection is described below.

Diaries

Staff working with case study residents were asked to complete a diary over a 24-hour period. This involved recording the care given to the residents and how they responded. The exercise reminded staff that residents behaved differently during the day from at night. They discovered, through completing activity diaries, recording what each of the case study residents was doing and how they were occupied, that the activities routinely available in the home were not engaging the case study residents.

Staff found the diary exercises time-consuming. In turn the project team found that the diary content was recorded erratically and some staff lacked confidence in writing. Many staff found it hard to record achievements and instead reported the failings of residents to achieve goals that were unrealistic to start with. They tended to focus on organised activity rather than the daily tasks that comprise being part of a home. For example, a resident successfully pulling up a bedcover or replacing a toothbrush in a holder was disregarded as too insignificant a detail to acknowledge.

Life stories

In one home a small group of staff developed a list of topics to guide their history-taking interviews with resident and carer. Others developed a questionnaire for completion by the family carer, covering the same domains as the topic guide. Both were used and life stories were written up by the key workers. In spite of a routine-oriented regime, staff were supported by managers to find the space in which to undertake this work.

Key workers found this activity very rewarding. It encouraged them to see the residents in context and they developed a new respect for them. Development of the life stories also gave pleasure to the residents as they had undivided attention from staff, and the carers felt their role was acknowledged. As the ideas for the topics were developed by the staff it gave them a feeling of worth and achievement. For the project team the exercise reinforced the value of a bottom-up approach and the need for ownership of tools. It also reminded the team of the need to ensure that family carers were involved and that they agreed the final version of the life story and how it was to be used.

Workshop

Partway through the project staff from the care homes attended a half-day workshop. The overall aim was to identify how the care being delivered to people with dementia could be improved. The specific objectives were to:

- enable staff to recognise what providing better care involves
- enable managers to:
  - recognise what staff need in order to provide better care
  - give commitment to facilitating necessary change
- identify staff development needs.

The workshop activities were broken down into three exercises in which groups considered:

- what they had learned about residents from different methods of information gathering

- what conclusions they had reached about what residents need by using the methods tried

- how these needs could be met.

Up to this point the work of the project had focused on a person-centred approach to people with dementia and ways of improving the knowledge of all staff about their residents as the basis on which to plan care. The discussions of different methods of information gathering brought out the benefits and disadvantages of the diaries and life story work already described. The strongest message to come from the workshop discussions was confirmation of their recognition of the need for person-centred care. One participant said that 'each resident should be viewed as unique, as a person, rather than as a set of diagnoses which included dementia'.

In discussing how to meet residents' needs, all groups considered that one-to-one staff–resident quality time was important: this was also a key finding from the information-gathering exercises that they had undertaken. Staff compiled a 'wish-list' of what they felt was necessary to meet the needs of all residents, but especially those with dementia. The list covered practice organisation, communication, staff skills and commitment, interagency collaboration and environment. It was noticeable that most of the ideas were dependent upon management leadership and additional resources, for example: 'staff to be used more effectively as care staff and not domestic work', 'more overlap in shifts to improve communication and team work', 'resources to access research updates on dementia and drugs development', 'to ensure better pre-admission procedures' and 'to work in an environment that is both functional and safe'.

The final part of the workshop was to create the action plan for moving forward, focusing on keeping observation logs, assessment and reviewing care plans. This re-energised the project staff, who were flagging by this stage and feeling somewhat overwhelmed. The workshop provided a vehicle for the collective review of the project and highlighted, as follows, the issues that had to be addressed in developing care-planning in the homes. In particular it:

- confirmed that life stories were a valuable vehicle for enabling better understanding of residents and for clarifying strategies for action plans

- highlighted that work needed to be done on assessments

- highlighted the perception that an individualised approach to care needed resources, i.e. staff time, that were rarely available

- highlighted that a change in attitudes by most staff, towards a greater involvement with residents and careful observation, would take some considerable time to achieve.

Enhanced assessment

A small group of staff reviewed the assessment section of the care plan and developed detailed prompts for each topic. The document was then tested on newly admitted and current residents. The staff found the modifications useful because they helped them to pursue topics such as 'values and beliefs' that they had previously been unable to frame. New and more relevant information was uncovered.

The input from relatives

Relatives of the case study residents were very willing to become involved and played an important role in the project. They were provided with verbal and written outlines of the study purposes and objectives, and the protocol for data collection, and subsequently consent to participation was obtained. The relatives' involvement included interviews with the researcher, interviews with staff as part of life story building, providing photographs and memorabilia, and testing questionnaires.

Relatives' views were sought about the care environment, their perceptions of the needs of their relative and whether or not those needs were being met, and their aspirations for the future of their relative. For some, sharing an account of the admission process was important as it gave them an opportunity to express some of their feelings of loss. Relatives helped staff by agreeing to be interviewed. In one case this involved two semi-structured interviews that included the resident. In another example several interviews were conducted by telephone and another participant, living at a greater distance, wrote up their version of their relative's life story.

Review

The review process was ongoing throughout the duration of the project. It was supported by the care-planning group of managers and the research team, the workshop, and ongoing informal discussions. In-depth interviews were conducted with all levels of staff who had participated, with family carers and with some care managers.

Did action research improve care-planning?

We observed some small but important adjustments in the attitudes of individual staff and their practice over the course of the project. The advantages of the case study approach were that it gave a picture of both the changes in the condition of the person with dementia and the ways in which care staff responded to changing needs. Of the ten case study residents, over a period of twelve months two residents died and one was moved to a nursing home. The dementia-related conditions of three residents worsened considerably, three residents deteriorated to the extent that they required hospitalisation, and one went on holiday and was so disturbed by the experience that staff found difficulty in coping with her and felt that her personality had changed.

By focusing primarily on the case study residents the variability in the quality of care by different staff became very apparent. Although in early discussions care assistants and senior staff identified person-centred care as synonymous with good practice, they illustrated their views by focusing on the care needed for personal hygiene and safety, seemingly giving lesser priority to the emotional and spiritual needs of residents. This prioritising, which was driven by the needs of the group as well as the individual, emphasises caring as doing things to and for people rather than with them. We endeavoured to address this imbalance by encouraging staff to reflect on their total experience. Whilst we do not suggest that reflection was a new experience for all care staff their comments indicated that a few key workers were challenged by the project to review their care and, in particular, some recognised the extent to which residents' lives had become routinised.

Key observations about the outcome of this approach are shown in Boxes 3.3, 3.4 and 3.5. Whilst Box 3.6 identifies the challenges to achieving change.

Box 3.3 Impact of project on staff and their care practices

- Care staff found it was useful to be involved in modifying the tools.
- Some care staff reported being challenged to think more carefully about their practice.
- There was some evidence of more positive recording in daily notes and new goals being identified that were specific to the person and recognised his or her dementia.
- Less positively, several staff who initially expressed interest opted out: explanations for doing so included lack of time, lack of practical management support and problems with writing.
- Other staff complained that the project was taking staff time away from non-case study residents.
- The project asked staff to become engaged with activities that some felt were outside their contractual remit.

Box 3.4 Impact on residents

- Residents seemed to enjoy the extra attention. For example, one male resident looked forward to the time with a key worker spent looking at a book of photographs of the town where he lived as a young man; a female resident took pleasure in sharing her life story book, completed with pictures and mementoes up to the present time.
- For others, the quality of their lives was enhanced through more appropriate attention to details of care such as wearing a hearing aid that had previously been overlooked, or having someone sit and share viewing a television programme with them.

Box 3.5 Impact on families

- Most families who became involved did so willingly and said that they benefited from getting to know the key worker better.
- A positive result of the project for some residents and their families was the recognition, in one of the homes in particular, of the need to involve families much more actively, especially at admission.

Box 3.6 Challenges to achieving change

- Major organisational change within the provider authority, a seemingly perpetual feature of the sector, had an unsettling effect on the homes throughout the lifetime of the project.
- Because of fixed-term employment contracts some staff did not feel motivated towards the project; those who were willing to invest in it often did so in their own time, showing great commitment to the residents.
- A key observation in the feedback given in each home was the importance of management support and leadership in encouraging staff to effect changes to practice.
- Home managers were often torn between meeting the needs of the many as opposed to the needs of the few.
- Care managers, who were members of work teams, did not generally see residential care homes as the appropriate placement for people with dementia. Their level of involvement with people varied as dementia progressed. Apart from reviews, they had little role in the detail of care-planning within the homes.
- Care managers' expertise seemed to be offered erratically. Care staff asked for it usually only at the point where managing a resident's behaviour became too difficult within the home and a new placement was sought.

Clearly it is unrealistic to assume that changes can be implemented without considering the range of factors that influence the context in which day-to-day care is delivered. This context includes structural factors, staffing issues, relationships with external interests and management culture as key features. The various ways in which these factors were found to impact on care-planning for people with dementia within the current project are shown in Table 3.1.

Table 3.1 Factors influencing the implementation of person-centred care-planning for people with dementia within care homes

Factor type	Factor	Rationale
Structural factors	Type of home (e.g. personal care or nursing care, specialist dementia care, integrated dementia unit)	Different types of home may have different approaches to professional accountability and views about the role of the written record. Integrated units within a larger home may require a different approach to care-planning and this might be difficult to implement.
	Size of home	In general the larger the care units the more staff will need to rely on good care-planning documentation to transmit information.
	Type of provider organisation	Homes that are part of a larger organisation are likely to have organisation-wide documentation with which they have to comply.
Staffing	Staff ratios	Staff ratios have a significant impact on the amount of time that staff have available to plan and document care, as well as impacting on the nature and quality of care that they are able to deliver.
	Shift patterns	Shift patterns have a significant impact on continuity of care. Sharing information between day and night staff is an important issue.
	Roles and responsibilities	Roles and responsibilities between different grades of staff vary considerably between homes, for example, the extent to which care staff are involved in drawing up care plans.
	Staff stability	Stability of staff is good for continuity of relationships but can result in patterns of work becoming entrenched and inflexible. High staff turnover makes it difficult to undertake development work.

Factor type	Factor	Rationale
	Staff development	This is central to the development of care-planning but there is considerable variation between homes in their capacity to access the funding and expertise needed to support staff development.
Management culture	Service models	Homes have different models of service underpinning their activities (e.g. social care model, nursing model), and this influences care-planning.
	Values and philosophies	Homes operate in line with different sets of values and philosophies. Most homes espouse person-centred care but this is interpreted and implemented differently in different places.
	Management style and leadership	A demonstrated commitment on the part of a manager makes it more possible for staff to develop and implement new approaches.
	Staff morale	To make progress with care-planning. development staff must feel valued and not be preoccupied with the effects of other organisational changes.
External relationships	Principally with social services, a range of health services and the registration and inspection systems.	The initial care management assessment makes an important contribution to in-home care-planning Most residents in homes have some contacts with external health services and it is important that care-planning arrangements address communication at this interface.

Conclusions

There is evidence that the true percentage of people with dementia in residential homes is considerably higher than identified by the staff in the study sites. Matthews and Dening (2002) suggested that within residential and nursing homes in the UK dementia prevalence may be higher than 60 per cent and that such levels must have implications for the type of care that these homes provide. Social settings are both powerful and fragile environments (Moos 2003) where the interaction between individuals and their social contexts is often characterised and constrained by notions of risk balanced against rights, responsibilities and individual freedoms. This is never more true than in institutional settings and it is the responsibility of provider organisations, home managers and their staff to harness that power and maintain that balance in a positive, emancipatory way for the advantage of their residents.

An important first step in achieving these goals is to ensure appropriate assessment prior to entry into care homes. Challis *et al.* (2004) commented on the benefits of identifying undiagnosed conditions and improving care managers' decision-making through timely specialist assessment. Furthermore, and in support of staff reports from the study sites, Mozley *et al.* (1999) provide one of many studies confirming that a high proportion of older people are able to talk about their quality of life, in spite of having significant cognitive deficits.

People with dementia require not only attention to their physical needs but also to their emotional and spiritual needs. In particular they need:

- individualised planned care that pays attention to the details of their life history and is based on thorough and ongoing assessment

- ongoing and appropriate responses to their mood changes

- sensory stimulation and exercise

- a safe environment

- maintained links with family and community

- support of sufficient skilled and dedicated staff with an interest in them and an empathy with their experience.

Recognition of these needs implies a value base for the service that is empowering to all residents. In this respect the needs of older people with dementia are the same as those without dementia. However, the *way* in which their needs are met may have to be different. The project highlighted some changes that could be adopted and built into everyday practice.

Care plans need to be achievable and encompass both social care and health needs. They should be frequently reviewed and updated as needs change. In order to improve continuity of care across shifts key workers should work together with other staff, relatives and the person with dementia to determine goals of care and strategies for achieving them. They should prioritise plans that emphasise the uniqueness of the individuals and their special wishes and inclinations as well as their physical needs.

They should take a collective, consultative approach to identifying care needs and residents' wishes prior to formulating care plans.

Care plans should be kept in a safe but accessible location. Homes vary in the extent to which, and how, residents 'own' their care plans. For example, some homes keep care plans in residents' rooms whilst others see them as documentation that is held in the staff domain. Similarly, some homes permit relatives' to have easy access to them and others do not. The approach of homes in this respect is often related to the extent to which they adopt a truly person-centred model of care and their overall approach to service-user and relative involvement in influencing life within the home.

Whilst it may be axiomatic to suggest that the role of the care assistant is pivotal to residents' experience of care, individuals varied in their aptitude for caring for people with dementia. Recruiting staff with the needs of people with dementia in mind appears to be a necessary strategy if homes are to provide appropriate care. In the view of one informant this meant being prepared to take risks and being able to recognise the individuality of each resident and desire to maximise their potential. Within this project, many staff seemed unsure of their ability to fulfil the care needs of people with dementia. They felt ill-equipped in terms of knowledge of the disease and skills in communicating and managing changes in behaviour. Training courses that not only provide a theoretical overview but also introduce problem-solving strategies are essential for staff development.

The experience from this study suggests that if we are to develop care-planning successfully, there needs to be a move beyond the focus on written plans. It is also necessary to ensure that the development of care-planning is empowering for all concerned and embedded within the organisational context. Action research is an inclusive activity. As such its approach reflects some of the basic principles of person-centred care by trying to uncover the perspectives of participants.

Whilst there are inevitable questions of resources, this project did demonstrate the extent to which incentivising, motivating and empowering staff could be achieved within a reappraisal of existing resources. Care-planning for people with dementia should be about individual rather than generic plans and should start from the uniqueness of each person. In particular, the project reinforced the need for a more positive attitude to people with dementia within provider policy and for staff to be valued and to feel that they can make a contribution to developmental activities. There must, therefore, be opportunities for staff to develop skills and knowledge.

Of course, it can always be argued that staffing levels need to be more generous to allow staff time to be with residents, but real differences can be made by reappraising priorities and roles. However, most importantly, the right staff must be recruited: those who are able to develop the 'us' relationship, who have empathy with the people they care for, and who share and reflect upon their practice.

Acknowledgements

With acknowledgements to Caroline Cantley, former Professor of Dementia Care and Monica Smith, former Research Associate, Dementia North, Northumbria University.

References

Challis, D., Clarkson, P., Williamson, J., Hughes, J. *et al.* (2004) 'The value of specialist clinical assessment of older people prior to entry to care homes.' *Age and Ageing 33*, 1, 25–34.

Hart, E. and Bond, M. (1995) *Action Research for Health and Social Care: A Guide to Practice.* Buckingham: Open University Press.

Matthews, F.E. and Dening, T. (2002) 'Prevalence of dementia in institutional care.' *The Lancet 360*, 9328, 225–226.

Moos, R. (2003) 'Social contexts: Transcending their power and fragility.' *American Journal of Community Psychology 31*, 1–2, 1–13.

Mozley, C.G., Huxley, P., Sutcliffe, C., Bagley, H. *et al.* (1999) "Not knowing where I am doesn't mean I don't know what I like": Cognitive impairment and the quality of life response in elderly people.' *International Journal of Geriatric Psychiatry 14*, 9, 776–783.

National Audit Office (2007) *Improving services and support for people with dementia. Report by the Comptroller and Auditor General.* London: The Stationery Office.

OECD (2005) 'The OECD Health Project: Long-term care for older people.' *OECD Social Issues/Migration/Health Volume 2005*, 11, i-140(141). OECD Publishing.

Patton, M.Q. (2002) *Qualitative Research and Evaluation Methods* (3rd edn). London: Sage.

Silverman, D. (2006) *Interpreting Qualitative Data: Method for Analyzing Talk, Text and Interaction* (3rd edn). London: Sage.

Vreven, L. (2006) *Advancing International Long-term Care Initiatives through Cross-Atlantic Exchange.* AARP Global Report on Ageing, special issue. Available at www.aarp.org/research/international/gra/fall2006/from_the_editor.html, accessed November 2007.

Wortley, S. (2000) 'Business as usual or action research in practice?' *Action Research E-Reports 6.* Available at www.2fhs.usyd.edu.au/arow/arer/006.htm, accessed August 2007.

CHAPTER 4

The Use of Narrative in Developing Relationships in Care Homes

Christine Brown Wilson, Glenda Cook and Denise Forte

Introduction

With the move to a care home, older people face significant changes in their social relationships. While there is the possibility of developing new relationships as they meet and get to know fellow residents and staff in the home, they may experience difficulty in sustaining the same quality of relationship with family, friends and acquaintances (Cook 2006; Hubbard, Tester and Downs 2004). Older people invest considerable emotional energy in maintaining and developing relationships following the move to a home. However, what they achieve often goes unrecognised by care home staff, the danger being that residents can remain unsupported in their efforts. As relationships develop, older people may share stories about themselves containing key messages that have the potential to influence care delivered by staff. For this to happen, staff need to be able to hear what older people are saying and distil these key messages in order to identify any implications for their practice.

This chapter uses narratives derived from three research studies carried out by the authors and others, to draw attention to the social relationships that develop in the context of care homes. The chapter begins with a discussion of narrative research as an approach that has the potential to privilege the views of older people and illuminate possibilities for developing the relationships that older residents experience. We then move on to present and analyse a number of narratives, and conclude with some recommendations for practice development based on this analysis.

Uses and challenges of story-telling in care homes research

In Western society, there has been a renewed interest in story-telling in recent years. This is evident in media accounts of daily news where the human interest story takes centre ground to poignantly tell the story of an event, natural disaster or personal tragedy. Through the story, events are portrayed from the individual's point of view and the meaning and impact of that experience is made available publically. Narrative study is becoming increasingly recognised as a powerful vehicle for understanding unique human experiences in a range of social conditions (Hurwitz, Greenhalgh and Skultans 2004; Zaner 2003). This is also evident in care homes research, where there is increasing recognition of the need to understand individuals' perception of their experiences through narration (NCHRDF 2007). Accessing these experiences, however, is not always straightforward. Older people who have moved to a care home often encounter situations where they are marginalised from decisions that affect their lives and living conditions (Reed *et al.* 2003; Sandberg, Lundh and Nolan 2001). They are disempowered when their views and concerns are ignored. The context of the care home has the potential to influence the way older residents respond to a research encounter. They may hesitate in agreeing to participate in research and, when they consent to take part, they may be concerned that their views will be disregarded or rejected. Hence, older people need continuous reassurance that their views are important and will be taken seriously.

Chamberlayne, Bornat and Wengraf (2000), in their discussion of biographical methods, have argued that the social context of the research encounter and the participants' perceptions of their role in this shape dialogue and the data elicited: 'life story, as told, may be a product of a life made ready for public consumption in a situation where identity is at risk from the negative stereotypes of frailty and the processes and procedures of caring' (p.10).

These ideas are particularly relevant to the field of care homes research. Older residents live with the impact of stereotypes of frailty, old age and being a recipient of care, and this can influence what they disclose to others. Even when the social context has been taken into consideration, older residents face other challenges when they attempt to participate in research. Communication problems, sensory impairment(s) and/or cognitive constraints may limit their ability and confidence to take part in data collection processes. In these circumstances it is important that individuals feel comfortable and confident to express their views. During everyday interaction, residents use a range of strategies to communicate their views to others. Amongst these, story-telling is a comfortable, non-threatening approach that enables dialogue to take place. Through story-telling older people readily discuss everyday events and reflect on the feelings, sentiments, images, desires and thoughts that were associated with those stories. In the context of research, story-telling has been adapted to enable older people to enter into a narration of their experiences, thoughts, ideas and desires for the explicit purpose of eliciting data (see for example, Biggs *et al.* 2000; Jovchelovitch and Bauer 2000; Plummer 1997).

When older residents are invited to give accounts of their life and its events through story-telling, careful attention is required to overcome the practical and social barriers to participation. For example, individuals with expressive dysphasia will be supported to tell their story if a strategy of waiting or pausing whilst they search for the words to describe their experience is negotiated with them. Similarly, careful planning of the location is important to those with hearing impairment to ensure that there is minimal background noise that may interrupt the discussion. Practical issues such as these need to be recognised and addressed in order to support older people in telling their stories.

Privileging the voice of older people requires more than good will; it demands considerable thought and planning. Prolonged engagement between the participant and researcher is important to build trust. In the main, care home studies have adopted methodologies that require limited engagement with older people such as single interviews to investigate a particular aspect of care home life. When researchers complete their brief episodes of data collection they leave. Residents, however, live in the home prior to and following data collection, and this may adversely affect disclosure during the research encounter. Methodologies such as narrative interviewing over an extended period of time provide the opportunity for researchers to build trust with their participants. Importantly, this opens up the possibility that discussion may move beyond issues that were made ready for public consumption. It also challenges the moral responsibility of the researcher to balance the needs of the research process with the rights of residents to privacy and to disclose only information that they want to impart.

In the field of care homes research narration is now being used as a way of highlighting the views of older residents to reveal how care home life is experienced. The voice of older residents has been almost silent for far too long, the danger being that current knowledge of life in a care home may not reflect the experience of residents. By accessing the perceptions and experiences of those who live in care homes, widely held views can be questioned, reaffirmed or challenged. This is also important in influencing the development of practice and services in ways that ensure their appropriateness and acceptability to older people.

The narratives

This chapter draws upon narratives from three studies (see Study A – Cook 2007; Study B – Brown Wilson 2007; Study C – Forte, Cotter and Wells 2006 for in-depth details of each study). The studies were carried out in geographically diverse areas of England. Each study utilised a hermeneutic approach, which Rodwell (1998) describes as a circle of information created between participants and the researcher to enable the sharing of perspectives to support the development of shared meanings. This dialectic process enabled the perspectives of the participants to be checked and refined, supporting older people, families and staff to talk about everyday situations that may not always be considered important. These situations were often recounted through informal stories related to everyday events within the care homes. From these stories, more formal accounts or narratives emerged.

Many of the narratives from these studies revealed how older people, their families and friends worked hard to reconstruct their life and relationships following the move to a care home, and as they continued to live there. The narratives that will be presented in this chapter affirm the importance of relationships in the older person's experience of care home life. Ronch (2004) describes narration as a powerful tool in communicating the values within a home and the narratives within this chapter demonstrate how the use of story-telling enables residents' voices to be heard within a communal setting. Extending this approach from research to practice may encourage staff to find practical ways for improving the experience of residents and families by listening to stories of everyday events.

From the analysis of narratives from the three studies, a range of factors that may influence the development and maintenance of relationships have emerged. The following sections in the chapter consider what these narratives have revealed about relationships in care homes and suggest ways in which the understandings that were developed from the narratives can be used to develop practice.

Changes in social relationships

Changes in existing relationships occur immediately on entry to a care home. Meetings with family and friends, for example, now always take place always within the context of visiting, which alters the nature of the relationship. Residents are now dependent on the willingness and ability of family and friends to visit them. When they do meet, the nature of their interaction may differ as the balance of giving and receiving within their relationships changes. Familiar patterns of interaction may no longer exist and residents may be less able to make a contribution to their relationships in their accustomed manner, for example offering food and refreshment. Nevertheless, older residents want to keep in touch with family and friends and they strive to develop ways to achieve this:

> ...and another friend she comes nearly every day... I have not got many left now and two are away at the moment and my friend in D, she had a fall. She is about 20 years younger than me. She was in hospital for a while so she couldn't get over. I rang my friend and could not get in touch, so I thought that I had the wrong number as I couldn't get hold of her... you see I don't use the phone very much you know. I am not at all good on the phone now [as a consequence of her speech difficulties following a stroke]. I find that writing to my friends is a good way to keep in touch. But I manage, that is the main thing.
>
> Edna, resident (Study A)

Following the move to the care home Edna wanted to maintain long-term friendships and achieved this through enlisting the support of care staff to take dictation from her, enabling her to send and receive letters from friends.

This example highlights the difficulties one woman experienced in maintaining existing relationships following the move to a care home and is indicative of older residents' constant struggles to maintain their social relationships. Many residents experience communication, sensory, physical and cognitive problems that exacerbate their difficulties in maintaining relationships, yet they invest considerable emotional energy in developing ways to continue to engage with other people (Cook 2006; Davies 2003). This suggests that relationships between family, long-term friends, residents and staff are important to older residents and evidence is increasingly pointing to the impact of the older person's engagement in social relationships on self-perceived quality of life and life satisfaction (Bowers, Fibich and Jacobson 2001; Murphy *et al.* 2004). Staff listening to residents speaking about their past lives may provide insight into the significant relationships residents have enjoyed with those outside of the care home and help them to find ways of supporting residents in maintaining these relationships:

> I have a good friend who lives in the next village but there is no public transport so it is difficult for her to come and see me. The staff will take me there in a car about once a month, then some friends will drop me back, so that's how we keep in touch.
>
> Beatrice, resident (Study B)

As well as the intrinsic problems that residents encounter in maintaining their relationships, the time that residents spend with people is also subject to various restrictions. Visiting is usually flexible in care homes, but there are often implicit agreements between residents, staff and visitors whereby visiting usually takes place between late morning and early evening. Relatives and friends also have constraints on their time which in turn impacts on visiting. Factors such as the geographic locality of the home and access via public transport also influence how frequently family and friends visit those living in a care home:

> I didn't realise how lucky I was to be in here because it is so handy for everybody, well all of my people who visit me. It is so handy for them – well my sister lives in H [5 miles away], and she gets the bus right to the door.
>
> Charles, resident (Study A)

Families and friends also work very hard at maintaining a special relationship with residents by continuing routines or rituals they had at home, although staff may often be unaware of this activity (Brown Wilson 2007; Sandberg *et al.* 2001). New routines are also established to maintain regular and meaningful interaction. Telephone calls at a set time and day, going out for meals together, and participation in social events enable the older person to experience enjoyment. Archibald (1999) suggested that when relatives and friends were encouraged to work with the older person in developing a life story book or other activities the quality of the visit could improve, enhancing their relationship. Staff could also contribute to this type of activity, with stories shared with them by the resident being included in a life story book. This type of practice would assist staff to get to know residents as individuals and the knowledge gained could be used to tailor care-planning to individual needs.

The stories highlighted in this section affirm the importance of residents maintaining involvement with family and friends, which is an important link to their personal history and enhances the quality of their life when living in a care home. While this has been reported in the care home literature, these stories shed light on the subtle changes that older people experience and their responses (Friedmann *et al.* 1997; Rowles and High 1996; Sandberg *et al.* 2001).

The social context of care home life

Care homes are complex social environments. They are places where people live, work and visit; and those people are continually changing. Hence social relationships are in a constant state of flux. This can be difficult for older residents who want to get to know other people and interact with them as there are many features of this environment that mitigate against this. The previous discussion highlighted some of the difficulties that residents face in maintaining long-term friendships and relationships with family. When they move to a care home they work to develop relationships with staff, fellow residents and visitors to the home and this often starts with the sharing of personal stories. Staff could use these stories to identify areas of common interest with other residents and so facilitate introductions and opportunities for meaningful activity within the home:

> She [resident] told me how she used to attract birds to her garden, so now I think to do something with her like with the nuts and the bird things… She'll talk to me the next time she sees me that the birds haven't come yet…then she'll talk to her son and daughter-in-law about it when they come, and she tells them what we've been doing…in a way you could almost say it was a spiritual kind of care really.
>
> Ann Marie, care worker (Study B)

Developing relationships with others can be made easier with a welcoming environment in which the older resident is made to feel part of the care home community. For example, staff attitudes such as smiling and spending the time getting to know the residents and their needs can do much to offset some of the less positive aspects of moving into a care home.

Furthermore, staff recognising the value of an older person's experiences in his or her life prior to coming into the home can also facilitate the development of relationships within the home.

Care homes are environments for living in as well as working in, and they can be isolated from local communities. Consequently, developing and sustaining relationships can be complex. Care staff can support older people by:

- ensuring the environment is open and welcoming to family, friends and the local community
- valuing the development of meaningful relationships between staff and residents as well as supporting functional interaction
- implementing staff assignment processes that enhance continuity in social interaction between staff and residents.

Relationships with staff are often valued by residents and provide opportunities for sharing mutually enjoyable times:

> Oh I had every faith in her. Every faith she could have taken me anywhere and I would have gone. You don't meet many people in life like that and know so early on in the relationship... I might take years to get to that stage with somebody else but with her it was just natural from the beginning. Just natural she would talk about her family and she wanted to know all about mine. What made them go to Australasia and all the rest of it. So sympathetic when I told her about my sister dying out there.
>
> Anne, resident (Study A)

Residents often attempt to remember names, personal details and interests of other people as a way of initiating interaction. This is not easy in an environment where the routines of the home operate in ways that determine the extent that people can interact with each other and in situations where there is a rapid turnover of staff:

> You never know who is going to walk through the door when you wake up in the morning and when they bring your breakfast in. You ask their name and you ask that half a dozen times during the day because you have forgotten and the next thing you know they have gone and they don't even say goodbye – they just disappear.
>
> Anne, resident (Study A)

Such comments point to the constraints that exist within care homes, yet older people value the relationships that they form with fellow residents, staff and visitors following the move to a home. While their stories high-light the difficulties residents encounter they also point to aspects of practice that staff could develop to improve the quality of experience for residents.

Developing new relationships with fellow residents

Although the importance of relationships between residents is now being recognised, (Cook, Brown Wilson and Forte 2006; Hubbard *et al.* 2004), this subject has been largely neglected in the care home literature (Reed and Payton 1997). Residents interact with each other mainly at pre-determined points during the day focused around care home routines such as meal times and organised activities. This is not suggesting that social interaction lacks spontaneity. Chance meetings do occur as residents move about the care home; however, routines and rituals contribute to a pattern of the same people meeting regularly. These 'coming togethers' promote social interaction, which provides the foundation for the development of relationships within the care home setting:

> Well it was that I just happened to sit there, near her and she said, 'You're the only one I can hear,' and she kept saying 'Is Freda down yet?' … In the course of talking of course it came out we were both teachers.

> Freda, resident (Study B)

As residents become increasingly frail and dependent, they may be unable to nurture relationships actively, which suggests that there is a greater role for staff in supporting residents to develop new relationships within the care home setting:

> …it did evolve, as time has gone on, Gwen's mental state has improved and obviously you want to put two like-minded people together and it just crept up on us really that they could talk to each other, and then you want to put people where they can converse with each other, and she can hear Freda.

> Jane, deputy matron (Study B)

Care workers sometimes assume that older people are unable to make or sustain relationships with each other and this means that a central feature of communal living for older people is largely neglected by staff (Reed and Payton 1997). This may have a significant impact on the daily experience of older people in care homes. For example, Murphy *et al.* (2004) found that residents' quality of life was improved when care staff supported relationships between residents. In Study B, staff recognised the importance of relationships with other residents through listening to the stories residents shared with them and consistently seated residents to facilitate these relationships. One resident commented on the importance of having other residents seated nearby due to her vision and hearing impairment:

> There are two people I sit near and I can hear to talk with, everyone else is so far away. I would be lost without them. I can talk to Freda because I can hear her. She keeps me up to date. I usually have to ask her what's for dinner. I should feel lost if there wasn't the three of us.
>
> Gwen, resident (Study B)

Social interaction between people living and working in a care home is qualitatively different to engagement between family and friends. Interaction between family members develops from familial ties, shared history and common bonds, whereas interaction between friends is grounded in intimacy, mutual understanding and reciprocity (Jerrome 1993). In contrast, those living and working in care homes come together out of the need to receive and give care. The prominence of these factors tends to focus interaction on the functional aspects of life rather than emphasising social preferences, experiences and the interests that people share. Developing relationships within the care home setting can therefore be difficult as the following narrative illustrates:

> Cause I am not a good mixer. I'll tell you what happens. I used to go down to the sitting room which is beautifully decorated with lovely armchairs and lovely furnishings and photographs. Really nice, you couldn't get it more homely. They keep changing things around which makes things worse for me. Never mind... I have been talking to a woman for ages and the next day I wheel myself past her because I cannot see her and I don't recognise her.
>
> Anne, resident (Study A)

Throughout many of the stories that Anne told about her life in the care home she highlighted the various ways that her visual problems led to difficulty in establishing and maintaining relationships with other people who lived in the home. Her story about her earlier life is one of an outgoing sociable woman. In her narrative she discusses the problems she faces when trying to mix with others who are living in the care home. She feels embarrassed because she is aware that she continually breaches normal social conventions when she fails to acknowledge others following initial introductions and discussions.

In summary, older people in care homes value the opportunity to develop relationships with other residents. However, physical or cognitive frailty may create barriers to developing relationships. Therefore, staff need to be supported to:

- listen to the stories residents tell about their lives

- introduce residents who may have shared interests to each other and arrange for those with common interests to sit together

- be aware of the difficulties some residents may have in developing relationships and find practical ways to support them if they wish.

In addition to sensory problems, residents may experience difficulty in communicating with each other:

> I am about the only one here that can speak. Unfortunately everybody else has had a stroke and their speech is a bit affected… It is really difficult when there is nobody that you can converse with except for the people who come to see you… I know everybody here but there is nobody that I can go and talk to.

> Charles, resident (Study A)

Situations such as this suggest that being together does not always guarantee friendships or intimacy. Similarly, a shared environment does not necessarily imply shared interests (Abbott, Fisk and Forward 2000). Consequently, residents may experience social and emotional isolation within the care home environment (Nolan, Grant and Nolan 1995; McKee *et al.* 2005). Abbott *et al.* (2000) suggest that the experience of social participation for older people in care homes is perhaps one of adjustment rather than friendship. This was echoed in the comments of a participant in Study A:

> You are not forced to mix. It is just as well because I haven't anything in common with these [residents] as far as I can make out. I am just as happy to be on my own and see my friends when they call.

> Charles, resident (Study A)

Adjustment is also required when residents experience deterioration in their health and when a resident dies. If close relationships have been formed this may be a source of grief and mourning:

> I would say that there is no family atmosphere as far as I am concerned…

People die and they are all ancient that are in here and you no sooner get to know somebody just through being in the dining room together and somebody goes, you always getting changed. You hardly get to know somebody and then someone else is there you know.

Florence, resident (Study A)

These stories suggest that residents are keen to develop relationships with other residents but may experience difficulties due to sensory impairment or the fear of losing people who have become friends. Prior to entry into a care home many older people have faced a series of losses and developing new relationships with other residents may feel too much of a challenge. Consequently a resident may withdraw to his or her room, only engaging with staff in any meaningful way. When staff become aware that residents are choosing this avenue, sensitive listening to residents' stories may provide insight into how to support them in developing meaningful relationships with others.

The findings presented in this section suggest that it is important for staff to be aware of residents' needs and desires and to support them to develop relationships with others living in the home. Often this support is simply achieved by introducing residents to each other, and organising the environment in such a way as to promote interaction. The following section continues to examine the theme of relationships between residents. Using narratives from staff, it provides insight into how practice may be developed to support intimate relationships within the care home setting.

Maintaining a sense of identity and developing intimate relationships

As discussed in previous sections, the move to a care home brings with it many disruptions to an older person's life and can threaten his or her sense of identity. The maintenance of previous relationships and intimacies is key to providing a sense of biographical continuity for the older person (Archibald 1998; Wells 2000). Any move to a care home has the potential to disrupt residents' intimate relationships, which may impact on their sense of self. Staff need to be aware of this and actively support an environment that encourages both the relationships that the person brings to the home and any new relationships. However, there may be little recognition among staff that relationships and intimacy form an important aspect of the psychological backdrop for older people and their relatives/friends/ significant others at this transitional time.

Story-telling can help to develop relationships that provide residents with a sense of identity in a number of ways. For example, a better under-standing of the person may enable staff to provide a wider choice of sensitive care respecting dignity and cultural identity. Use of biography provides the opportunity for residents to feel valued for who they are and what they have done. This is particularly important for people with cogni-tive difficulties. Recognising that residents retain a need for intimacy also supports their sense of identity. Davidson and Fennell (2004) suggest that to love and be loved is arguably one of the most powerful and fundamental driving forces for sustaining self-esteem and self-identity, and the need for reciprocal loving does not necessarily diminish with age. Indeed, the need for intimate relationships, and the friendship and acceptance that accom-pany such relationships, is vitally important to the well-being of older people entering or living in a care home (Forte *et al.* 2006; Heath and White 2002). In the previous section examples were given of how staff rec-ognised the relationships residents developed with each other. This section draws on excerpts from staff narratives in Study C to describe the choices made by a couple with dementia and the support they received from their relatives and staff to help them sustain their intimate relationship. Using narratives from staff within this care home provides insights into the ways in which staff were able to develop their practice. They provided an envi-ronment that supported the intimate relationship formed by this couple and in turn managed to support their sense of self at a time of increasing losses due to the move and their dementia.

George and Rosie were both suffering from moderately severe demen-tia with impaired verbal skills. They first met in hospital and formed a close relationship, supporting each other to maintain the degree of independ-ence they had. This suggests that the need for intimacy, love and a variety of relationships does not cease simply because people are labelled 'old' or experience cognitive impairment. Some staff members, together with relatives of the couple, recognised the importance of this relationship in maintaining George and Rosie's sense of self and identity and were keen to support their move to the same care home. However, other staff at the hospital were less aware of the importance of their relationship and did not take it into account when discharging George. It was only when it seemed likely that Rosie might also be discharged to the home that they thought to mention it. As the senior care manager says:

I don't think there was an intention for her to be placed here; it just happened that this was where the first vacancy came up.

Senior care manager (Study C)

This highlights the vulnerability of relationships when the older people involved are not able to communicate their needs verbally. George and Rosie could easily have found themselves permanently separated, with negative consequences for their relationship and their individual sense of self. They were already vulnerable to a loss of identity because of their dementia and it could be argued that the fact that they had developed an intimate relationship was essential to enhancing their self-esteem and protecting them against any further loss.

Staff members in the unit were supportive of the couple but were surprised at how George and Rosie immediately recognised each other despite being separated for some weeks. The first night in the home Rosie slept in her own room but the next night she simply moved into George's room. Initially staff members were taken aback but were sensitive enough to support Rosie's decision:

She moved in there. It seemed almost natural for her to do that. I remember the staff at the time…it rather took them aback at first… Here were two people who seemed relatively confused but were making very closed decisions, there was no messing, you know, for them, there was no questioning.

Senior staff member (Study C)

Although George and Rosie both experienced severe cognitive impairment they were able to gain support and comfort from their relationship. Which partner took the lead in the relationship oscillated between George and Rosie depending on the circumstances. From their interactions it became apparent that they were drawing on each other's strengths to function as a couple. However, to support residents in maintaining an intimate relationship staff need to possess a range of skills, particularly the ability to see the relationship as 'normal'. For example, how should staff react when the couple seem to be upset with each other?

I think we all found that difficult; what's happening? Are they breaking up? What should we be doing? And what we realised was do nothing. They are having a tiff, what relationship doesn't?

Senior staff member (Study C)

The above narrative points to the difficulty of enabling the couple to have the privacy they need. Their cognitive impairment made this couple particularly vulnerable and, if staff had not recognised the importance of providing a supportive environment where they were able to develop and maintain intimacy, their relationship could have been jeopardised. Davies, Aveyard and Norman (2005) suggest that staff need to develop empathic understanding and work imaginatively and creatively with people experiencing dementia. Maintaining privacy and dignity were particular areas where staff felt challenged in working with George and Rosie:

> I had to involve the staff as well...because they both needed a level of input, assistance with washing and dressing... There were issues, particularly at the beginning, if we tried to work with one or the other, the other person would very much want to be there, be involved and that created some problems I think for the staff. They found that quite difficult, how do we separate them?

> Senior staff member (Study C)

This story highlights the dilemmas staff might face when supporting such intimate relationships and enabling a couple to share the same room but at the same time affording them privacy. The need for creativity in working practices and sensitivity on the part of staff is evident in the narratives about George and Rosie. Support from relatives and home managers as well as trained staff sensitive to the needs of residents are essential if older people are to be able to develop the types of intimacy they desire and live fulfilling lives within a care home. In particular, in order to provide an environment where intimate relationships can be sustained staff need to:

- feel supported in helping residents to regain or sustain a mutually supportive relationship
- be flexible in care delivery to meet the expected and unexpected needs of residents
- ensure that a couple, whether heterosexual or same sex, have the privacy they need
- be vigilant that the relationship is mutual and that both residents are continuing to consent to it
- establish a forum where all concerns for staff and residents can be discussed openly
- be prepared to support both partners if the relationship ends.

The previous sections have illustrated the importance of supporting residents in developing and maintaining relationships within care homes. Extracts from narratives captured within the context of three care homes suggest the skills needed by staff when working with residents, their families and each other to enable residents to develop and maintain their important relationships as well as fostering their sense of identity. Not all residents wish, or are able, to develop relationships with other residents. These residents, however, often value their relationships with friends, families or staff and should be supported to maintain them.

Using stories to develop practice in care homes

In this chapter stories have been used to derive general principles in relation to supporting residents to develop and sustain relationships. Ronch (2004) suggests that putting the spotlight on the everyday practice of staff has been found to be a powerful way of setting the process of change in motion. Care staff can use stories they hear and tell every day to develop their practice. This calls for a re-evaluation of communication strategies in care homes so that stories between residents, families, friends and staff are encouraged and valued and each person's sense of identity is fostered.

In care settings staff can also use strategies that involve narration or story-telling to understand the relationships that are important to individual residents. These may include reminiscence, life plans, life story, life review and life diaries (Clarke, Hanson and Ross 2003; Kenyon, Clark and Vries 2001; McCormack 2004). These approaches can be used to develop a rich picture of the older person and his or her social networks, providing care staff with a good understanding of the relationships that older people consider to be important. Furthermore, these approaches can be used to examine the nature of the relationships within an individual's social network. Older people do not lose the need for intimacy because they move to a care home, and therefore it is essential that these intimate relationships are identified and supported. The evidence provided by these studies suggests that staff do not always recognise the relationships that are valued by older people; therefore this is an important step toward improving practice in care homes.

The use of story-telling has the potential to enhance practice in care homes but is not without its challenges. Residents have different, complex health and social care needs, and communication, sensory and cognitive problems which can impede their abilities to make and sustain relationships.

However, an individual's personal narrative of his or her life can be developed from many sources, including the resident, family, friends and staff members, each bringing a different perspective on the resident's life. When these perspectives are combined, they can be used to enhance the quality of experience for the older person. Through careful consideration of the stories that individuals share, practical and simple measures to address each resident's needs and problems can be identified. Some of these approaches will require little more than continuous application of effective communication strategies, such as staff introducing themselves and others in the care home setting to initiate dialogue; whereas other strategies, such as transcribing letters for residents to send to family and friends, do have resource implications. It is beyond this discussion to describe every strategy that may be used to support relationships. Perhaps the most important message is the need to listen to residents and to negotiate and resource practical, relevant and achievable strategies that enable them to fulfil their aspirations.

Conclusions

Staff in care homes can help older residents to maintain and develop relationships by:

- identifying the relationships that are important to residents

- enabling staff to discuss alternative strategies with residents for 'keeping in touch' with family and friends

- ensuring the environment is open and welcoming to family, friends and the local community

- valuing the development of meaningful relationships between staff and residents as well as supporting functional interaction

- implementing staff assignment processes that enhance continuity in social interaction between staff and residents

- listening to the stories residents tell about their lives

- introducing residents who may have shared interests to each other

- arranging for those with common interests to sit together

- being aware of the difficulties some residents may have in developing relationships and finding practical ways to support them if they wish.

References

Abbott, S., Fisk, M. and Forward, L. (2000) 'Social and democratic participation in residential settings for older people.' *Ageing and Society 20,* 327–340.

Archibald, C. (1998) 'Sexuality, dementia and residential care: Managers' report and response.' *Health and Social Care in the Community 6,* 2, 95–101.

Archibald, C. (1999) *Activities and People with Dementia: Involving Family Carers.* Stirling: Dementia Services Development Centre, University of Stirling.

Biggs, S., Bernard, M., Kingston, P. and Nettleton, H. (2000) 'Lifestyles of belief: Narrative and culture in a retirement community.' *Ageing and Society 20,* 6, 649–672.

Bowers, B.J., Fibich, B. and Jacobson, N. (2001) 'Practice concepts. Care-as-service, care-as-relating, care-as-comfort: Understanding nursing home residents' definitions of quality.' *Gerontologist 41,* 4, 539–545.

Brown Wilson, C. (2007) 'Exploring relationships in care homes: A constructivist inquiry.' Unpublished doctoral dissertation. University of Sheffield.

Chamberlayne, P., Bornat, J. and Wengraf, T. (eds) (2000) *The Turn to Biographical Methods in Social Science. Comparative Issues and Examples.* London and New York: Routledge.

Clarke, A., Hanson, E.J. and Ross, H. (2003) 'Seeing the person behind the patient: Enhancing the care of older people using a biographical approach.' *Journal of Clinical Nursing 12,* 697–706.

Cook, G. (2006) 'The risk to enduring relationships following the move to a care home.' *International Journal of Older People Nursing 1,* 3, 182–185.

Cook, G. (2007) 'Life as a care home resident in later years: "Living with care" or "existing in care".' Unpublished doctoral dissertation. Northumbria University.

Cook, G., Brown Wilson, C. and Forte, D. (2006) 'The impact of sensory imparment on social interaction between residents in care homes.' *International Journal of Older People Nursing 1,* 216–224.

Davidson, K. and Fennell, G. (eds) (2004) *Intimacy in Later Life.* London: Transaction Publishers.

Davies, S. (2003) 'Creating community: The basis for caring partnerships in nursing homes.' In M.R. Nolan, U. Lundh, G. Grant and J. Keady (eds) *Partnerships in Family Care.* Maidenhead: Open University Press, pp.218–237.

Davies, S., Aveyard, B. and Norman, I. (2005) 'Person-centred dementia care.' In S. Redfern and F. Ross (eds) *Nursing Older People.* London: Churchill Livingstone Elsevier.

Forte, D., Cotter, A. and Wells, D. (2006) 'Sexuality and relationships in later life.' In S. Redfern and F. Ross (eds) *Nursing Older People.* London: Churchill Livingstone Elsevier, pp.437–455.

Friedmann, M.L., Montgomery, R.J., Rice, C. and Farrell, L. (1997) 'Family involvement in the Nursing Home: Family oriented practices and staff–family relationships.' *Research in Nursing and Health 20,* 527–537.

Heath, H. and White, I. (2002) *The Challenge of Sexuality in Health Care.* Oxford: Blackwell Science Ltd.

Hubbard, G., Tester, S. and Downs, M. (2004) 'Meaningful social interactions between older people in institutional care settings.' *Ageing and Society 23,* 1, 99–114.

Hurwitz, B., Greenhalgh, T. and Skultans, V. (eds) (2004) *Narrative research in health and illness.* Oxford: Blackwell Publishing Ltd/BMJ Books.

Jerrome, D. (1993) *Good Company: An Anthropological Study of Old People in Groups.* Edinburgh: Edinburgh University Press.

Jovchelovitch, S. and Bauer, M.W. (2000) 'Narrative interviewing.' In M.W. Bauer and G. Gaskell (eds) *Qualitative Researching with Text, Image and Sound.* London: Sage. pp.57–74.

Kenyon, G., Clark, P. and Vries, B. (2001) *Narrative Gerontology: Theory, Research and Practice.* New York: Springer Publishing Company.

McCormack, B. (2004) 'Person-centeredness in Gerontological Nursing: An overview of the literature.' *International Journal of Older People Nursing* in association with *Journal of Clinical Nursing 13*, 3a, 45–53.

McKee, K., Downs, M., Gilhooly, M., Gilhooly, K., Tester, S. and Wilson, F. (2005) 'Frailty, identity and the quality of later life.' In A. Walker (ed) *Understanding Quality of Life in Older Age.* Buckinghamshire, PA: Open University Press. pp.117–129.

Murphy, J., MacDonald, C., Downs, M., Hubbard, G. and Tester, S. (2004) 'What does quality of life mean for frail residents?' *Nursing and Residential Care 6*, 2, 89–92.

NCHRDF (2007) *My Home Life: Quality of Life in Care Homes. A Review of the Literature.* London: Help the Aged.

Nolan, M.R., Grant, G. and Nolan, J. (1995) 'Busy doing nothing: Activity and interaction levels amongst differing populations of elderly patients.' *Journal of Advanced Nursing 22*, 528–538.

Plummer, K. (1997) *Telling Sexual Stories. Power, Change and Social Worlds.* London: Routledge.

Reed, J. and Payton, V. (1997) 'Understanding the dynamics in care homes for older people: Implications for de-institutionalising practice.' *Health and Social Care in the Community 5*, 4, 261–268.

Reed, J., Cook, G., Sullivan, A. and Burridge, C. (2003) 'Making a move – residents in care homes' experiences of re-location.' *Ageing and Society 23*, 225–241.

Rodwell, M.K. (1998) *Social Work Constructivist Research.* New York: Garland Publishing.

Ronch, J. (2004) 'Changing institutional culture: Can we re-value the nursing home?' *Journal of Gerontological Social Work 43*, 1, 61–82.

Rowles, G. and High, D. (1996) 'Individualising care. Family roles in nursing home decision making.' *Journal of Gerontological Nursing 22*, 3, 20–25.

Sandberg, J., Lundh, U. and Nolan, M.R. (2001) 'Placing a spouse in a care home: The importance of keeping.' *Journal of Clinical Nursing 10*, 3, 406–416.

Wells, D. (2000) 'Introduction.' In D. Wells, D. Clifford, M. Rutter and J. Selby (eds) *Caring for Sexuality in Health and Illness.* Edinburgh: Churchill Livingstone. pp.1–8.

Zaner, R. (2003) 'Sisyphus without knees: Exploring self–other relationships through illness and disability.' *Literature and Medicine 22*, 188–207.

CHAPTER 5

Older People with Learning Disabilities: A Quality Initiative in Caring

Robert Jenkins

Introduction

The aim of this chapter is to explore the introduction of clinical governance into a residential care home for older people with learning disabilities. This pioneering action research project took place over a one-year period, commencing in 2000. The initial discussion in the chapter will set the scene by highlighting some issues concerning services and health needs of older people with learning disabilities. An overview of the project will be provided which will include some personal reflections from two of the participants.[1] The latter part of the chapter will consider whether the introduction of clinical governance had any lasting effects in the home and highlight some of the future challenges and issues in caring for this client group.

Services for older people with learning disabilities

In recent years there have been noticeable changes in services for, and lifestyles of, people with learning disabilities (Jenkins 2005a). Most of the large hospital or institutional type of provision has now been replaced with community-based housing schemes, and the majority of people with learning disabilities now live in the community with their families and, in later life, usually with their mother (Hubert and Hollins 2000). They are now

---

1   This chapter was based on the journal article 'The Shaw Healthcare Project' in *Learning Disability Practice 6*, 10, 30–33. Adapted with kind permission of RCN Publishing. Copyright © RCN Publishing 2003.

also outliving their parents when in the past this was not the case. This trend towards care in the community is supported by 'normalisation' and social role valorisation philosophies (Wolfensberger 1972, 1992), which highlight the devaluing effect of living in segregated institutional types of residence. It is argued that people with learning disabilities gain 'social value' by engaging in normal life experiences such as shopping, going to work and undertaking the usual leisure and socialising activities such as going to the pub or cinema (King's Fund Centre 1980) and there is evidence to suggest that this can lead to improvements in quality of life (Dagnan, Ruddick and Jones 1998).

It is unclear whether people with learning disabilities should move into generic older people services when they reach old age, stay with their current learning disability service or have some specialist service. Northway and Jenkins (2007) argue that as a result of the wide adoption of normalisation principles, older people with learning disabilities should be encouraged to use ordinary generic older people services. However, Thompson's (2002) aptly named report 'Misplaced and forgotten' suggests that there are real concerns regarding the suitability of placing older people with learning disabilities in residential homes for older people. These concerns have been identified as care staff having limited knowledge and training to meet the specific needs of people with learning disabilities. There has been a tendency to place older people with learning disabilities in residential services at a much younger age, with 40 per cent aged under 65 years. Evidence has also highlighted that there are few activities for this client group, little contact with family and friends, and the other residents in the home are not always welcoming towards this group of people (Thompson, Ryrie and Wright 2004). Currently, there are few residential homes that cater exclusively for older people with learning disabilities (Jenkins 2005b). However, there is some consensus over the need for: better healthcare and quality services; involving service users; promoting healthier active lives, partnerships and integrated care; person-centred planning; and advocacy for those with learning disabilities (DoH 2001a; Welsh Assembly Government 2006). Barr (2001) suggests that it is important that health and social services should be aware of the needs of older people with learning disabilities in order to make appropriate services available. However, a lack of collaboration between specialist and primary care services has been noted (Rodgers 1994). In particular, the need for nurses to work in collaboration with nurses from other specialisms has been highlighted (Northway and Walker 1999).

Health needs of older people with learning disabilities

People are generally living longer due to improvements in social conditions, improved access to healthcare and advances in medical care (Holland 2000) and the numbers of older people with a learning disability are also likely to increase in the future (Northway and Jenkins 2007). Nonetheless, there is an average ten-year difference in the life expectancy of people with learning disability compared to the general population (Jenkins 2005a). It is difficult to be precise as life expectancy may be influenced by a number of factors such as biological traits, types of employment, social class, geographical location, disability, lifestyle choices, income, etc., which also affect the general population. However, some of the particular factors that impact on the life expectancy of people with learning disabilities are unemployment, genetic syndromes, degree of learning disability and susceptibility to particular health-related problems.

Older people with learning disabilities are more at risk of physical disorders and diseases such as sensory defects, cancer, diabetes and fractures (Jenkins, Brooksbank and Miller 1994). Higher risks have also been identified in areas such as cardiovascular and respiratory diseases, hypertension, arthritis, immobility, urinary incontinence and cerebrovascular disease. Some genetic disorders, for example Down syndrome, bring additional problems, such as increased prevalence of vascular disease and hypothyroidism (Cooper 1998). Psychiatric disorders are also common amongst older people with learning disabilities due to additional risk factors stemming from old age and a learning disability (Cooper 1999). It is reported by Hubert and Hollins (2000) that the higher rates of psychiatric disorders include dementia, anxiety and depression, together with affective and delusional disorders. Dementias usually affect people with learning disabilities in the same way as other older people, except for people with Down syndrome (Wilkinson and Janicki 2002). Individuals with Down syndrome have a greater chance of developing dementia, especially Alzheimer's disease. Janicki and Dalton (2000) report rates of Alzheimer's disease for people with Down syndrome at around 22 per cent for those aged 40 years and over and 56 per cent for those over 60 years. They also tend to develop the condition at an earlier age and the course of the condition and loss of skills is more rapid, compared to the general population (Hutchinson 1999).

A significant contributing factor to the development of physical illness is the individual's lifestyle. People with learning disabilities often lead unhealthy lifestyles (Barr *et al.* 1999; WHO 2001), due in part to health promotion initiatives ignoring this client group. Despite this, there have been attempts to include people with Down Syndrome in developing strategies to improve health status (DOH 1995, 2001a). Thus it can be seen that, as a result of increasing health problems, older people with a learning disability may require the intervention and support of professionals such as nurses. However, Jenkins (2000) suggests that little attention has been paid in the nursing literature to the needs of older people with a learning disability. Demand for services and the assistance of nurses is likely to increase in future years (Barr 2001; DoH 1998a, 2001a), including nurses who specialise in working with people with learning disabilities and/or other nurses working in primary care. Indeed, the Department of Health (1999a) has set a vision of maximising the contribution of nurses in healthcare delivery to this client group and the Welsh Assembly Government (2002) aims to strengthen the role of learning disability nurses. However, an area that has been overlooked is the contribution that learning disability nurses make in the independent, voluntary and private sectors. A large and growing number of learning disability nurses work in these areas.

Clinical governance and the role of the nurse

At the time of the study, the adoption of clinical governance in the health service was viewed as a key feature through which excellence in clinical care could be achieved (DoH 1997, 1998b, 1999b). However, initiatives in the NHS were not necessarily extended to the independent, voluntary and private sectors.

Clinical governance is defined as 'a framework through which NHS organisations are accountable for continuously improving the quality of their services and safeguarding high standards of care by creating an environment in which excellence in clinical care will flourish' (DoH 1998b, p.33) and the Royal College of Nursing (1998) highlights the particular contribution that nurses can make to this endeavour. However, Currie and Loftus-Hills (2002) argue that while organisations must embrace the notion of clinical governance, it also needs to be seen by front line staff as an integral part of their workload rather than being viewed as an optional extra. They suggest that there need to be stronger partnerships between clients, managers and staff if clinical governance is to be successfully implemented.

Background to quality improvement initiative

Shaw Healthcare (at the time of the study a national charitable friendly society, but now a commercial healthcare organisation) provides housing and staffing to meet the needs of a variety of vulnerable adults including people with learning disabilities. At the beginning of the Millennium, Shaw Healthcare approached the School of Care Sciences (now the Faculty of Sport, Health and Science) at the University of Glamorgan to develop a project to introduce clinical governance into four of its group homes in South Wales. Three of the homes catered for people with mental health needs and one (the subject of this chapter) provided services for older people with learning disabilities.

Shaw Healthcare wanted to introduce clinical governance in order to develop a culture where quality of care would be at the heart of everyone's business at all levels within the organisation. Recent strategies and key papers in Wales such as *Realising the Potential* (National Assembly for Wales 1999) and *Quality Care and Clinical Excellence* (Welsh Office 1998) had provided impetus for organisations to review their aims for care delivery. It was felt that nursing within Shaw Healthcare needed to move toward providing excellence in care by focusing on a number of key areas (see Box 5.1). Through the process of action research, Shaw Healthcare Homes aimed to raise standards of service delivery and promote innovative practice. A number of quality improvement objectives were identified for the homes and action research was identified as a suitable way of learning from the implementation of proposed changes.

Box 5.1 Focused areas for excellence in care

- improving the environment of care and managing risk
- ensuring a high standard of service for all and facilitating the implementation of good practice through a shared commitment to quality
- encouraging independent and reflective practice
- developing life-long learning and client need-based education
- recruiting, retaining and developing excellent staff
- demonstrating the value of nursing
- client involvement and empowerment

Action research

Action research has gained popularity in nursing as a means of improving care due in part to its 'hands-on' and problem-focused approach (Badger 2000). For example, it has been used to develop a specialist practitioner role in accident and emergency departments (Jones 1996), identifying older people in need (Moyer *et al.* 1999) and improving health visitor parenting programmes for parents of pre-school children with behaviour problems (Kilgour and Fleming 2000). Greenwood (1994) states that action research appeals to nurses because the central purpose of nursing is to bring about positive change in health through social practice. Action research is seen to be an approach, rather than a specific method (Meyer, Spilsbury and Prieto 1999), with Reason and Bradbury (2001) defining it as:

> a participatory, democratic process concerned with developing practical knowing in the pursuit of worthwhile human purposes, grounded in a participatory worldview which we believe is emerging at this historical moment. It seeks to bring together action and reflection, theory and practice, in participation with others, in the pursuit of practical solutions to issues of pressing concern to people, and more generally the flourishing of individual persons and their communities. (p. 1)

Morton-Cooper (2000) identifies some specific key principles of action research in relation to healthcare, which may be helpful in the development of a study (see Box 5.2). Action research is not without its difficulties, par-

---

Box 5.2 Key principles of action research

- generated by the practitioners and aims to improve practice
- starts with a problem shared and experienced by colleagues and/or patients
- workplace orientated
- aims to validate any claims it makes by rigorous justification processes
- utilises a flexible trial-and-error approach
- examines key assumptions held by researchers and challenges their validity
- accepts that there are no final answers

Adapted from Morton-Cooper 2000, p. 19

ticularly in areas such as informed consent and addressing the power relationships between the researcher and participants (Meyer 1993). In spite of these difficulties, action research has the potential to bring research and practice closer together. An essential feature of action research is the use of reflection by participants. Jasper (2006) suggests there are three basic requirements for reflective practice:

- the need to have experiences from which to learn

- the use of reflective processes to help 'unlock' such experiences and their meaning

- the need to take action as a result of the learning and understanding that has taken place.

Why use action research for the project?

For this project action research was felt to be appropriate for a number of reasons. First, it shared an emphasis on partnership, efficiency and excellence. Second, it could be easily incorporated within the clinical governance framework as a vehicle for bringing about organisational change. Third, it had the potential to meet the organisational aims of moving towards excellence, raising standards and ultimately improving the well-being of clients in the home. Finally, it was believed that the problem-focused orientation of action research would allow the researcher to deal with problems in a direct way and offer solutions.

An important goal of the project was to develop a sustainable model of action in which the staff would feel very much part of the change process. As part of the research project it was agreed that a senior lecturer in nursing based at the university would assist each home in their bid towards excellence. This required the lecturer to commit to working in the home for a period of one year, for no more than two days per month (four half days). Each home also appointed a practice development nurse to assist with the project. A six-stage plan was devised to implement the necessary changes in each home (see Table 5.1).

An audit tool was developed and a number of additional measures were also used to gather data. These were: the Index of Adult Autonomy (Raynes and Sumpton 1992), the Index of Participation in Domestic Life (Raynes, Sumpton and Pettipher 1989a), the Index of Community Involvement (Raynes, Sumpton and Pettipher 1989b) and the Minnesota

Table 5.1 Quality improvement objectives

Stage	Aim	Action taken
One	Educate managers regarding quality improvement via clinical governance	A one-day workshop was held with all the managers to discuss issues related to the project.
Two	Implement baseline audit in each home	The managers and their teams conducted an audit over a two-day period. The audit focused on areas such as quality of life, staff development, staff satisfaction and value for money.
Three	Agree an action plan	Following the baseline report, areas of strength were built upon and areas of weakness were addressed.
Four	Implement the necessary changes to move towards excellence	Areas focused upon were: nursing knowledge and competence, risk assessment, environment of care, record keeping, user involvement, evidence-based care, clinical supervision and team working.
Five	Revisit the baseline and raise the standards	One year after the first audit the same areas as in stage two were re-audited.
Six	Set an annual contract for quality improvement with each manager and his or her team	Where significant improvements were made, new standards of practice were developed. Where no improvements were made a new action plan was developed. An annual contract was made to maintain the quality of care.

Job Satisfaction Scale (Weiss 1967). The audit involved gathering evaluative data from a number of sources such as:

- records, including care plans
- structured interviews with staff and clients
- observation of the home environment and care practices
- discussion with home manager and staff regarding philosophy of care, objectives and care practices.

Regular meetings took place with the project team (all the care home managers, two senior managers from Shaw Healthcare and seven university lecturers and researchers) to discuss and monitor progress. Each home had to set a number of specific objectives (see Table 5.2).

Table 5.2 Group home project objectives

Objective	Rationale	Actions	By whom
Introduce an independent advocacy scheme into group home	For residents in the home to have their views and wishes expressed through an independent agency	Contact and invite independent advocacy scheme into home Welcome and support independent advocates in the home	Home manager and designated staff
Develop a resource area for staff	To improve evidence-based practice	Area set aside in the treatment room to have up-to-date literature in specific files Practice development nurse to write a report justifying the need for such a facility Practice development nurse to keep files tidy and to update regularly	Practice development nurse
Utilise a suitable model of care and review current care plans	To ensure that the United Kingdom Central Council (UKCC) standards for record keeping and best practice are adhered to	Working party to be set up to look at the current model of care and care-planning All care plans to be reviewed and problems to be identified Seek advice and support from organisation's specialist nurse Staff to attend study day on the Tidal Model[1] Consider introducing new documentation and new model of care	Home manager and all staff
Introduce an appropriate Quality of Life measure	To seek to improve the quality of life of the residents in the group home	Staff to review current Quality of Life measurement tools Seek advice and support of the organisation's specialist nurse Adopt the most suitable measure for the residents of the group home	Practice development nurse and designated staff
Introduce clinical supervision	Improve staff support and professional practice	Consider the various forms of clinical supervision Seek advice and support of organisation's specialist nurse Adopt a suitable form of clinical supervision for staff	Home manager and all staff

1 The Tidal Model is a philosophical approach used in mental health which is focused on helping people recover their personal story or journey so that they may be enabled to regain some control in their lives.

All four lecturers working in each of the homes were required to make field notes and also complete a personal diary in which they would reflect on their practice and the development of the project. The following accounts were the personal reflections of the senior lecturer and the home's practice development nurse at the time.

Lecturer's perspective

This was a refreshing project for me because it ensured that time was set aside which allowed me to become more involved in clinical practice. It can be difficult for lecturers to find and be allowed time to work in clinical settings, and take an active part in the drive to improve quality of life for people with learning disabilities. The project also enabled me to develop insight into a residential service providing care exclusively for older people with learning disabilities. Thompson (2002) has raised concerns regarding the poor quality of life of many individuals with learning disabilities who currently reside in residential homes for older people. This highlights the importance of seeking to ensure quality of care in settings such as the home involved in this project.

The first months of the project were spent orientating myself to the workings of the home and getting to know staff and residents. There seemed to be some discontent around pay, which is not unusual in the caring professions. I had previously spent many years as a trade union activist and was well aware of the low pay and poor conditions of many of the front line workers in both health and social care, especially in services for older people and learning disability. One of the reasons for low pay in these areas is because much of the work is given little value or status. Dealing with incontinence, nutritional needs, laundry, bathing and communicating with residents are essential and vital tasks but can be negatively viewed as either unpleasant or mundane. Carnaby and Cambridge (2002) highlight that care staff suggest that friends and family also devalue their work. However, these areas of personal care can make a huge difference to the way people with learning disabilities feel about themselves. It is difficult to feel good about yourself if you are left soaking in urine or people ignore you. It is often at this interface of intimate caring where many of the personal relationships between staff and residents develop. The warmth of human interaction can foster trust, sensitivity, affection and understanding between a resident and staff members. On many occasions

I witnessed good practice in these areas where residents were well cared for; however, staff often underplayed their work as 'just' caring for the individual. This is perhaps why Davies (1998) advocates for a revaluation of caring work, which recognises the skills, competence and therapeutic relationships involved.

A clear advantage of having a lecturer on site is that staff members have an ideal opportunity to discuss their educational needs. Some of the qualified members of staff indicated that there was now more 'pressure' on them to gain higher qualifications. An important element of clinical governance is to raise standards of care and this is unlikely to happen unless staff raise their own level of knowledge and skills. The move towards an all-graduate profession in Wales at the time was clearly acting as a motivating factor for those who were academically minded. However, others felt that an all-graduate profession was a retrograde step and believed that more value should be placed on experience and practical skills.

One of the ways in which the home wished to improve client involvement and empowerment was to encourage the use of an independent advocacy scheme. Initially there was some concern and suspicion by the staff about having independent advocates in the home. There is often a fear that advocates will go out of their way to complain about various aspects of care. Ivers (1998) feels that it is important that staff support the notion of independent advocacy or it will not be effective. Jenkins and Northway (2002) highlight that registered learning disability nurses have an important role to play in modifying negative stereotypes of independent advocates. The practice development nurse and I promoted the use of independent advocates and tried to ensure that staff worked in an open and cooperative manner. In spite of their initial concerns the staff made the advocates feel welcome and they were afforded as much support as possible. A smile, a cup of tea and a pleasant manner made a world of difference in making independent advocates feel welcome. Ironically after a period of time some staff felt that the advocates were not making enough noise on behalf of the residents! Clearly much confusion surrounded the concept of advocacy. For example, there is evidence that older people living in residential care had little understanding of the term 'advocacy' and the role of the independent advocate was also poorly understood by residents, staff and relatives. Interestingly both family members and staff felt that there would not be a conflict of interest in advocating on behalf of their relative or resident in their care (Northway et al. 2004). This was in stark contrast to the literature which suggests that there would be a conflict of interest due to the close nature of their relationships (Braye and Preston-Shoot 1995; Dalrymple and Burke 1995).

Practice development nurse's perspective

I commenced my role as a practice development nurse at the start of the project, and a key role was to develop a 'partnership' with the lecturer to take the project forward. At first much of my time was spent allaying the fears of the staff who were suspicious about having a lecturer on site. I became a bit of a 'buffer' and had to temper some extreme views that there might be an ulterior motive for the study. One way of allaying such fears was to provide regular meetings and feedback to staff and clients. Surprisingly, I found myself having to defend my role in the project and it was difficult at times to balance the everyday demands of working in the home while trying to maintain the project's impetus.

The government White Paper *Valuing People: A New Strategy for Learning Disability for the 21st Century'* (DoH 2001a) provided the key principles of rights, independence, choice and inclusion, which guided the project. The person-centred approach to care-planning advocated in the *National Service Framework for Older People* (DoH 2001b) was also viewed as being essential in delivering real change in the lives of people with learning disabilities. The home had always embraced the Roper, Logan and Tierney (1996) model of nursing care, which, we decided, generally focused too much on physical needs. It also seemed that the clients had to in some way fit into the plan rather than the plan developing around the individual. We eventually opted for implementing Essential Lifestyle Planning (Sanderson *et al.* 1997) as a way of building the caring team around individual clients. There was some resistance and tension amongst some of the staff to this proposed change. Parley (2001) highlights this issue by stating that 'when tension occurs between an old care plan and a new one, an issue of power comes into play. Do staff then opt for the approach best suited to the individual or go with the service strategy in the problem solving plan?' (p.306). It can be difficult for individuals to change ways of working particularly if this involves changing attitudes. Adopting a person-centred approach to care helped us to meet one of our objectives by shifting power away from professionals and creating a more empowering environment for the client. It was also helpful that the organisation embraced person-centred planning in its other homes and the clinical nurse specialist for Shaw Healthcare Homes provided an invaluable link, support and encouragement in developing this area.

In partnership with the lecturer, a resource room was set up in the home and a small library was developed. The library contained recent journals and relevant articles, posters, information leaflets and completed projects undertaken by the staff team. Registered nurses found it especially useful in ensuring that their practice was evidence-based (NMC 2004).

Key lessons from undertaking the project

- The involvement of a lecturer worked best when linked with a nominated staff member such as a practice development nurse. This 'partnership' can be an effective use of time, help to bridge the theory-practice gap and provide support and encouragement for clinical staff.

- A suitable framework for organising care such as Essential Lifestyle Planning needs to be adopted, which requires positive commitment from all those involved.

- The use of independent advocacy schemes can help to empower clients as long as it is supported and understood by staff.

- It is evident that there needs to be more value placed on the intimate and personal care undertaken by care staff in meeting the needs of older people with learning disabilities.

Developments since the end of the project: 2002–2007

The first thing to report is that clinical governance remains 'a dominant influence in health policy in the UK and is imperative for safe, effective service delivery and professional practice' (Pridmore and Gammon 2007, p.723). The influence of clinical governance seems to have remained, which is significant as some policies can fade away after a couple of years. Pridmore and Gammon (2007), however, argue that there are differences in the application, interpretation and monitoring of clinical governance in the four countries that make up the UK. Unfortunately there is little evidence of uptake of clinical governance in the voluntary, independent and private sectors. In relation to the specific home objectives set out in

Table 5.2, there have been some improvements that have been maintained. One of the main successes is that the independent advocacy scheme is still running and the independent advocates continue to visit residents on a fortnightly to monthly basis. As highlighted in the lecturer's reflections, staff were at first a little uneasy about having 'outsiders' adopting the role of advocate. However, the advocates are now seen as having an important role to play by providing an independent voice in ensuring that the opinions and wishes of the clients are heard. They have represented residents at care review meetings and hold regular residents' meetings in the home. Staff being supportive towards independent advocates is seen as crucial to its success (Ivers 1998; Jenkins and Northway 2002).

The resource area has been preserved and the files containing relevant literature are still available to staff and students on placement. Unfortunately the practice development nurse responsible for maintaining the resource area has moved on and the role has not been retained. However, a computer and some new literature have been added to the resource area over the years and a new post of activity coordinator has been established to increase the activity levels of the residents. Essential lifestyle planning has been maintained and has worked well in ensuring that the residents are at the centre of the planning process. The NMC (2007) advise that there should be documented evidence of discussions and consultation between all members of the care team including clients. A number of the quality of life measures are currently being used as a direct result of the project, particularly as a result of the initial audit of the home. Involvement in the project acted as a motivating factor for the author and colleagues at the university to develop a quality of life model of care which can be used by learning disability nurses in residential care for people with learning disabilities (see Jenkins, Wheeler and James 2006). This model is also suitable for use with other groups of vulnerable adults, such as older people and people with mental health needs. Clinical supervision is now well established in the home and all staff regularly engage in this process. In terms of recruiting and developing staff there has been a noticeable trend. A number of the support staff have undertaken student nurse training in learning disability, child, mental health and general nursing at the University of Glamorgan. A number of students who had placements in the home while undertaking the learning disability branch programme have managed to find employment in the home. Overall, there has not been a net loss of staff and the level of academic achievement has increased as student nurses in Wales undertake degree-level pre-registration nurse education. While it can not be claimed that these changes were directly linked to the project, these developments are nonetheless interesting.

Future challenges and issues in caring for older people with learning disabilities

Jenkins' (2008) recent research highlights some challenges and issues likely to face nurses caring for the increasing number of older people with learning disabilities. Although learning disability nurses are ideally placed to care for older people with learning disabilities, there is a need for other specialist nurses to become involved in the care of this client group as a result of increasing complexity of need. For example, mental health nurses and palliative care nurses have an important role in dementia care and supporting older people at the end of life respectively. This should not prevent learning disability nurses from developing expertise in these areas. Similarly, generalist trained nurses should consider specialising in the area of learning disability.

Growing numbers of people with learning disabilities are developing dementia, particularly people with Down syndrome, and this poses challenges for all health professionals. For example, it is particularly problematic to diagnose or detect dementia in individuals who have severe and profound learning disabilities due to their poor cognitive, behavioural and verbal skills. Sadly, dementia is often well advanced in this client group before it is detected and this leads to an inevitable delay in treatment. Watchman (2003) highlights that dementia is less likely to be detected in older people with learning disabilities owing to the different assessments tools being utilised, lack of training and the high turnover of care staff. There is little research to suggest that the palliative care needs of people with learning disabilities are being met. It is not known whether this client group utilises general palliative care services or whether they require specialist provision. In the nursing home, older people with learning disabilities who were dying had their needs met by the nursing staff in the home although, on some occasions, staff utilised the support of the local palliative care services. Interestingly, there has been an increase in the number of deaths and referrals to the home in the last five years of life.

Another important challenge relates to evidence beginning to emerge regarding the suitability of using Percutaneous Endoscopic Gastronomy (PEG) as a way of dealing with serious reflux problems. There is no clear rationale or guidance on the use of PEG feeding for older people with learning disabilities, particularly those with advanced dementia. In some areas there is a reluctance to use this method while in others it seems to be a growing trend. There also appears to be conflict between relatives' and care staff's perceptions in terms of whether having a PEG fitted improves the quality of life of the individual or not. For example, in one particular case, care staff felt that having a PEG reduced the risk of choking, while a relative believed that it would reduce the quality of life of her brother by restricting his mobility and enjoyment of food. The client in this study, when asked, had no strong feelings either way (Jenkins 2008).

One final issue is the relevance of the label 'learning disability' as people grow older. For most, if not all of their lives, people with learning disabilities tend to be defined by this diagnosis. However, as a result of age, or some debilitating conditions such as dementia, their learning disability may assume less importance. Some carers even feel that these individuals have the same care needs as any other older person and that the label of learning disability is not relevant. In practical (physical) terms this may well be the case, and indeed some individuals who have been labelled in this way may welcome the 'loss' of such a stigmatising term. However, nurses need to take into consideration the effects of having such a label on the formation of individuals' self-concept and their health. Their memories, learning history, experiences, opportunities, relationships (psychological, social and spiritual, etc.) will all have been affected by the way in which people have applied the learning disability label to them in the past and this cannot be ignored. In a legal sense, then, the diagnosis of learning disability is an important consideration when dealing with issues such as capacity and consent. The skill for nurses is deciding when the label is relevant and when it is not. The most important thing to remember for all staff in working with this client group is that they are people first who just happen to find it difficult to learn as quickly and as effectively as others – a condition that may affect any of us at some stage in our lives.

Conclusion

The project described in this chapter has gone some way to demonstrating how clinical governance can be introduced within the independent sector to improve the quality and standard of care. It has also shown how some of these positive changes can be sustained and built upon to enhance quality of life for older people with learning disabilities. However, the growing numbers of older people with learning disabilities with complex needs is likely to increase, with a resulting demand for specialist provision for this client group. The challenge for services lies in providing suitable environments and staff with the necessary skills and knowledge to meet the needs of older people with learning disabilities.

References

Badger, T.G. (2000) 'Action research, change and methodological rigour.' *Journal of Nursing Management 8*, 201–207.

Barr, O. (2001) 'Towards successful ageing: Meeting the health and social care needs of older people with learning disabilities.' *Mental Health Care 4*, 6, 194–198.

Barr, O., Gilgunn, J., Kane, T. and Moore, G. (1999) 'Health screening for people with learning disabilities by a community learning disability nursing service in Northern Ireland.' *Journal of Advanced Nursing 29*, 6, 1482–1491.

Braye, S. and Preston-Shoot, M. (1995) *Empowering Practice in Social Care*. Buckingham: Open University Press.

Carnaby, S. and Cambridge, P. (2002) 'Getting personal: An exploratory study of intimate and personal care provision for people with profound and multiple intellectual disabilities.' *Journal of Intellectual Disability Research 46*, 2, 120–132.

Cooper, S.A. (1998) 'A clinical study of the effects of age on the physical health of adults with mental retardation.' *American Journal on Mental Retardation 102*, 582–589.

Cooper, S.A. (1999) 'The relationship between psychiatric and physical health in elderly people with intellectual disability.' *Journal of Intellectual Disability Research 43*, 1, 54–66.

Currie, L. and Loftus-Hills, A. (2002) 'The nursing view of clinical governance.' *Nursing Standard 16*, 27, 40–44.

Dagnan, D., Ruddick, L. and Jones, J. (1998) 'A longitudinal study of the quality of life of older people with intellectual disability after leaving hospital.' *Journal of Intellectual Disability Research 42*, 2, 112–121.

Dalrymple, J. and Burke, B. (1995) *Anti-oppressive Practice, Social Care and the Law*. Buckingham: Open University Press.

Davies, C. (1998) 'Caregiving, carework and professional care.' In A. Brechin, J. Walmsley, J.S. Katz and S. Peace (eds) *Care Matters: Concepts, Practice and Research in Health and Social Care*. London: Sage.

Department of Health (DoH) (1995) *Learning Disability: Meeting Needs Through Targeting Skills*. London: HMSO.

Department of Health (DoH) (1997) *The New NHS: Modern, Dependable*. London: HMSO.

Department of Health (DoH) (1998a) *Our Health Service*. London: HMSO.

Department of Health (DoH) (1998b) *A First Class Service: Quality in the New NHS Health Services*. London: HMSO.

Department of Health (DoH) (1999a) *Making a Difference. Strengthening the Nursing, Midwifery and Health Visiting Contribution to Health and Healthcare*. London: Department of Health.

Department of Health (DoH) (1999b) *Clinical Governance: Quality in the New NHS*. London: HMSO.

Department of Health (DoH) (2001a) *Valuing People: A New Strategy for Learning Disability for the 21st Century* (Cmnd 5086). London: The Stationery Office.

Department of Health (DoH) (2001b) *Modern Standards and Service Models: National Service Framework for Older People*. London: Department of Health.

Greenwood, J. (1994) 'Action research: A few details, a caution and something new.' *Journal of Advanced Nursing 20*, 13–18.

Holland, A.J. (2000) 'Ageing and learning disability.' *British Journal of Psychiatry 176*, 26–31.

Hubert, J. and Hollins, S. (2000) 'Working with elderly carers of people with learning disabilities and planning for the future.' *Advances in Psychiatric Treatment 6*, 41–48.

Hutchinson, N.J. (1999) 'Association between Down's syndrome and Alzheimer's disease: Review of the literature.' *Journal of Learning Disabilities for Nursing, Health and Social Care 3*, 4, 194–203.

Ivers, V. (1998) 'Advocacy.' In Y.C. Craig (ed.) *Advocacy, Counselling and Mediation in Casework*. London: Jessica Kingsley Publishers.

Janicki, M.P. and Dalton, A. (2000) 'Prevalence of dementia and impact on intellectual disability services.' *Mental Retardation 38*, 3, 276–288.

Jasper, M. (2006) *Professional Development, Reflection and Decision-making*. Oxford: Blackwell Publishing.

Jenkins, R. (2000) 'The needs of older people with learning disabilities.' *British Journal of Nursing 9*, 19, 2080–2089.

Jenkins, R. (2005a) 'Older people with learning disabilities Part 1: Individuals, ageing and health.' *Nursing Older People 16*, 10, 30–34.

Jenkins, R. (2005b) 'Older people with learning disabilities Part 2: Accessing care and the implications for nursing practice.' *Nursing Older People 17*, 1, 30–34.

Jenkins, R. (2008) 'Meeting the needs of older people with learning disabilities: The role of nurses.' Keynote address. Yorkshire Universities Learning Disability Nursing Research and Development Forum conference. University of Hull, 23 January.

Jenkins, R., Brooksbank, D. and Miller, E. (1994) 'Ageing in learning difficulties: The development of health care outcome indicators.' *Journal of Intellectual Disability Research 38*, 257–264.

Jenkins, R. and Jones, M. (2003) 'The Shaw Healthcare project.' *Learning Disability Practice 6*, 10, 30–33.

Jenkins, R. and Northway, R. (2002) 'Advocacy and the learning disability nurse.' *British Journal of Learning Disability 30*, 2, 8–12.

Jenkins, R., Wheeler, P. and James, N. (2006) 'Care planning in residential settings.' In B. Gates (ed.) *Care Planning and Delivery in Intellectual Disabilities Nursing*. Oxford: Blackwell.

Jones, S. (1996) 'An action research investigation into the feasibility of experienced registered sick children's nurses (RSCNs) becoming children's nurse practitioners.' *Journal of Clinical Nursing 15*, 1, 13–21.

Kilgour, C. and Fleming, V. (2000) 'An action research inquiry into a health visitor parenting programme for parents of pre-school children with behaviour problems.' *Journal of Advanced Nursing 32*, 3, 682–688.

King's Fund Centre (1980) *An Ordinary Life*. London: King's Fund Centre.

Meyer, J.E. (1993) 'New paradigm research in practice: The trials and tribulations of action research.' *Journal of Advanced Nursing 18*, 1066–1072.

Meyer, J.E., Spilsbury, K. and Prieto, J. (1999) 'Comparison of findings from a single case in relation to those from a systematic review of action research.' *Nurse Researcher 7*, 2, 37–59.

Morton-Cooper, A. (2000) *Action Research in Health Care*. Oxford: Blackwell Science.

Moyer, A., Coristine, M., Jamault, M., Roberge, G. and O'Hagan, M. (1999) 'Identifying older people in need using action research.' *Journal of Clinical Nursing 8*, 1, 103–111.

National Assembly for Wales (1999) *Realising the Potential: A Strategic Framework for Nursing, Midwifery and Health Visiting in Wales into the 21st Century.* Cardiff: Welsh Assembly.

Northway, R., Ameen, J., Coll, A.M., Jenkins, R., Cornthwaite, F. and Evans, S. (2004) *Information, Advice and Support for Older People Living in Residential Care: An Exploratory Survey of Advocacy.* Pontypridd: University of Glamorgan.

Northway, R. and Jenkins, R. (2007) 'Specialist learning disability services.' In B. Gates (ed.) *Learning Disabilities Toward Inclusion* (5th edn). Edinburgh: Churchill Livingstone.

Northway, R. and Walker, G. (1999) 'Promoting collaboration within community health care nursing.' *Journal of Community Nursing 13*, 4, 4–8.

Nursing and Midwifery Council (NMC) (2004) *The NMC Code of Professional Conduct: Standards for Conduct, Performance and Ethics.* London: Nursing and Midwifery Council.

Nursing and Midwifery Council (NMC) (2007) NMC Record Keeping Guidance. Available at www.nmc-uk.org/aFrameDisplay.aspx?DocumentID=4008, accessed 6 July 2008.

Parley, F.F. (2001) 'Person-centred outcomes: Are outcomes improved where a person-centred care model is used?' *Journal of Learning Disabilities 5*, 4, 299–308.

Pridmore, J.A. and Gammon, J. (2007) 'A comparative review of clinical governance arrangements in the UK.' *British Journal of Nursing 16*, 12, 720–723.

Raynes, N.V., Sumpton, R.C. and Pettipher, C. (1989a) *The Index of Participation in Domestic Tasks.* Manchester: Department of Social Policy and Social Work, University of Manchester.

Raynes, N.V., Sumpton, R.C. and Pettipher, C. (1989b) *The Index of Community Involvement.* Manchester: Department of Social Policy and Social Work, University of Manchester.

Raynes, N.V., Wright, K., Shiell, A. and Pettipher, C. (1994) '*The Cost and Quality of Community Residential Care.* London: Fulton.

Reason, P. and Bradbury, H. (2001) 'Introduction: Inquiry and participation in search of a world worthy of human aspiration.' In P. Reason and H. Bradbury (eds) *Handbook of Action Research: Participative Inquiry and Practice.* SAGE: London. pp.1–14.

Rodgers, J. (1994) 'Primary health care provision for people with learning disabilities.' *Health and Social Care in the Community 2*, 1, 11–17.

Roper, N., Logan, W. and Tierney, A. (1996) *The Elements of Nursing* (4th edn). Edinburgh: Churchill Livingstone.

Royal College of Nursing (1998) *Guidance for Nurses on Clinical Governance.* London: Royal College of Nursing.

Sanderson, H., Kennedy, K., Richie, P. and Goodwin, G. (1997) *People, Plans and Possibilities.* Edinburgh: SHS Ltd.

Thompson, D. (2002) 'Misplaced and forgotten: People with learning disabilities in residential homes for older people.' *Housing, Care and Support 5*, 1, 19–22.

Thompson, D., Ryrie, I. and Wright, S. (2004) 'People with intellectual disabilities living in generic residential services for older people in the UK.' *Journal of Applied Research in Intellectual Disabilities 17*, 2, 101–107.

Watchman, K. (2003) 'It's your move.' *Learning Disability Practice 6*, 8, 14–16.

Weiss, M. (1967) *Manual for the Minnesota Satisfaction Questionnaire.* Minneapolis, MN: University of Minnesota.

Welsh Assembly Government (2002) '*Inclusion, Partnership and Innovation' A Framework for Realising the Potential of Learning Disability Nursing in Wales.* Cardiff: Welsh Assembly Government.

Welsh Assembly Government (2006) *National Service Framework for Older People in Wales.* Cardiff: Welsh Assembly Government.

Welsh Office (1998) *Quality Care and Clinical Excellence. NHS Wales, Putting Patients First.* Cardiff: Welsh Office.

Wilkinson, H. and Janicki, M.P. (2002) 'The Edinburgh Principles with accompanying guidelines and recommendations.' *Journal of Intellectual Disability Research 46,* 3, 279–284.

Wolfensberger, W. (1972) *The Principle of Normalisation in Human Services.* Toronto: National Institute of Mental Retardation.

Wolfensberger, W. (1992) *A Brief Introduction to Social Role Valorization as a High-Order Concept for Structuring Human Services.* Syracuse, NY: Training Institute for Human Service Planning, Leadership and Change Agency, Syracuse University.

World Health Organisation (WHO) (2001) 'Healthy ageing – Adults with intellectual disabilities: Summative report.' *Journal of Applied Research in Intellectual Disabilities 14,* 4, 256–275.

PART 2

The Organisation

The Living Edge: Connection to Nature for People with Dementia in Residential Care

Garuth Chalfont

Introduction

This chapter describes an example of how a research project created a positive experience for residents in a residential care home through participatory engagement between people with dementia, the researcher and the natural world. The research is concerned with connection to nature for people with dementia and included three studies by the author over a two-year period. Study One was a user needs analysis consisting of interviews and focus groups (Gibson and Chalfont 2007). Study Two was a comparative examination of the potential for connection to nature provided within 14 different care home settings, focusing on the architecture and landscape (Chalfont 2006). This chapter draws primarily from Study Three, which investigated the potential benefits of 'edge spaces' of buildings by bringing people into contact with nature while engaging them in conversation. Sensory stimulation was experienced from a comfortable location either just inside or outside the building. The research aimed to answer the following question: given the opportunity to sense the natural environment and to engage with someone socially at the same time, in what ways might a person use this experience to enhance his or her well-being?

The study reported here drew upon the concepts of personhood and the maintenance of self, and the methods of psychological therapies, horticultural therapy and meditation. Theoretically, engaging people with the natural world could reinforce their sense of self. The usual question-and-answer interview format was rejected. Instead, given opportunities for self-direction, people used nature as a tool for self-expression, with some creative and unexpected results. Furthermore, when participants connected to nature and to another person, they used the experience to reinforce their identity.

Within participatory engagement is an assumption that certain values and principles are important. This study demonstrated the importance of one principle in particular:

- engagement – ensuring that all people involved have the opportunity to participate as they would like.

This was achieved by empowering participants during dialogue to lead the discussion. Giving the time and space to explore areas they found meaningful, and issues they felt to be important, ensured that all participants had the opportunity to participate as and how they wished.

The objectives of the chapter are to:

- present an example of research in care homes that addresses connection to nature for people with dementia

- give a brief overview of why connection to nature is beneficial

- introduce the concept of 'edge space' in care environments

- give examples of how people enjoy the natural world

- demonstrate a person-centred methodology that enabled creative uses of nature by participants, some with fairly advanced dementia

- demonstrate how both the social and physical environment enhance well-being

- show how people with dementia use nature creatively

- give environmental design guidance to include a connection to nature

- recommend caregiving and research methods that help people express and maintain their identity through social engagement.

The chapter is organised in five sections. 'Connection to nature' contains the rationale for the research, a brief overview of relevant literature, and some of the barriers to providing nature in care homes. 'Edge space study' gives the background and theoretical framework for the approach. It then describes the study, sites, participants and methodology. 'Findings' reports some of the nature-related activities people enjoyed. Excerpts from the edge space dialogues show how people with dementia used nature creatively to express themselves and to reinforce their identity. The penultimate section explores the implications of the study and recommends good practice within care homes to improve quality of life, including improvements to environmental design, caregiving and research methods. A concluding section presents a summary of the chapter.

Connection to nature

This section reviews the benefits a connection to nature might provide for a person with dementia, and the barriers to providing such a connection in residential care environments.

Benefits of connection to nature

Connection to nature has multiple human benefits which can be gained both actively and passively. Walking, gardening and lawn sports provide the benefits of physical exercise, fresh air, sunshine and social interaction. Even visits to the outdoors have proved beneficial. A study by Rappe and colleagues described the relationship between the reported frequency of visits to an outdoor green environment and self-rated health in 45 female nursing home residents. A strong positive association was established between the reported frequency of visiting outdoors and self-rated health (Rappe, Kivelä and Rita 2006). Environmental support for older peoples' outdoor activities has been shown to have a positive effect on their well-being and quality of life (Sugiyama and Thompson 2005).

Studies have also investigated passive interactions such as viewing a garden. Lowered blood pressure and heart rate were shown to be correlated with increased health and well-being of elderly women from simply viewing a landscape (Tang and Brown 2005). In a controlled study of older people, blood pressure, pulse rate and the power of concentration were influenced significantly by a period of rest in a garden (Ottosson and Grahn 2005). These researchers found that a garden can restore an elderly person with low psycho-physiological balance to a state of better harmony. An outdoor visit was important for recovery from stress and fatigue and the improvement was especially significant for the most susceptible. Receiving massage is also a relatively passive connection to nature and one that has been found to benefit the person. Sensory stimulation from aromatherapy massage with lemon balm (Melissa officinalis) essential oil resulted in an overall improvement in agitation for 35 per cent of subjects (Ballard *et al.*

2002). In a randomised controlled trial examining the effects of aromatherapy massage and conversation on behavioural disturbance reported by Smallwood and colleagues (2001), significant improvement was found in the motor behaviour of persons with severe dementia. Behavioural disturbances were reduced with the combination of aromatherapy and massage by as much as 34 per cent.

The meaning and benefit of 'edge space'

The concept of 'edge space' has been explored in various fields including architecture, geography and environmental psychology. An edge is a boundary or a transitional space, such as between public and private space, between indoors and outdoors, and between domesticated and wild. According to Christopher Alexander the edge is a lively place:

> When it is properly made, such an edge is a realm between realms: it increases the connection between inside and outside, encourages the formation of groups which cross the boundary, encourages movement which starts on one side and ends on the other, and allows activity to be either on, or in the boundary itself. (Alexander *et al.* 1977, p.755)

Alexander said that buildings are generally thought of as turning inward but must be rethought as also 'oriented toward the outside' (p.753). Edges are often attractive places: for example, in cities we can see the popularity of pavement cafes. Edges are where a person can spend time, where actions can develop and where the person becomes stimulated by, and oriented towards, the outside natural world (Chalfont and Rodiek 2005).

Barriers to connection to nature in residential care

The care environment includes people being cared for, people providing that care, the physical aspects (architecture and nature) and the organisational and policy framework. Any of these factors may prevent a connection between the person with dementia and the natural world. Because so many factors must align, even a simple walk outside is a challenge in many long-term care facilities.

The barriers to outdoors are related to social or policy aspects, physical environment aspects or the person's physical condition and mobility. Social or policy aspects include insufficient staff help; lack of awareness of benefits of outdoors; lack of planned activities outdoors such as walks; staff not available to assist; no use of volunteers; lack of family involvement in outdoor events or visits outdoors; policies not permitting residents outside alone; and lack of regulations for outdoor space (Cutler and Kane 2005; Kearney and Winterbottom 2005). Physical environment barriers are shown in Box 6.1 below.

Box 6.1 Physical barriers to the use of outside spaces by older people with dementia

- lack of shade or protection from weather
- gradient changes at entrances (step or threshold at door)
- limited access to the garden
- no direct route from a person's rooms
- no unlocked route
- no hard surface walking paths leading to amenities
- no seating or covered seating
- lack of tables
- outside areas not secured or enclosed
- lack of edge spaces
- boring spaces
- no view to real life
- residents on upper floors
- no direct access off the unit
- not conducive to privacy or to social relationships
- seating and tables not clean, dry and in good repair
- too far to go from indoor areas to outdoor spaces

(Chalfont 2006)

The architecture also plays a role in facilitating sensory stimulation from nature. Factors include how well the building lets in light and fresh air, provides views, orientates the person to time of day and year, provides green nature, encourages walking, attracts wildlife and connects to the local neighbourhood. Accomplishing these depends on being able to move about freely. The building design or care practice may limit movement by residents, by urging residents to sit down, and locking or camouflaging doors to outdoor areas.

Edge space study

The edge space study was chosen for this book because it demonstrates that caregiving and the physical environment can mutually engage a person, and by so doing, bring a creative approach to person-centred care. This section will provide the background for the study and outline the theoretical framework for the approach. It will then describe the study, the sites, the participants and the methodology.

Laying the groundwork

In the five years prior to carrying out this and other studies, the author visited 30 dementia care facilities in the UK, 5 in Norway, 2 in Sweden and 6 in the USA, examining their potential to provide residents with a connection to nature. He also carried out a prolonged observational study of daily life in two care homes in the UK as part of the Engineering and Physical Sciences Research Council (EPSRC)-funded INDEPENDENT Project. This included an analysis of the physical features of the rooms and buildings where the participants spent most of their time. Some of these results can be found elsewhere (Chalfont 2006, 2008). Of particular interest were how the building and landscape were designed and how the residents used them. Inventories were made of the built and natural elements and the activities such elements afforded. The situation of the building on the site and within the neighbourhood, and its proximity to local area natural resources were also considered, to gain an understanding of the potential for connection to nature at various scales.

Theoretical framework

Theoretical support for the edge space study comes from the areas of personhood and the maintenance of self, psychotherapy, social and therapeutic horticulture and meditation.

PERSONHOOD AND THE MAINTENANCE OF SELF

The concept of positive personhood draws on the work of Kitwood, Gilleard and others. Gilleard first conceptualised dementia in terms of 'personhood' (Gilleard 1984), specifically 'the loss of the person' (p.18) and the 'fading of self' (p.10). Kitwood and Bredin expanded this concept by saying that 'the key psychological task in dementia care is that of keeping the sufferer's personhood in being' (Kitwood and Bredin 1992, p.41). Gilleard's conceptualisation connects the physical environment and the sufferer's personal reality, and most importantly, this is accomplished through interaction. The quality of the interaction largely determines the positive or negative effect on personhood, which is by definition social, because it 'emerges in a social context...guaranteed by the presence of others...' (Kitwood and Bredin 1992, p.272). By 1997, Kitwood had defined personhood as 'a standing or status that is bestowed upon one human being by others, in the context of relationship and social being' (1997, p.8). Others have also said that 'the threatened loss of self does not appear to be linked to the "progress" of the disease but rather to the related behaviour of significant others' (Bond and Corner 2001, p.104). There is a link between engagement with others and well-being that in dementia is specific to a person's ability to maintain a coherent sense of self.

Discourse analysis of conversations by people with dementia has provided insight into their maintenance of self. Sabat and colleagues have been developing the various 'selves' of a person with dementia and the support or threat posed by the focus of the attention of others (Sabat and Collins 1999; Sabat and Harré 1992; Sabat, Napolitano and Fath 2004). Characteristic of this area of research is the analysis of conversations between a researcher and a person with dementia with whom the researcher had developed a long-term, trusting relationship. This is not one characterised by a dynamic such as 'researcher–patient' but rather by one of 'person-to-person' (Sabat 2002, p.28). The participants had been known by the author for at least two years at the time of the edge space dialogues. These associations were ones of acceptance and trust.

Evidence from a study involving people with dementia in residential care supported the relevance of a socio-biographical theory of self (Surr 2006) through the use of unstructured interviews with 14 people with dementia:

> Relationships with family, other residents and care home staff were important for maintenance of self. Social roles related to work, being part of a family, caring for others and being cared for, were particularly significant for self in this group. (Surr 2006, p.1720)

Surr's work drew upon theories of interpersonal relationships for maintenance of self. One such theory, Winnicott's caring environment (Davies and Wallbridge 1981), suggests that 'quality of interpersonal relationships is an essential component of preservation of self and therefore should be considered a crucial element in dementia care that aims to uphold self' (Surr 2006, p.1721). According to Surr, Goffman argued that institutional living held great potential for loss of self (p.1723). One reason cited for this was restriction on access to the outside world.

PSYCHOTHERAPY

The second area lending support to the study is an approach to well-being through psychological therapies, which is becoming more widely practised. A review of psychosocial interventions for people with dementia described current methods, including the psychodynamic approach, reminiscence and life review, support groups and cognitive/behavioural therapy, behavioural approaches, memory training and reality orientation (Kasl-Godley and Gatz 2000). Cognitive stimulation therapy (CST) has been shown to significantly improve cognition and quality of life in older people with dementia. CST has similarities with the edge space study. For instance, it involves 'gentle non-cognitive exercises to provide continuity and orientation...multi-sensory stimulation where possible and encouraged the use of information processing rather than solely factual information' (Spector *et al.* 2003, p.253).

Psychological therapies involve engaging the person psychologically and emotionally. The edge space study showed people engaging with their environment psychologically and emotionally, and communicating with a listener. As engagement and communication are key ingredients for a therapeutic encounter, the interactions in edge space were potentially of therapeutic benefit for the participants.

SOCIAL AND THERAPEUTIC HORTICULTURE

The third area of theoretical support is drawn from the practices of social and therapeutic horticulture (STH), in particular the triangular dynamic in which the person is engaged both with natural elements and with another person. The general model for the interactions that occur in STH is for the client and the therapist to converse while engaged in horticultural activities. The plant becomes the focus and clients are able to use nature as a metaphor to communicate their feelings and work through the emotions they may be experiencing. During this process, nature is used as a therapeutic tool and human interaction in relationships is the mechanism by which this occurs. Actual participation in activities of horticulture, such as planting, potting or caring for plants, is normal practice during a session of STH. This interaction occurs indoors or outdoors by using a range of different plant materials and activities in various settings. Similar to STH, the proposed experiments in edge space were designed to see if nature might be useful to people with dementia as a tool to facilitate personal communication. This study draws from the theory and practice of social and therapeutic horticulture the concept of human engagement in proximity to nature for therapeutic benefit.

MEDITATION

Theoretical support for the study also draws upon recent work in the area of meditation for people with dementia. People with advanced cognitive impairment can be instructed in meditation, can practise with support and guidance, and can benefit by decreased agitation, increased group participation, improved self-control and increased relaxation (Lindberg 2005). Meditation or spiritual practices can be learned because guided imagery is not dependent on stored memory. Guided imagery allows for creative use of the senses which serves to diminish the person's sense of isolation. During the meditation or spiritual practice the person is fully active and directive. In this way, participation promotes relational, emotional and spiritual well-being (Lindberg 2005). Meditation and guided imagery provided further theoretical support for the study by demonstrating creative use of the senses during social interaction.

Study description

The study investigated interactions between people and nature, facilitated by the built and social environment, with the expected outcome of contributing to the well-being of the participants. 'Edge spaces' of buildings seemed promising places where this might occur. The study required sensory stimulation from nature and dialogue with another person to occur simultaneously. Sensory stimulation indoors through a window might include sights and sounds, while outdoors it would also include temperature, fragrance and the feeling of sunlight and air on the skin.

The dialogues were held in an indoor or outdoor edge space which afforded connection to nature, and where the participants felt comfortable to spend time talking to someone. Similar to leading a guided imagery session or a meditation, the researcher acted as a catalyst to the interaction by empowering the participant to be fully active and directive (Lindberg 2005). The edge space provided sensory stimulation from nature to which the participant could respond. Facilitating an enjoyable and potentially beneficial interaction was the intended outcome, similar to a guided imagery session. For this to be possible for a person with dementia, the researcher must 'meet them where they are' psychologically. Hence, the protocol involved a gentle and flexible approach to communication. Essentially, the dialogue was intended to be an informal friendly chat, putting the clients in charge so they could lead the dialogue wherever they wished.

Study sites

The two residential care homes in the study each had a dementia care unit providing enhanced care to ten residents. The homes were similar in age, size and style of the building. One was in a built-up residential neighbourhood and the other was more isolated with larger areas of open space surrounding it. They were also different in terms of the organisational running of the home, with each place being a reflection of the skills, style, personality and experience of the staff members and the individual managers. The study sites were edge spaces inside or outside the homes.

An indoor edge space is near a window (or a door) with furniture for two people to sit (or a clear space to stand) within hearing and speaking distance of each other. Indoor edge spaces were located in bedrooms, dining rooms or lounges. An outdoor edge space is an outdoor space adjacent to the exterior wall where two people can sit or stand not far from (and within view of) the entrance. Outdoor edge spaces were located in an enclosed garden or patio area.

Participants

Eleven residents in the two homes participated in the study by meeting these criteria:

- having a diagnosis of dementia of any type
- expressing a willingness to talk to the researcher
- able to stay alert, awake and aware for at least 15 minutes
- able to comprehend and respond to verbal communication

- able and willing to give verbal consent to participate

- able and willing to give written consent to participate (or advocate).

One person had mild dementia, one had severe dementia and the rest were in the mild to moderate stages. One participant was male and all were white British. The ages ranged from 66 to 89 with a median age of 82.

Methodology

When considering methods and tools for human–environment research, existing studies in dementia care settings are more often comparative than exploratory. The comparative approach requires methods for looking at differences in the effect of the intervention on a person. It also makes some preliminary assumptions about what can be improved and how. Such studies adopt a clinical trials approach to carrying out and measuring interventions, both care interventions and those in the physical environment. For instance, a study may look at the effects of sensory stimulation on the person with dementia, such as aromatherapy massage, as described previously. A study by Ottosson and Grahn (2005) compared effects on people after two different stimuli: viewing a garden or viewing a wall. The possible ways these stimuli might affect the person were determined beforehand. For instance, increased well-being can be measured by various physiological factors (heart rate, blood pressure, etc.). This is valuable work which gives us much-needed quantitative data and conclusive findings on the value of garden environments.

Another type of comparative study might explore effects on behaviour by modifying the environment. An example of a redesign of the physical space can be found in a study on the effect of an enhanced nursing home environment (Cohen-Mansfield and Werner 1998). In this study a home environment and an outdoor environment were enhanced with benches and additional visual, olfactory and audible stimuli. As a result, participants spent more time in the enhanced environments, used the benches and experienced a positive impact on their mood and behaviour: 'less trespassing, exit-seeking, and other agitated behaviour in those who pace' (p.199). Residents found it more pleasurable. Staff and family also preferred the enhanced environment.

Both sensory stimulation (Ballard *et al.* 2002; Smallwood *et al.* 2001) and sensory environment interventions (Cohen-Mansfield and Werner 1998) involving people with dementia were to some degree effective in reducing so-called 'negative' behaviours, including agitation, shouting, wandering (*sic*) and behavioural disturbances, as well as providing an increase in positive behaviour and effects. But such studies, whether about an intervention in care or in the physical environment, take as their starting point the desire to modify what is seen as problem behaviour or negative well-being. Conversely, an exploratory approach might seek to generate an experience that is not pre-determined, but open to potential synergy of the intervention itself. In the exploratory study reported in this chapter, sensory stimulation through a connection to nature benefited a person with dementia in ways that were not pre-determined. Essentially, the experience of the research exercise provided the space and time in which the participants could determine for themselves how that time was spent and could direct the course of the conversation accordingly. By adopting this exploratory approach the outcomes were determined by the individuals, demonstrating an innovative person-centred research methodology.

This exploratory approach also positioned the research within an environmental framework. In other words, it was not research about care environments. It was research of environments themselves. People were not asked to reflect upon or think about how they use space, what the home meant to them or how satisfied they were, etc. The person's use of the space was central to the research, which was carried out in the environment it was investigating, and included enabling the person's use of it.

Dialogues were audio-taped and the primary data were gathered during these social interactions. 'The commitment to understanding participants' perspectives implies investigating the experience, meanings, intentions and behaviour of people with dementia on their own terms. This inevitably means using fieldwork methods which get the investigator close to the subject of study' (Bond and Corner 2001, p.106).

Unlike a semi-structured interview with pre-determined discussion topics, this study endeavoured to generate dialogue with no particular agenda. This shifted the intention from gathering data to initiating social interaction for its own sake, the interaction being the object of interest, rather than the topic being discussed. Support for this approach was found in Surr's (2006) work with people with dementia in residential care, in which she allowed participants 'to direct the interview and set the agenda' (p.1724).

The methodology for the edge space study also included photographing the building; taking notes about how the residents, staff and visitors used it; measuring rooms and distances to outside, etc. Floor plans of the buildings and site details such as landscape elements, outdoor areas, and neighbourhood were also gathered.

Ethical approval for carrying out the research was gained through both the university and the Central Office for Research Ethics Committees (COREC). Ongoing consent was gained from participants throughout the research and written consent was gained prior to the dialogues, either from the residents or their relative/advocate. Verbal consent was achieved by asking the participants prior to and during the dialogues if they wished to continue to participate.

Findings

This section shows some of the ways three participants identified themselves through enjoyment of nature-related activities, both presently and in the past. From the edge space dialogues, examples are given of people using nature creatively in order to express themselves, and how such engagement supported their sense of themselves by reinforcing their identity. This is one of the key dimensions of quality of life in care homes as identified in *My Home Life* (Owen and NCHRDF 2006).

The natural world had previously played a role in the lives of many participants, and some believed they still continued to participate in these ways. Activities people identified with included crown green bowling, swimming, going away on holiday, playing golf, walking in the countryside, gardening, walking around the garden or just 'pottering' in the garden. Social relationships with neighbours were developed in conversations 'over the fence'. Having a warm sunny 'sitting out' place was identified as a positive aspect of the garden. Some people fondly remembered older relatives whom they associated with the greenhouse, the allotment, farm animals, pets or walks in the country. Particular plants, flowers and fruit trees were mentioned. A nearby park was identified for the sporting activities it offered.

In the following examples of dialogue, PwD = the person with dementia, and GC = the researcher.

Sporting in the countryside

One gentleman in the study had led a very active life and still clearly identified himself as carrying on an outdoor life, although that was not the case.

GC: What can you see out there?

PwD1: I can see all that...all that...where the football pitches used to be and caravans at the top there, and come in and come down. There's the church on the left hand side... See that church?

GC: Yup.

PwD1: St Aidan's Church. You used to come through into the park where you used to play football, everything, cricket. Well, schools used to use it you see. And then further on...all sorts of sporting activities going on, you know, netball for ladies, bowls, you know things like that...

GC: Do you get outside very much?

PwD1: Yeah, we go into Derbyshire quite a lot and that... Play sports, things like that...winter time...indoor games.

Caretaking in the neighbourhood

In this next example, a woman was able to retain her identity as a compassionate and generous neighbour, long after she no longer cared for 'everybody and their mother's cat'. The conversation was with a professional carer (PC) who was able to reinforce the person's identity through shared knowledge of the person she had been in the past, even if in care the person with dementia was no longer able to participate in that activity.

PC: You used to look after cats, didn't you?

PwD2: Oh, he did he used to look after mine. Don't I look after them now?

PC: I don't know.

PwD2: No, I don't think I do. Oh I used to look after everybody and their mother's cat. Didn't I?

PC: Every cats on main road.

PwD2: They all come up to my place.

PC: I know you feed 'em, that's why.

PwD2: I know we did. We fed 'em all. Still, if summat's hungry and you've got summat to feed it, let it have it I say. May be wrong.

Visiting the garden

In this example the woman identifies herself as a garden person by saying that she still goes out into the garden 'many a time of day'. This daily routine from the past, even though it no longer occurs in the care home where she lives, is a fondly remembered activity that reinforces her identity, she being a person who likes 'a little bit of garden'.

> GC: What did you like about that garden?
>
> PwD2: I don't know. I liked it. I like this one and all. I like a little bit of garden.
>
> GC: When do you go out into the garden?
>
> PwD2: I go out many a time of day. Walk through garden and have a look at things.
>
> GC: What sort of things do you see?
>
> PwD2: Oh little bits of flowers. Daffodils and all sorts. Not elaborate, not an elaborate garden.

Later on, she identifies herself as independent in terms of this activity, because she can do it 'on me own'.

> GC: Do you go out into the garden on your own?
>
> PwD2: Sometimes I walk round it if it's a nice day.
>
> GC: Did you go out with somebody else?
>
> PwD2: Nobody to go out wi' when everybody's gone to work. So I have a walk round on me own.
>
> GC: What can you see from that garden?
>
> PwD2: Not a lot. Just an ordinary garden with some garden next door, and flowers and things. It's alright.

Helping Father

In the following dialogue another woman began on the topic of gardens and quickly moved to her relationship with her father.

> GC: Did you used to have a garden?
> PwD3: Two.
> GC: Two! Tell me about them.
> PwD3: We were always in the garden.
> GC: What was it like?
> PwD3: Oh garden was alright except when he started having us 'it's your turn to this and it's your turn to that'.

Caretaking the chickens

While on this topic, she was looking out of the window...

> GC: What did you like to do in [the garden]?
> PwD3: I wasn't bothered about ought [anything] in garden. One of me [?] coming through now.
> GC: What's coming through? Show me. [She points out the window to a blackbird on the hill.]
> Oh, right. What is it?
> PwD3: It's one of the chickens. Don't know which one it is.
> GC: One of the chickens? (Mm) How many chickens do you have?
> PwD3: I don't know, it's got two or three. Sometimes they alright, sometimes they's difficult, run away.
> GC: Is that your job? What did you have to do with the chickens?
> PwD3: Sometimes you have to, you know, feed 'em first, and wash 'em.

Her experience of caring for chickens was reawakened by the sight of a blackbird outside the window. The moment was also made possible through engagement with a listener who encouraged sensory stimulation from nature. During such stimulation this dialogue became meaningful. By recalling her chicken caretaking experience she identified herself as responsible, adept, caring and knowledgeable.

Being with someone

In this next example, a woman quoted earlier began by discussing a small hill in the view out of the dining room window. This led rather quickly to her revelation of an intimate relationship.

GC: Have you ever been up on top of that hill?
PwD2:   I don't think so. I think Tommy has but I haven't.
GC: Who has?
PwD2:   Tommy.
GC: Tommy? Who's Tommy?
PwD2:   Used to be with me.

The natural world for some participants provided a language of metaphor with which they were able to communicate spiritual matters. In the following example this same woman who was in the last year of her life was able through a connection to nature in the presence of another person to raise moral and ethical issues.

Personifying the blackbird

GC: There was a bird a few minutes ago you told me you saw up on that hill.
PwD2:   Ay. Has he gone?
GC: I don't know, can you see him?
PwD2:   No.
GC: Do you remember what he looked like?
PwD2:   Oh I do, a tan, dark coloured bird.
GC: What was he doing?
PwD2:   Just looking at us lot, thinking when are we going to throw him any grub. Did we give him something?
GC: I don't think we did.
PwD2:   He'll think we're so many miserable boogers. Well he would, wouldn't he. Wouldn't you, if you were hungry and we didn't give you a bit of nought to eat? You'd think to your sen [self] you're a miserable sod, wouldn't you? And I would.

Predicting her future

After about a ten-second pause she began to raise the issue of her own mortality.

> PwD2: How much more have you to do?
> GC: Today...
> PwD2: Only today? I've more than today I think. I think I have more than today to do.
> GC: More than today?
> PwD2: I think so...

In this brief and extraordinary exchange, a person with dementia moved fluidly from discussing wildlife to commenting on her life expectancy. Nature opened the door for this to occur. But it also required a listener to allow moments of silence in the dialogue. During such a moment, this person with dementia was able to shift the topic to a more profound and perhaps spiritual level.

The edge space dialogues enabled people with dementia to use nature to express themselves and to maintain personal identity through interaction with others. Edge spaces can be locations for social interaction and sensory stimulation from nature, with the potential to stimulate and enhance communication. This use of a person-centred research method in a specifically enabling space resulted in maintenance of self which is a contribution to the well-being of people with dementia (Gillies 2001; Harman and Clare 2006; Harris and Sterin 1999).

Implications

Efforts to provide a participatory experience within a therapeutic framework can improve quality of care by contributing to a person's sense of self and personal identity. Working to help residents maintain their identity is a key dimension of quality of life according to *My Home Life*. The study described above was a creative approach to person-centred care as it allowed people with dementia to identify themselves through the recalling or re-imagining of favourite or meaningful activities. Social interaction enabled them to maintain their identity in spite of limited participation.

The research has quality of life implications for design, caregiving and methodology.

Design implications

A care environment involves both physical elements and human interactions. The building and the contributions of individuals are equally important in providing optimal quality of life. This study demonstrated that views from edge spaces stimulated dialogue for people with dementia, and helped to reinforce personal identity by providing opportunities for creative self-expression. The following design guidance can help care environments to facilitate connection to nature.

BUILDING ORIENTATION AND DESIGN

The height and physical positioning of the building on the land will impact the sensory experience of people using the home. The yearly path of the sun and how light and air enter the building largely determine the patterns of sun and shade inside and out, as well as the microclimates of spaces adjacent to the building.

USE OF SPACE AND TIME

Consider the times when rooms are used. They are best when well lit with sunlight when they are more likely to feel warm and inviting. Consider the views at different times of day. Is there local activity to stimulate conversation or a peaceful green view for relaxing? Where possible, plan the use of the room for when the lighting and views are optimal.

STRUCTURE AND FURNITURE

What a person is capable of doing in a space depends partly on physical features. Tables and chairs are often necessary for activities. The proximity of furniture to windows determines view potential. For useful outdoor spaces, provide access for mobility, comfortable sheltered seating, proximity to the entrance, manageable walks, beauty and sensory stimulation. Will the effort to go outside be rewarded by the experience that awaits a person?

ROUTINE DOMESTIC NATURE-RELATED ACTIVITIES

Increasingly, the therapeutic role of normal domestic activities in the lives of people with dementia is being recognised, valued and promoted (Knocker 2007). Participation can generate meaningful conversation and bring purpose and useful occupation to people's lives, as well as structure to their day. Nature-related activities can also provide exercise and fresh air, and can connect people to their local community and neighbourhood. Examples include hanging out the washing, pottering in the garden, sweeping the path, picking fruit and preparing vegetables for a meal.

Caregiving implications

Spending time talking to people with dementia is therapeutic as it provides necessary social interaction. This remedies the often short task-orientated exchanges between residents and caregivers which are unfortunately too common in many care settings. Meaningful conversation with a person provides him or her with opportunities for self-expression. Furthermore, the caregiver becomes aware of the self-identity roles that the caregiving process and activity interventions could then be designed to support.

Research implications – person-centred methods

People do not operate in a spatial or a social vacuum. Their response and interaction emerges out of the social and physical context of the moment. In this study, a research space, which is also a person's living environment, empowers and enables that person's interactions within it. A research exercise can potentially provide an environment and investigate it at the same time. In this way human–environment interaction reflects a methodology of participatory engagement – a creative approach to person-centred care.

Design, care and research implications were briefly mentioned. To *design for nature in dementia care*, by addressing the physical and social aspects of the care home environment, consult the book by that title (Chalfont 2007b).

Conclusion

This study supports the importance of maintaining identity in later life and offers one research method to achieve it within the context of care homes. While personal identity can survive through late stages of dementia, social identity depends on interaction with others (Sabat and Harré 1992). Therefore, failure to recognise people's identity and provide them with the necessary tools and opportunities to maintain it will reduce their well-being. On the contrary, according to Cohen-Mansfield, Parpura-Gill and Golander (2006), 'understanding and enhancing a person's identity can improve overall care for people with dementia, resulting in more individualized care and thereby enhancing the person's well-being…[furthermore] long-term care settings must strive to provide avenues for identity expression' (p.211).

The following points illustrate the key messages and implications of this chapter for work within care homes:

- A care home involves the residents, the staff, the building and the natural world – successful improvements involve both people and place.

- Connection to nature depends on physical and social elements.

- The building orientation, furniture, physical elements, and the schedule of daily use affect the lighting, ambience and views of any room, impacting the person's experience within it.

- A view to nature can stimulate the senses, prompt social interaction, provide topics of conversation, nurture spirituality, improve caregiver interaction and enhance family visits.

- Edge spaces of buildings can potentially contribute to well-being.

- A person's ability to engage in nature-enhanced dialogue seems undiminished by even advanced levels of cognitive impairment.

- The natural world provides a language of metaphor to communicate spiritual matters.

- The research process can be a creative experience for the participant.

This chapter provides evidence that recognising and attending to each of these points can help to maintain the identity of older people with dementia living in care homes, and enhance the care experiences of their families and staff working with them.

References

Alexander, C., Ishikawa, S., Silverstein, M., Jacobson, M. *et al.* (1977) *A Pattern Language.* New York: Oxford University Press.

Ballard, C.G., O'Brien, J.T., Reichelt, K. and Perry, E.K. (2002) 'Aromatherapy as a safe and effective treatment for the management of agitation in severe dementia: The results of a double-blind, placebo-controlled trial with Melissa.' *Journal of Clinical Psychiatry 63,* 7, 553–558.

Bond, J. and Corner, L. (2001) 'Researching dementia: Are there unique methodological challenges for health services research?' *Ageing and Society 21,* 1, 95–116.

Chalfont, G.E. (2006) 'Connection to Nature at the Building Edge: Towards a Therapeutic Architecture for Dementia Care Environments.' PhD thesis. Sheffield: University of Sheffield.

Chalfont, G.E. (2008) 'Wholistic design in dementia care: Connection to nature with PLANET.' In S. Rodiek and B. Schwarz (eds) *Outdoor Environments for People with Dementia.* New York: Haworth.

Chalfont, G.E. (2007b) *Design for Nature in Dementia Care.* London: Jessica Kingsley Publishers.

Chalfont, G.E. and Rodiek, S. (2005) 'Building Edge: An ecological approach to research and design of environments for people with dementia.' *Alzheimer's Care Quarterly, Special Issue – Environmental Innovations in Care 6,* 4, 341–348.

Cohen-Mansfield, J., Parpura-Gill, A. and Golander, H. (2006) 'Utilization of self-identity roles for designing interventions for persons with dementia.' *Journal of Gerontology: Psychological Sciences 61B,* 4, 202–212.

Cohen-Mansfield, J. and Werner, P. (1998) 'The effects of an enhanced environment on nursing home residents who pace.' *Gerontologist 38,* 2, 199–208.

Cutler, L.J. and Kane, R.A. (2005) 'As great as all outdoors: A study of outdoor spaces as a neglected resource for nursing home residents.' In S. Rodiek and B. Schwarz (eds) *The Role of the Outdoors in Residential Environments for Aging.* New York: Haworth. pp.29–48.

Davies, M. and Wallbridge, D. (1981) *Boundary and Space. An Introduction to the Work of D.W. Winnicott.* Middlesex: Penguin.

Gibson, G. and Chalfont, G. (2007) 'Housing and connection to nature for people with dementia: Findings from the INDEPENDENT Project.' *Journal of Housing for the Elderly 21,* 1/2, 55–72.

Gilleard, C.J. (1984) *Living with Dementia.* London: Croom Helm.

Gillies, B. (2001) 'The experience of living through dementia.' *International Journal of Geriatric Psychiatry 16,* 1, 111–112.

Harman, G. and Clare, L. (2006) 'Illness representations and lived experience in early-stage dementia.' *Qualitative Health Research 16,* 4, 484–502.

Harris, P. and Sterin, G. (1999) 'Insider's perspective: Defining and preserving the self of dementia.' *Journal of Mental Health and Aging 5,* 3, 241–256.

Kasl-Godley, J. and Gatz, M. (2000) 'Psychosocial interventions for individuals with dementia: An integration of theory, therapy, and a clinical understanding of dementia.' *Clinical Psychology Review 20,* 6, 755–782.

Kearney, A.R. and Winterbottom, D. (2005) 'Nearby nature and long-term care facility residents: Benefits and design recommendations.' In S. Rodiek and B. Schwarz (eds) *The Role of the Outdoors in Residential Environments for Aging.* New York: Haworth. pp.7–28.

Kitwood, T. (1997) *Dementia Reconsidered: The Person Comes First.* Buckingham: Open University Press.

Kitwood, T. and Bredin, K. (1992) 'A new approach to the evaluation of dementia care.' *Journal of Advances in Health and Nursing Care 5*, 41–60.

Knocker, S. (2007) 'Capturing the magic of everyday, purposeful activities.' *Journal of Dementia Care 15*, 2, 20–21.

Lindberg, D.A. (2005) 'Integrative review of research related to meditation, spirituality, and the elderly.' *Geriatric Nursing 26*, 6, 372–377.

Ottosson, J. and Grahn, P. (2005) 'Measures of restoration in geriatric care residences: The influence of nature on elderly people's power of concentration, blood pressure and pulse rate.' In S. Rodiek and B. Schwarz (eds) *The Role of the Outdoors in Residential Environments for Aging.* New York: Haworth. pp.227–256.

Owen, T. and NCHRDF (eds) (2006) *My Home Life: Quality of Life in Care Homes.* London: Help the Aged.

Rappe, E., Kivelä, S. and Rita, H. (2006) 'Visiting outdoor green environments positively impacts self-rated health among older people in long-term care.' *Hort Technology 16*, 1.

Sabat, S.R. (2002) 'Surviving manifestations of selfhood in Alzheimer's disease.' *Dementia 1*, 1, 25–36.

Sabat, S.R. and Collins, M. (1999) 'Intact social, cognitive ability and selfhood: A case study of Alzheimer's disease.' *American Journal of Alzheimer's Disease* January/February, 11–19.

Sabat, S.R. and Harré, R. (1992) 'The construction and deconstruction of self in Alzheimer's Disease.' *Ageing and Society 12*, 443–461.

Sabat, S.R., Napolitano, L. and Fath, H. (2004) 'Barriers to the construction of a valued social identity: A case study of Alzheimer's disease.' *American Journal of Alzheimer's Disease and Other Dementias 19*, 3, 177–185.

Smallwood, J., Brown, R., Coulter, F., Irvine, E. and Copland, C. (2001) 'Aromatherapy and behaviour disturbances in dementia: A randomized controlled trial.' *International Journal of Geriatric Psychiatry 16*, 10, 1010–1013.

Spector, A., Thorgrimsen, L., Woods, B., Royan, L. *et al.* (2003) 'Efficacy of an evidence-based cognitive stimulation therapy programme for people with dementia.' *British Journal of Psychiatry 183*, 248–254.

Sugiyama, T. and Thompson, C.W. (2005) 'Environmental support for outdoor activities and older people's quality of life.' In S. Rodiek and B. Schwarz (eds) *The Role of the Outdoors in Residential Environments for Aging.* New York: Haworth. pp.167–185.

Surr, C.A. (2006) 'Preservation of self in people with dementia living in residential care: A socio-biographical approach.' *Social Science and Medicine 62*, 1720–1730.

Tang, J.W. and Brown, R.D. (2005) 'The effect of viewing a landscape on physiological health of elderly women.' In S. Rodiek and B. Schwarz (eds) *The Role of the Outdoors in Residential Environments for Aging.* New York: Haworth. pp.187–202.

CHAPTER 7

Establishing 'Friends of Care Home' Groups

Sheila Furness and Bren Torry

Introduction

This chapter presents key findings from a year-long study where two 'friends of care home' groups were established, monitored and evaluated. The authors are both qualified social workers and one has worked as an inspector of care homes whilst the other has worked as a nurse in both residential and nursing homes. Working as researchers we wanted to draw upon our experiences and understanding of care homes to develop and provide a practical contribution that could be used to raise standards in these environments. Although the notion of setting up 'friends of care home' groups is not new, the lessons learnt from setting up such groups have not been shared through research.

The objectives of this chapter are:

- to identify ways of engaging relatives and friends in care homes for older people that will help to develop a greater sense of community and provide a forum for more meaningful engagement and activity

- to provide exemplars of how 'Friends of Care Home' (FCH) groups influence the quality of life of those living in the care home that will be of use to managers, staff and visitors to the home

- to examine how an FCH group can promote a culture of openness so that suggestions to improve care practices are welcomed and encouraged by all staff and will positively affect well-being.

The chapter begins with the rationale and background to the study and includes the profiles of each of the care homes. Following this, an outline of the methodology used to collect the data is included. Examples are used from each home to show how each group was set up, along with our observations of what seemed to work and some of the difficulties encountered along the way. Next, the key functions of the FCH groups in promoting social and leisure activities, empowerment and advocacy, and influencing care standards are described. The chapter concludes by considering the implications for practice and providing a summary of the main points.

Rationale

In response to ongoing criticisms and concerns about the quality of care and quality of life for those living in care homes in England, the government introduced national minimum standards for care homes for older people (DoH 2003) under Section 23 of the Care Standards Act 2000. Several of these national minimum standards relate specifically to the involvement of relatives and friends in the running of the home. Care home managers are required to ensure that effective quality assurance and quality monitoring systems are in place (standards 31–38). 'A competent manager is adept at fostering an atmosphere of openness and respect, in which residents, family, friends and staff all feel valued and that their opinions matter (DOH 2003, p.31). Establishing an FCH group is one way in which this requirement can be met. Regular meetings in the home with family and friends can provide a healthy forum in which to raise any concerns and also provides an opportunity for positive feedback. An FCH group also signifies that the home is prepared to engage and work with relatives. Individual care homes can only benefit from shared and collective efforts to engage and learn from each other in order to enhance the quality of life for those living and dying in the home.

A study by Levy-Storms and Miller-Martinez (2005) examined the relationship between the caregivers' involvement and its effects on their level of satisfaction in a care home. They found that it was not how often a family visited a relative but what they did during their visit that affected their satisfaction with the care. They suggest that family well-being could be one way to evaluate the quality of care.

A number of studies suggest that the role of relatives has been undervalued and is an underdeveloped resource that can be utilised to provide mutual benefits for all parties (Davies 2001; Ryan and Scullion 2000; Wright 2000). However, it must also be recognised that some residents may receive infrequent or no visitors. This may be because their families lose contact or become distant, their relatives and friends become infirm and not able to visit or die, or they have no known close relatives. However, statistics published as part of the Health Survey for England 2000 found that 64 per cent of all residents in care homes surveyed received visitors at least once a week; 20 per cent at least once a month; 9 per cent every two to three months to one year; and only 6 per cent had no contact (Bajekal 2002). Relatives and friends who are prepared to engage with FCH groups can play an important role in supporting and advocating for others who have no visitors to look after their interests.

Background to the study

In the context of the study described within this chapter, a Friends of Care Home (FCH) group is defined as a voluntary group of people, whose membership to this group is united as a result of some form of current, past or even anticipated future connection to the home. The basis could be either as a relation, through friendship, via a shared interest (such as faith, previous group/club membership, hobby), through voluntary work (such as on behalf of a religious group) or because of previous employment (an ex-staff member, or someone who previously worked with one of the residents in a former employment). The group may have many roles (for example, informal inspection, monitoring of care, fundraising or even therapeutic support for members); however, the main purpose is to promote the well-being of residents and to support staff in this process. A healthy FCH group will continually evolve and change in response to the energies and aspirations of its members.

The 'Friends of Care Home' concept is not necessarily a new one; there is evidence that informal support groups within healthcare provision have been in existence for many years. For example, many charitable groups have existed to raise funds for elderly care, such as Age Concern, hospice groups and hospital fundraising groups. The Relatives and Residents Association was founded back in 1992 to promote the support and well-being of people living in care homes within England and the wider UK. They have published a helpful booklet that sets out some guidance about how to establish a relatives group within a care home (The Relatives and Residents Association 1996).

The idea for this project stemmed from a research study conducted with 19 care homes in one region in the north of England (Furness 2006). The impetus was driven by an advisory panel, established by one of the researchers, made up of local people who either had been carers or were professionals involved with care homes. The advisory panel expressed an interest in working together to promote good practice in care homes and organised a workshop with care home managers, staff, relatives, members of the public and other professionals to explore the purpose and benefit of setting up FCH groups (Furness 2007). Participants at this workshop identified the following benefits:

- Demonstrates a shared commitment to providing good care.

- Provides a forum to consult others on changes/issues affecting the care of residents.

- Acts as a way of giving general feedback to the care home and facilitates information exchange.

- Indicates to visitors that the management is prepared to listen and value their views.

- Assists the transition from being a carer and to find a new supportive role.

- Shows respect for each others' views and experiences of caring for each resident.

- Offers a way of maintaining and developing a different kind of relationship between relatives/friends and the care home staff.

- Visitors may instigate new activities thus taking some pressure off staff and allowing them to make a positive contribution to the home.

- The group can challenge or lobby to change external factors impacting on the home, for example care home fees set by government and lengthy waiting times at hospital, particularly when accompanying residents who have dementia.

Methods

The motivation to undertake this comparative study between two FCH groups resulted from the perceived advantages for residents, relatives and care home staff. Data were collected using interviews with care home managers, residents and relatives, and observations were undertaken during FCH meetings and events. We also distributed a questionnaire to staff and to visiting relatives and friends. Additionally, information was collected through various sources of relevant correspondence including minutes of FCH meetings, care home policies and procedures, and newsletters.

Permission to conduct the research was granted by the care home owners and managers. Care home managers consulted with residents and relatives prior to granting us approval and access. In compliance with good ethical practice the study proposal was peer reviewed by a university research ethics committee. Informed consent was sought from all participants prior to their involvement in the study, and anonymity, confidentiality and privacy were assured. An information sheet about the study was made available for participants with clear statements that they could withdraw at any point without adverse effect.

Only those residents identified by each care home manager as able to take part in the study were approached; residents with dementia or end stage terminal illness, or anyone unwell at the time of the study were excluded.

Care home profiles

CARE HOME A

This was a privately owned care home housed in a large adapted property. The home was able to accommodate three service users aged under 65 years of age with dementia and one additional service user under 65 years. The home had been extended to provide purpose-built ground floor accommodation for 37 residents in total. There were four lounges and a dining room. The owner had two other care homes. The manager had worked at the home for 21 years and had been the registered manager for 19 years.

At the start of the project there were 34 residents. Twenty-six residents tended to use one of the four lounge areas. Eight residents stayed in their bedrooms and did not have any contact with other residents because of their health and mobility needs.

In terms of visiting patterns, the manager estimated that 6 relatives visited on a daily basis; 20 on a weekly basis; 4 or 5 visited each month and 3 residents did not receive any visitors at all. On average most visitors tended to stay for approximately 30 minutes. One relative came every morning and stayed for about two hours and another relative spent about two hours there every afternoon.

CARE HOME B

This was a privately owned care home for older people with dementia or other mental health issues. The home was able to accommodate up to 39 people over 65 years of age with dementia, one of whom may have past or present alcohol dependence; up to three with mental disorder, excluding learning disability or dementia; three service users under 65 years of age with dementia; and one additional service user under 65 years. Similarly to Care Home A, this was an old building adapted for healthcare provision, including nursing. The accommodation was arranged over four floors and there were two lounges, a dining room and conservatory. The home could accommodate up to 39 residents in total. There was a new owner in place, who also owned two other care homes, and a new manager.

At the start of the project there were 35 residents. All of the residents were mobile and therefore free to make use of the rooms available to them. The manager estimated that four relatives visited daily, seven relatives visited weekly and four residents did not receive any visitors. The manager was unable to estimate average lengths of visits, suggesting that visits varied.

The two care homes were similar in size but there appeared to be two key differences. The first difference related to how long the owner and manager had been in place, with the owner and manager in Care Home A being much longer established than that of Care Home B. The second difference related to the mental health of the residents; in Care Home B all residents displayed some degree of dementia and therefore their contribution to the FCH group was seriously limited.

Both care homes formed a Friends of Care Home group. Care Home A's group lasted 12 months and held seven meetings. Care Home B's group lasted nine months and held five meetings; during this time the group tried to influence social and leisure activities for the residents but a change in management disrupted their plans.

Lessons learned

In this study the following key lessons were identified in relation to the 'process of setting up an FCH group' and the recognition of 'the potential use of the FCH group'.

Setting up the FCH groups

Beginning is easy…continuing is hard

Japanese Proverb

We found that there were three key stages involved in setting up an FCH group: engaging the manager, engaging relatives and friends and then getting started with the first meeting.

STAGE ONE: GETTING THE MANAGER ON BOARD

The key learning points discovered were:

- The manager needs to be *committed* to setting up and supporting an FCH group in order to develop its potential and for the group to flourish in the longer term. Motivation will have an impact upon commitment.
- The manager needs to allocate *adequate time to support and promote* the group and to determine how best to make sure that all relatives are invited to meetings, kept informed of activities and included as much as possible. Although there are many demands on the manager, setting up and facilitating an FCH group needs to be a priority.
- It is vital that the manager or a delegated member of staff *recognise that it is their responsibility to communicate with relatives* otherwise attendance at meetings can be poor and affect others' commitment.

We found it easy to engage the managers because in both homes they had volunteered to participate in the study. Neither of the care homes had tried to set up an FCH group before, although the manager of Care Home B had previous experience of working with an FCH group in a similar setting.

The researchers met each care home manager to discuss the project and to determine their expectations and the commitment involved. Managers outlined their expectations of the group, the degree that relatives were currently involved in the home's activities, visiting practices, existing social activities and their views about relatives' involvement in monitoring and quality assurance.

Care Home A had previously attempted to involve relatives in social evenings and care-planning; however, uptake was limited. At the time of the initial interview the manager of Care Home B had only been in post for three months; it was hoped by the manager that relatives would become involved in care-planning.

When asked about the objectives of the FCH group manager A stated:

> I'd like relatives to come in and discuss any issues they've got...their expectations of the relative when they're here, anything that...they feel we do well, the things that they're not so keen that we could improve on and just really get a better...relationship and more input from them 'cause obviously they know the service user better than we do so it's better really.

Manager B, however, identified that:

> ...one is the area of advocacy that people with dementia often lose out... I think also it is a way of getting feedback other than through question-naires and inspection reports. I also think it is a very traumatic and very difficult process for people to adjust to having a relative with dementia... So I do see that it can be a self-support group as well...but also it brings new ideas and new developments into the home... I quite like different perspectives.

Although both had different objectives the important factor here is that they both had a vision about what they wanted to achieve from an FCH group.

Residents and relatives were informed of this planned initiative either in person or by letter. A poster was displayed at each home to advertise an inaugural meeting and there was an open invitation for everyone to attend.

It cannot be stressed enough that thorough planning and preparation are key aspects for successful participation. It may have been more benefi-cial if further canvassing of potential interest had taken place before the first meeting date was established.

STAGE TWO: GETTING THE RELATIVES ON BOARD

The key learning points to promote relative engagement were found to include:

- The manager or a delegated member of staff needs to invite all relatives and friends to join the FCH group. The manager should *check out the most convenient date and time to hold a meeting which is suitable for the majority* of relatives and friends.
- All *staff need to be made aware of the purpose* of establishing an FCH group and should be encouraged to promote the group actively by speaking to relatives and other visitors.
- *The first meeting needs to be well publicised* by displaying posters about the meeting, inviting relatives verbally as well as sending written invitations to the meeting.
- Initially, the meeting should be informal and could be a social activity.
- Some form of *'incentive' should be provided,* for example, light refreshments.
- *Involvement of any kind, whether active or passive, should be encouraged.* A simple form could be devised that contains information about contact details, times available to attend FCH group meetings, interest in membership and interest in receiving further details about the group's activities.
- Group *objectives need to be realistic and achievable.*

At the first FCH group meeting group members were asked to identify a purpose for their group. Their key aims were:

- Care Home A FCH group members' views about joining the group were categorised into one main theme: *to support the care home.* One participant revealed that he wished 'to give something back to the home', but overall, it was agreed by the relatives that the group should 'support the work of the staff'. It was observed that the manager did not contribute towards the formulation of this aim, consequently previous expectations and ideas for the group were lost at this point.

- Care Home B FCH group members' views about joining the group were categorised into three themes:

- *improving life for the residents*, for example 'to make things better for the resident', 'contribute to helping', 'to make a contribution'
- *to improve the home*, for example, 'to make a better home'
- *to deal with own personal feelings*, for example, guilty feelings 'to lessen my own feelings of being unable to care'.

In comparison to Care Home A, the manager in Care Home B appeared to share ideas and key aims for the group. If ownership of the group and its activities is to be fostered, it is important that members are able to express their ideas and identify their own goals.

The first meeting was also used to explore the views about members' involvement in the group, with respect to timing, length and frequency of meetings. FCH members in Care Home A shared contact details and discussed a range of topics for future meetings; ideas included educational events, social events and ways to involve others and keep them informed of the FCH group's activities via the home's newsletter. Relatives also took the opportunity to praise staff and provide feedback about the positive atmosphere in the home and recognition of the demands placed upon staff. In comparison Care Home B FCH group used the occasion to share personal information with each other, as well as provide feedback about a recent refurbishment. The manager provided an update about future plans for the home. Also discussed were ideas for future activities for residents.

It is important that those attending the first meeting are made to feel welcome by the manager. This can be achieved by facilitating introductions and discussion, and by making sure the environment is comfortable.

STAGE THREE: GETTING STARTED

Key learning points:
- It is useful for any FCH group to *regularly revisit and review their aims* to confirm that new and existing members agree and subscribe to these. This will help to ensure that the group maintains a focus and will allow new members to better understand the purpose and be able to shape the group's identity.

- It will be important to attract new members *to bring fresh ideas and energy* to the group.
- An FCH group *can meet informally* without having a formal chair and minute taker because these roles may prevent people from actively participating.

Core membership of the FCH groups differed; Care Home A attracted three relatives and friends whereas Care Home B was attended by ten relatives and friends. Care Home A quickly adopted a formal approach with a rotating chair and minute taker; their agreed remit was to raise funds for the social well-being of residents.

Care Home B members adopted an informal approach and, by comparison, evolved more slowly in response to members' needs. The FCH group regularly increased membership by including relatives of newly admitted residents. This allowed members to support each other and provided an environment where they could advocate on behalf of residents, relatives and staff.

This informal approach allowed members to become more active and engaged within the group. As examples, one member suggested providing contact details to the manager, which could be distributed to other relatives of new residents. Another member interviewed relatives and recorded their views about their experiences and ways that had helped them to accept and cope more with the move of their relative into the home, with the aim of incorporating key messages into a leaflet to be given out to new relatives.

An FCH group can provide a helpful structure by facilitating direct support to relatives and friends, by validating their experiences and by helping them to adjust to the changes. A cross-national study carried out in the USA and UK by Nolan and Dellasega (1999) identified the need for interventions and better support systems to help carers adjust to their new roles before, during and after admission of their relative to a care home. Potentially the presence of an FCH group provides an organised approach that will indirectly benefit and support a new resident.

When interviewed at the start of the study, the manager of Care Home A expressed a desire to use the FCH group to obtain feedback from relatives about their views about care; however, this was never raised at meetings. Relatives have a right to feel that their views are respected and, where possible, action is taken to address concerns or issues in order to secure their confidence. Permission to comment and provide feedback appears to be an important feature that should be actively encouraged by staff.

At the first meeting at Care Home B, the manager requested feedback about care issues and a number of issues were raised by relatives. Disappointingly the manager did not report back on, or resolve any of these issues. The manager later left the home and this feedback was lost. Failing to respond to FCH group feedback could result in members experiencing disillusionment and they may think that attending meetings or providing feedback is a waste of time.

Realising the potential of the FCH group

Vision without action is a daydream…
action without vision is a nightmare

Japanese proverb

When summing up the achievements of both Friends of Care Home groups it is important to take into consideration the impact each group has had on the residents, as well as on the relatives, friends and staff. The overall aim is to have a positive influence on the residents' quality of life within the care home.

Several studies have identified the importance of finding out the views of those using a service about what matters to them, and their preferences in terms of their quality of life (Fry 2000; Gabriel and Bowling 2004; Gerritsen *et al.* 2004; Scharf, Phillipson and Smith 2005). In care homes quality of life and quality of care can often be confused and used interchangeably. Residents living in a care home providing a high standard of care may not necessarily perceive that their quality of life is also of a high standard. Quality of life is subjective and can be influenced and affected by quality of care but there are other factors that may shape their satisfaction. For instance, in *My Home Life*, Owen and NCHRDF (2006) suggest that we need to understand the connections between different physical and psychological or emotional dimensions to quality of life and how they interact with each other. They urge moving away from a view based on needs to one based on preferences.

In this study of FCH groups, relatives, friends, residents and staff were consulted to seek their views regarding their participation in and potential use of the FCH groups. In light of the feedback three main themes were identified where the FCH group could be used to enhance quality of life for residents:

- social and leisure activities
- advocacy and empowerment
- influencing standards of care.

We found the promotion of 'social and leisure activities' and 'advocacy and empowerment' were the main short-term achievements of the FCH groups. The capacity to 'influence standards of care' appeared to require longer timescales.

SOCIAL AND LEISURE ACTIVITIES

Key learning points:
- *Opportunity for leisure and participation* in social activities is key to ensure that residents *retain a motivation for life* which contributes to their overall satisfaction and well-being. FCH groups can facilitate these opportunities.
- FCH groups can play an important role by *encouraging relatives to become more involved* and thus encourage residents to *maintain and develop new relationships* and stimulate an interest in their immediate and wider environment.

DoH (2006) suggests that independence should be actively promoted for people who use a care home service, through access to leisure and social activities, both within and outside the home. Promoting and maintaining quality of life also involves encouraging and supporting residents to make the most of their capacity and potential, and to try new experiences. People need to feel secure and confident within and outside of the home (CSCI 2006).

The FCH group in Care Home A identified improving resident access to leisure and social activities as one of its main aims. Residents, relatives and staff were asked to rate their views about current access to and use of leisure and social activities. The findings showed some diversity in perspective within and across staff, relatives and resident groups. For example:

- The majority of residents graded access to leisure as good or average whereas the majority of staff rated opportunities to take part in activities as good or excellent.

- Residents were asked to rate their *actual involvement* in the home's activities. The majority of residents rated it as poor.

This insight provides an opportunity for the manager to explore further how to improve resident involvement.

Staff were asked to identify how residents were encouraged to take part in activities. Three strategies emerged:

- introducing activities into the home

- improving interactions with residents

- making the activities sound attractive and fun.

Staff and relatives were also asked how participation in leisure and social activities could be improved.

- Staff responses fell into one category: that 'better staffing levels' would help.

- Relatives' responses were more varied, falling into the following categories:

  o the need for staff education: for example 'carers [to have] more knowledge on dementia', to engage and sustain resident interest in activities

  o the need for more organised activities

  o the stimulation from a pet

  o a recognition that everyone has a role to play in facilitating leisure activities, not just the staff

  o a change in the expectations of a resident's abilities or capabilities. Low expectations are likely to exclude residents from participation.

It was suggested that an activities coordinator should be employed by the home. This could be instrumental in encouraging relatives to get more involved by sharing their interests and time with residents, or in FCH groups.

The Relatives and Residents Association have produced an excellent publication with useful tips on how to involve relatives and friends in care homes for older people (Burton-Jones 2001). The National Association for Providers of Activities for Older People (NAPA) list of '101 things to do when visiting a relative or friend in a nursing home' can also be used by FCH groups to discuss how relatives might spend their time at the care home and to identify different approaches to engaging residents (Perrin 2000).

ADVOCACY AND EMPOWERMENT

Key learning points:
- The 'advocacy' role of the FCH group could be an essential activity because *collective voices are likely to be able to inform change* to a greater extent than a lone voice and those residents who do not receive visitors are likely to benefit hugely from this. It is essential, therefore, that relatives and residents are aware of the FCH group, its aims and objectives and how to access this group or at least contribute items to the agenda.
- The capacity for 'empowerment' within the FCH group is also an opportunity for the care home to *promote and practise an open and shared culture.* The group provides opportunities for information to flow between relatives and staff, where views can be aired and listened to, and responses made. Improved communication should enhance informed decision-making processes.
- The FCH group needs to *identify ways to invite and sustain resident involvement and participation.*

CSCI (2006) specifies that people should be well informed about their rights, options and responsibilities, and encouraged to have as much choice and control over their lives as possible. Promoting maximum independence is important in helping residents to make their own decisions and manage risk in their personal life.

Care Home A FCH group decided to involve residents directly in group membership, thus attempting to enhance communication and shared decision-making. In Care Home B residents were free to wander in and out of the meeting but their contribution was more limited.

CSCI requires all care homes to offer regular meetings with residents and relatives to explore their views and experiences. The FCH group could provide a useful mechanism for this. However, consensus can be hard to achieve. For example, in this study it was noted that where residents made suggestions in the FCH group regarding preferences for activities there was often debate followed by a lack of agreement. However, the FCH group was still in its infancy and, as one resident pointed out, the advantages of the group were yet to be seen: 'can't tell yet...need to follow through on actions'.

Many care homes report difficulties in engaging relatives in activities within the home and we explored this further in the study. Relatives were invited to identify factors that prevented participation in the FCH groups. Some relatives reported that they declined to attend as they wished to spend their limited time at the home with the resident. Other relatives indicated that age and restricted mobility were the main reasons for non-attendance. From our observations it was clear that the lack of knowledge and publicity about the group were also significant barriers.

INFLUENCING STANDARDS OF CARE

Key learning point:
- The FCH group is in a pivotal position to *influence standards of care* within the home and to contribute towards managerial decision-making processes.

CSCI (2006) requires the environment of a care home to be 'healthy', whereby respect is conveyed to all people by recognising their qualities and abilities, and by providing appropriate personal care. The recognition that residents need to retain choice, control and independence in their lives can sometimes be overlooked by both staff and relatives. Residents can experience little freedom and autonomy to express their views about their care. Their views can provide valuable insights into how the home could change routines, ways of working and simple adaptations to promote a partnership approach to care. There needs to be an acknowledgement and acceptance that relationships should be based on mutual respect and consultation.

CSCI (2006) recommends that staff should understand how to provide good-quality care and how to make the service better. Seeking and listening to feedback are essential requirements in ensuring the effective management of the home.

In this study residents in Care Home A were asked to rate their views about:

- the care home's response in listening to their wishes about the care they receive

- their perceived experience of living in the care home

- their health and emotional well-being.

Overall the ratings were good; however some dissatisfaction was identified in relation to care-planning and the quality of food, and feedback was given to the care home:

- Most residents were unaware that care plans existed. Of those who did know, the majority rated the management of their care plan as poor.

- Although the majority of relatives and staff rated the food as excellent, the majority of residents rated it as average. Comments included:

  'no choice for main meals'

  'meals and drinks could be warmer'

  'get another chef'.

The manager of Care Home A invites relatives and residents to complete a questionnaire that allows them to comment on all aspects of the home. Generally this is good practice and a recommendation for all homes. In Care Home B the manager had indicated that it would be useful to involve the FCH group in menu planning because residents were not able to inform staff about their dietary preferences. Concerns have been expressed about the poor quality and sufficiency of food being provided in many care homes and hospitals (ENHA *et al.* 2006; West, Ouellet and Ouellette 2003). This is an important area that could provide a focus for an FCH meeting and reassurance that management regularly review the type and quality of meals prepared for residents.

Implications for practice, education and research

In 2009, a new 'super regulator', the Care Quality Commission, will take over the registration and inspection of all health and social care services in England and Wales, including care homes for older people. There will be a greater reliance on care homes to self-assess their care outcomes and involve relatives and residents in providing feedback and comments about their care. The frequency of inspections will be determined on the basis of star ratings, ranging from those care homes rated with no stars (poor), which will be inspected at least twice a year, through to three-star (excellent) homes to be inspected once every three years. The regulator will review their intelligence on each home every year by considering the annual quality assurance reports written by each home, the number and nature of complaints, feedback and comments made by others external to the home and reports from the commissioning authority. Relatives' presence and engagement within the home is set to play a critical role, not only in the assessment of care standards but also in influencing and enhancing care practices.

Currently there are many formal and informal strategies in existence to engage relatives: one-to-one meetings, the use of questionnaires, telephone contact and, in some instances, use of the complaints procedure. CSCI predominantly rely on feedback from questionnaires and inspection visits. Both methods have limitations, however. The FCH group offers an alternative approach as it can serve to acknowledge relatives' expertise and provide a forum to discuss and influence day-to-day routines and care practices. It also enables managers to acquire constructive feedback, allow people to share concerns and work as a collective to support staff. Further research would be useful to identify other productive and accessible ways of generating and collecting comments and views about care standards.

With the climate of re-organisation of health and social care legislation during the late 20th and early 21st centuries, care homes in England have had to respond continuously to the pressures and increased demands placed upon them. The rapid pace of change has included the introduction of new legislation and care standards, new requirements for staff training and the changing role of care delivery, and these have placed additional pressures on managers. With an increase in the ageing population, and a demand for care in the community for older people with more complex health needs and higher dependency, staff will increasingly have to spend more time attending to personal care and possibly carrying out nursing care tasks. In many homes, the residents' health needs can dominate and their social needs can be overlooked as care staff do not have time to promote activity and stimulation on a regular basis. This can quickly result in boredom and disengagement by residents. Homes need to counter this type of culture and promote some meaningful activities. Homes that employ an activities coordinator are more able to achieve this by developing and offering a regular programme of entertainment, tailored to meet the needs of individuals. Many relatives have specific talents and interests and would welcome an invitation to share, participate in, or even organise social events that would involve and interest residents so that life becomes more engaging. Any opportunities to strengthen relationships with others, including other residents and the wider community, need to be promoted and encouraged if we are to develop more meaningful attachments and enhance well-being within care homes.

The impetus for setting up an FCH group can originate from anyone, and our experience suggests that groups led by both managers and relatives can be successful; however, both need to be receptive to each others' ideas. In order to sustain relatives' commitment, they need to recognise some benefits from their involvement and enjoy the experience. This small study has identified some pointers that can be shared with others and the authors have hosted local events to inform and motivate other care homes to set up FCH groups. Other agencies, for example CSCI, local authorities, and not-for-profit organisations such as Age Concern, Help the Aged and The Relatives and Residents Association, can also take a lead in promoting greater relative involvement in care homes. Although we do not think that FCH groups should be mandatory, CSCI could recommend their establishment as good practice.

Recognised health and social care qualifications, including continued professional development for staff at all levels, need to include elements that acknowledge and value the role of relatives and friends in the care of older people. In our study the FCH groups identified training suggestions for care staff. For example, one group suggested it would benefit residents if staff had greater knowledge of dementia. It is necessary to train staff to help them to understand, not only how residents can be affected by a move into a care home, but also the impact such a move can have on relatives. A failure by staff to recognise the role and expertise of relatives may result in low expectations of their involvement. Staff should recognise and value the expertise the relative has developed as a 'carer' and this can be acknowledged by involving relatives in drawing up and reviewing care plans. Feedback from relatives and residents may provide useful information when managers are seeking to appraise their staff training needs.

Relatives of residents with some form of dementia appeared more willing to share their experiences and distress with other relatives at meetings. This suggests that support groups for carers, particularly for those caring for people with dementia, would be well received. All homes providing for this client group should try to facilitate opportunities to allow relatives to offer mutual support to each other. Relatives may welcome the opportunity to socialise outside of the home and make new friends.

Although this study only lasted for one year and was based in two care homes, the authors remain committed to promoting FCH groups in care homes. In our view, the benefits outweigh the costs associated with setting up such a group. There was clear evidence that 'social and leisure activities' and 'advocacy and empowerment' can be realised relatively quickly, but changes to care practices may require more time as it may be a matter of changing accepted cultures of care. This research has also shown that FCH groups can enhance relationships between staff, relatives and residents by facilitating opportunities to communicate in different ways; encouraging participation enables a mutual understanding and respect for each others' roles and the support that they can offer.

Conclusion

The small study reported within this chapter suggests that Friends of Care Home (FCH) groups have the potential to enhance experiences of care home life for all concerned. Experiences of setting up FCH groups within two care homes provide a number of pointers for those interested in establishing similar groups. In particular, the support and motivation of the care manager is an essential prerequisite to initiating an FCH group. An inclusive approach should be adopted whereby all relatives and friends, whether frequent or infrequent visitors to the home, are encouraged to attend FCH meetings or organised events. Staff, residents and visitors should be kept informed about the group's activities via notice boards, newsletters and notes of meetings.

It is important that managers reflect upon their aspirations and reasons for setting up the FCH group and share these provisional aims with the group. Revisiting the group aims should be an ongoing process to ensure focus and commitment by all members.

It is helpful to encourage relatives of new residents to attend FCH meetings to hear others' experiences and gain support whilst they are at the adjustment stage. This can help them to engage better in the home's activities; foster a bond between members; fulfil their needs for mutual support; and contribute to group maintenance. Social events, both inside and outside the home, can help relatives to bond, form friendships and contribute to the longevity of the FCH group.

Finally, our experience suggests that it is essential that managers listen to relatives and take appropriate action in response to any feedback. This helps to gain confidence and encourage open communication, as well as avoiding disillusionment.

With forthcoming changes in the way that care homes are inspected in the UK, relatives and residents are likely to play a more important role in monitoring standards. We propose that FCH groups provide a useful mechanism for ensuring that these voices are heard.

References

Bajekal, M. (2002) *Health Survey for England: Care Homes and their Residents.* London: TSO.

Burton-Jones, J. (2001) *Involving Relatives and Friends: A Good Practice Guide for Homes for Older People.* London: The Relatives and Residents Association.

Commission for Social Care Inspection (CSCI) (2006) *Inspecting for Better Lives: A Quality Future Consultation Document.* London: CSCI.

Davies, S. (2001) 'The care needs of older people and family caregivers in continuing care settings.' In M. Nolan, S. Davies and G. Grant. (eds) *Working with Older People and their Families: Key Issues in Policy and Practice.* Maidenhead and Philadelphia, PA: Open University Press, pp.75–97.

Department of Health (DoH) (2003) *Care Homes for Older People: National Minimum Standards Care Homes Regulations* (3rd edn). London: The Stationery Office.

Department of Health (DoH) (2006) *Our Health, Our Care, Our Say.* London: The Stationery Office.

European Nutrition for Health Alliance (ENHA) in association with British Association for Parenteral and Enteral Nutrition (BAPEN), International Longevity Centre UK (ILC) and The Associate Parliamentary Food and Health Forum (2006) *Malnutrition among Older People in the Community: Policy Recommendations for Change.* Available at www.european-nutrition.org/files/pdf_pdf_37.pdf, accessed 24 April 2007.

Fry, P.S. (2000) 'Whose quality of life is it anyway? Why not ask seniors to tell us about it?' *International Journal of Aging and Human Development 50,* 361–383.

Furness, S. (2006) 'Recognising and addressing elder abuse in care homes: Views from residents and managers.' *Journal of Adult Protection 8,* 1, 33–49.

Furness, S. (2007) 'Promoting control and interdependence for those living in care homes by establishing "friends of care home" groups.' *Quality in Ageing 8,* 3, 24–31.

Gabriel, Z. and Bowling, A. (2004) 'Quality of Life from the perspectives of older people.' *Ageing and Society 24,* 675–691.

Gerritsen, D.L., Steverink, N., Ooms, M.E. and Ribbe, M.W. (2004) 'Finding a useful conceptual basis for enhancing the quality of life of nursing home residents.' *Quality of Life Research 13,* 611–624.

Levy-Storms, L. and Miller-Martinez, D. (2005) 'Family caregiver involvement and satisfaction with institutional care during the first year after admission.' *Journal of Applied Gerontology 24*, 2, 160–174.

Nolan, M. and Dellasega, C. (1999) '"It's not the same as him being at home": Creating caring partnerships following nursing home placement.' *Journal of Clinical Nursing 8*, 723–730.

Owen, T. and NCHRDF (eds) (2006) *My Home Life: Quality of Life in Care Homes.* London: Help the Aged.

Perrin, T. (2000) *101 Things to Do when Visiting a Relative.* London: NAPA.

Relatives and Residents Association (1996) *Setting up Relatives Groups in Homes.* London: The Relatives and Residents Association.

Ryan, A.A. and Scullion, H.F. (2000) 'Family and staff perceptions of the role of families in nursing homes.' *Journal of Advanced Nursing 32*, 3, 626–634.

Scharf, T., Phillipson, C. and Smith, A.E. (2005) 'Social exclusion and the quality of life of excluded older people.' *Working with Older People 9*, 3, 32–36.

West, G.E., Ouellet, D. and Ouellette, S. (2003) 'Resident and staff ratings of food services in long-term care: Implications for autonomy and quality of life.' *Journal of Applied Gerontology 22*, 1, 57–75.

Wright, F. (2000) 'The role of family care-givers for an older person resident in a care home.' *British Journal of Social Work 30*, 649–661.

CHAPTER 8

The Importance of Staff Support in the Provision of Emotionally Sensitive Care

Cheryl Holman and Keith Crowhurst

Introduction

This chapter is concerned with research and practice development involving a group of care staff working in a National Health Service continuing care ward for older people (Willow Ward). The work was commissioned as an education project on Keith's (charge nurse) ward, with Cheryl in the role of senior lecturer, facilitating the ward staff's continuing professional development. Cheryl later drew on the work to inform her PhD. The study is relevant to those interested and involved in care homes because it focuses on the complexities of loss and grief in similar types of long-term care environments. The chapter links to the theme of supporting end of life care in the *My Home Life* programme (Owen and NCHRDF 2006). It concludes that in order to promote emotionally sensitive care in continuing care settings, it is essential to address the emotional demands of the care work itself and to support care staff, at all levels, to acknowledge their feelings, including those feelings perceived to be negative.

The chapter begins with a discussion of the complexity of living with loss and bereavement in a continuing care setting and highlights the need for emotionally sensitive social research. The next section describes the methods of participant observation and the reflective work groups that were used to generate and make meaning of the data collected in the research. The key findings from the research are then set out and conclusions are explained. We consider how the research findings informed the practice development initiated by the lead clinician (Keith). We will show how the research not only led to a deeper understanding of loss and grief in the setting, but also had a major influence on how the practice development was carried out. The chapter concludes by drawing out principles of good practice that emerged from the work in order to support and encourage staff in their provision of emotionally sensitive care.

Setting the scene

The quality of care being offered to older people has been subject to repeated scrutiny and policy development (DoH 1999, 2001, 2006). The emphasis on dignified care, particularly at the end of life, has become a central driver for those planning and allocating resources (DoH 2006). As a result of these policy changes, most long-term care now takes place in the community, with those in greatest need often being cared for in residential settings in the private sector (care homes) until they die.

It is now unusual for continuing care to be provided in an NHS hospital ward (Davies and Seymour 2002) and in this study, residents were only admitted to Willow Ward when their needs exceeded the local care homes' admission criteria. Consequently, the resident population had an unusually high level of dependence and challenging behaviours compared with some continuing care facilities. Nonetheless, we suggest that the findings will resonate with, and be useful to, many people who have been involved in long-term care provision for older people.

Willow Ward is located in a hospital providing in-patient care for older people. It is the only continuing care ward in the hospital and is situated on the ground floor. Other care provision includes rehabilitation services for older people on the second and third floors. The social context of the hospital is particular. Indicators of poverty such as unemployment, income deprivation, low levels of education, and poor standards of housing suggest that the local area is one of the most socially deprived in the country. The make-up of the population is complex and subject to rapid change. Patterns of immigration and social mobility have a significant impact upon the age and ethnicity of the people in the area. According to the 2001 Census, the borough has a small, dynamic population (196,106) that is ethnically diverse and relatively young. At the time of the research the majority of residents of Willow Ward were white and English. A few of the older people had cultural origins in African countries such as Nigeria and Somalia and Caribbean islands such as Dominica and Montserrat, and some were of Bengali, Irish, Scottish and Jewish heritage. In contrast, the staff group consisted of a very ethnically diverse group of people whose cultural roots were in places as far-flung as Bolivia, the Caribbean, China,

England, Ghana, India, Nigeria, the Philippines, Sri Lanka, Vietnam and Zimbabwe. The lack of social and economic resources in the area and the cultural mix of those living and working on the ward were important considerations in the research and practice development.

The original commission for this work aimed to provide practice-based education for staff in the continuing care unit, with an emphasis on improving team work and skills in personal and social care. The ward had a reputation for providing good physical care but staff seemed to lack the interpersonal skills to cope with the complex emotional and social problems experienced by residents and their families. The staff themselves suggested the focus of the education should be on *living bereavement*. Although no definitions of this term were found in the literature at that time, a working definition was established with the staff:

> The feelings and behaviours demonstrated by residents and their carers [both formal and informal] following loss in the continuing care unit.
>
> (Holman and Jackson 2001, p.99)

The concepts of loss and grief were considered an appropriate focus for the research because the care staff identified them as important. They are fundamental to issues of care because they are central to an understanding of the personal and social experience of being ill, dependent and dying (Robinson and McKenna 1998).

Loss and grief in continuing care for older people

The term 'loss' is difficult to define as its use has different nuances and emphasis depending on the context. Robinson and McKenna (1998) suggest that individuals experience loss only when they value the person, thing or experience that has been lost. It could be said that a loss has occurred when grief is a consequence (Robinson and McKenna 1998). The concept of loss is fundamentally linked with the process of grief (Cowles and Rodgers 1991).

Terms such as 'bereavement' and 'mourning' are often used interchangeably with loss and grief but they have evolved differently. The concept of bereavement is founded on attachment theory and is a process of recovery from external loss such as a death of a loved one, and grief is understood to be the process that follows the experience of loss. More broadly speaking, all three concepts (bereavement, loss and grief) are individualised, pervasive and normal, involving a non-linear complex of emotions, thoughts and behaviours (Cowles and Rodgers 1991). A wide range of emotional experiences constitute grief, which can include anger, denial, yearning, sadness, relief, bitterness and despair. Bereavement theorists have articulated the possible stages of processing bereavement, including shock, yearning, searching, falling apart and rebuilding one's life acknowledging the absence of the lost person (Parkes 1998). People not only go through bereavement following a death but they experience similar feelings through other losses such as divorce, and changes in health or social status (Parkes 1998).

Thompson (2002) highlights that traditional bereavement theories have been criticised for not acknowledging the complexity of the grieving process, especially its social dimensions. He argues that to describe the process in terms of phases or stages is too simplistic and supports the notion that people oscillate between emotional states following a loss. Some feelings are attached to the loss whilst others are orientated to moving on and rebuilding. These competing forces produce a tension and complicated internal struggle for the bereaved. Klass and Walter (2001) are critical of how bereavement theories have been interpreted in clinical practice. They suggest that there has been an overemphasis on 'letting go' rather than an acknowledgement of the continued importance of relationship bonds and the integration of the lost person into the survivor's ongoing life. It is important to bear these issues in mind while considering the care work related to loss and grief in continuing care for older people.

The idea that people in continuing care settings might simply work through stages of grief was rejected by participants in this study; living with bereavement was seen as an ongoing, ever-changing and demanding process. The complexity of the individual's experience was seen in the context not only of psychological factors, but also social factors such as the relevance of ageism and the importance of organisational culture within continuing care environments. This highlighted the need for an emotionally sensitive social research method to capture this complexity.

A review of the research literature in this field (Holman, Meyer and Cotter 2004) suggests that studies undertaken in continuing care facilities such as care homes often ignore the complexity and multiplicity of loss, depending on the methodological approach taken. Holman et al. argue that different methodological approaches fragment and hide some aspects of loss in these settings. For example, some methods capture the individual emotional component, while others focus solely on the social dynamic. This fragmentation and hiding of aspects of loss renders research findings of limited value to those working in practice. Researchers tend to blame practitioners for poor practice, without ever really understanding the complexity of the work with which they engage. The next section describes the emotionally sensitive social research method used in this study to overcome this limitation.

Emotionally sensitive social research

The research methods were founded on an understanding that given the right conditions it is possible to explore aspects of emotional life that lie below the surface of experience (Hunt 1989). The research aims were to find out about the emotional demands placed on the care staff as a consequence of their everyday work, to support them in trying to understand and deal with the emotional aspects of their care delivery and to make suggestions about how psychosocial care practices could be improved.

There were two main ways through which the researcher got involved in the continuing care ward in order to generate, collect and analyse data. Participant observation entailed working alongside the care staff, carrying out the usual activities of care and gaining insight into their social worlds. The researcher also took part in and facilitated a Reflective Work Group, which explored psychological aspects of the work. The group was designed to provide a safe environment where all members of staff could discuss issues related to caring for the residents and their families. This supported the practice development work by providing a forum for care staff to discuss and learn about the feelings stirred up by their work. This was achieved principally through the process of containment. Containment is one person's ability to take in and understand another person's emotional state in order to help him or her to learn and grow. In this study the researcher used herself as a research instrument to detect the emotions being projected onto her by the participants in the Reflective Work Groups. By being emotionally sensitive, she was then able to contain participants' anxiety, reflect back their emotions in a more digestible form and help participants to better understand the emotional demands of their work in order to recognise when feelings were being acted out in their everyday practice.

Containing processes were thus integrated into the research in order to achieve a deep level of data about the emotional aspects of continuing care work and to help the participating staff learn and grow.

DATA COLLECTION

Over the three-year data collection period, 147 hours of field work were recorded. Of those hours, 98 included participation that involved contact with staff, residents and residents' families and 49 were Reflective Work Groups with care staff (see Table 8.1).

Table 8.1 Time spent in different modes of data collection

	Year 1 hours	Year 2 hours	Year 3 hours	Total hours
Participant observation involving contact with staff, residents and their families	39	55	4	98
Reflective Work Groups	11	22	16	49
Total	50	77	20	147

PARTICIPANT OBSERVATION

Ethnographic methods such as participant observation can provide insights into symbolic clues embedded in culture (Fielding 2001). In ordinary life these remain undisclosed in discussion or tucked away out of sight of the casual observer. This research not only tried to be mindful of external symbols in customs and practices but also used the researcher's feelings as symbolic clues to the emotional experience. This meant the researcher observed and recorded observations of both the external environment and her internal experience.

Hunt (1989) suggests noting the conflicting and unusual feelings experienced whilst gathering research data in the field. In psychoanalytic terms this is referred to as paying attention to counter-transference feelings. Understanding counter-transference is an essential tool in psychotherapy which can be transferred to the research setting (Hunt 1989), observation of organisations (Hinshelwood and Skogstad 2000) and organisational consultancy (Obholzer and Roberts 1994). The participant observation in this study was informed by this principle. In order to ensure this process was within an appropriate framework, robust psychoanalytic supervision informed all aspects of data generation and analysis. The method of supervision followed the Tavistock approach where multidisciplinary groups work together to try to link the real-life experience of the work with relevant psychoanalytic concepts (Rustin 2003).

Each period of participant observation lasted between one and six hours. They occurred at different times of the day and were aimed at collecting data around significant events and activities that were assumed to contain aspects of loss and grief, for example discussing the care of a resident who was dying. The participant observation consisted of the researcher being involved in the delivery of personal care in the morning when residents were washed and dressed; over lunchtime; the two hours after lunch when special events, staff meetings and social activities took place; and the late evening, when relatives and friends visited and residents had their evening meal and went to bed. The selection of people in the field work was time and context specific and related to the care of residents whom the researcher was allocated to work with by the staff nurse in charge of each shift.

The time spent with residents' relatives and friends depended on their visiting patterns. Conversation with regular visitors enabled closer relationships with the researcher to be formed over time. However, it was interesting to note that the one-off conversations with a less regular visitor could also be very revealing. Topics occurred naturally and usually related to issues that were current for the visitor, the resident and/or member of staff.

REFLECTIVE WORK GROUPS

The Reflective Work Groups provided an emotional space where the needs of care staff could be prioritised and it was a private time when they could speak about the intimacies of their work in an open and honest way. This served three purposes. First, it meant their feelings could be contained; by this I mean they could be heard, understood and given back to them in a verbal and manageable form (Waddell 2002). Second, the groups allowed participants to try out new ways of thinking and working with the emotions involved in their work in a safe environment. Finally, it provided a different quality of data from those achieved in the social context of the participant observation.

Data were recorded from 49 Reflective Work Groups over the three-year period. They took place on alternate Wednesday afternoons and lasted one hour. Each took place in an allotted room which was kept as consistent as the structural changes would allow. The group membership was not fixed and all care staff on duty were invited to attend. Although equal numbers of staff nurses and nursing auxiliaries participated, six individual nursing auxiliaries attended more frequently. In effect there was a core group of nursing auxiliaries and a smaller group of staff nurses who attended as regularly as their shift pattern would allow.

DATA ANALYSIS

On completion of data collection, data were read for analytic themes, which were listed. Related items were placed together and condensed where possible (Fielding 2001). Themes were tested by returning to the analytic notes made during data collection, then themes were linked to form a cohesive whole. This process was repeated until a robust set of interlinked themes emerged. A psychoanalytic dimension was added to the research methods by the researcher participating in a supervision group at the Tavistock Clinic. This involved discussing the data in a group consisting of individuals from diverse disciplines such as psychiatric medicine and care home management. Under the supervision of a psychoanalyst it was possible to formulate tentative explanations about the data and then return to the Reflective Work Groups and try them out with the care staff. The process of listening to the care staff's experiences, discussing them in the Tavistock supervision groups and feeding back the new understanding in the Reflective Work Groups formed a cycle of containment. This cycle of containment was integral to the research method which synthesised the data and produced the research findings. Comparing the researcher's own emotional experience in the participant observation with the care staff's accounts allowed formulations about the emotional experiences that were spoken about as well as those that remained hidden. The next section sets out the care staff's accounts of living bereavement and suggestions as to what might lie beneath the surface.

Living bereavement in continuing care for older people

By observing and listening to the staff it was possible to uncover their perceptions of the emotional demands of their work and compare it with the views and experiences of the researcher engaged in the same care work. The staff articulated a trajectory of loss which they witnessed and experienced as part of their everyday work with dependent and frail older people. They called this living bereavement. Sometimes staff seemed to miss out or gloss over some aspects of the emotional work that were noted in the participant observation by the researcher. There seemed to be an emotional demand in the work that the staff were aware of and did talk about, and then a hidden aspect that seemed to lie below the surface. By adopting an emotionally sensitive social research method, the researcher was able to uncover both the conscious and unconscious components of the staff's emotional work with residents.

The staff described the emotional demand of working with the experience of living bereavement in the following areas:

- working with shocked residents
- working with grieving relatives
- working with anxious residents and relatives
- working with residents' degenerating bodies and minds
- working with dying residents.

WORKING WITH SHOCKED RESIDENTS

The most usual route of admission to a continuing care ward is via the acute sector. In the study, residents were frequently admitted to an acute hospital unit from their own homes or a care home. There followed a period of acute care, rehabilitation and assessment to establish how continuing care needs would be met. If the person was assessed and his or her continuing care needs could not be met by community care or care in a residential or nursing home, an admission to Willow Ward was considered. This meant that some residents had a series of acute admissions following a slow deterioration process (e.g. residents with dementia) and finally came to Willow Ward, while others were admitted following a single acute episode that left them profoundly dependent (e.g. a stroke). On some occasions residents were admitted following deterioration or death of a carer. In effect, the circumstances that necessitated admission to Willow Ward involved loss and trauma for the resident and this became part of the staff's work with newly admitted residents. The emotional demands of caring for a new resident who was already afraid, probably confused and needing practical care were complex. Staff members spoke of coping with the conflict between their human feelings for the resident and their feelings related to solving difficult practical problems.

For example, one resident experienced a sudden change in his health. He was an independent man who originated from the Caribbean and had been very fit prior to his admission. When he arrived on Willow Ward he was totally dependent on nursing care for his main activities of living. The staff described the resident as being in a daze. They found moving him around with the moving and handling equipment was distressing, both for him and for the individuals providing his care. They tried to explain to him what they were trying to do and reassure him that they knew what they were doing, but this had no effect. He seemed agitated and afraid as they helped him. The staff seemed primarily concerned with the practicalities of the use of manual handling equipment, but they did realise the resident's behaviour related to his emotions:

> Bruce is a big man and he had a stroke and is now completely paralysed. He is unable to get out of bed and when we try to get him out of bed he goes completely stiff [she demonstrates with her arms]... It's so hard to move him, he just won't bend and it makes it difficult to use the slings without pushing his arms. It's not nice. It's not good for him or our backs. They should get the physio to see him.
>
> Gloria, nursing auxiliary

Later the group discussed why they thought he went stiff.

> **Cheryl, researcher:** Do you think he goes stiff because he doesn't want to get out of bed and maybe he's cross with you?
>
> **Patience, nursing auxiliary:** No, I think it's because he's afraid of being moved and he doesn't trust us yet.
>
> Extract from a Reflective Work Group

The staff seemed frustrated and disturbed by the conflict of wanting to provide good care for new residents but they seemed unable to deal with the disturbing emotions this sometimes involved.

WORKING WITH GRIEVING RELATIVES

There was a wide range of relationships between the residents and their relatives. Relatives who feature in the data include spousal partners, adult children (many of whom were older people themselves), grandchildren, great grandchildren, siblings, nieces, nephews, friends, neighbours and visitors from voluntary organisations. Sometimes the level of relationship was superficial, for example, a distant family member may have been listed as next of kin and rarely made any contact with the resident. Mostly, those who visited a resident had known them for a long time and there was usually an emotional bond between the resident and the visitor. Frequently the relatives who visited had provided care for the residents before they were admitted and they grieved the loss of the pre-existing relationship they had with them.

Care staff often reported difficulties in making relationships with new residents' relatives. They often felt scrutinised and criticised by relatives who were worried and wanted to ensure the resident received an adequate level of care. For example, the staff discussed the daughter of a newly admitted resident who frequently asked the staff to move her mother's position in the bed when the care staff felt it was unnecessary. The care staff expressed frustration at not being able to satisfy the relatives' expectations and were angry at being given too much responsibility. The staff went on to suggest that people seemed to blame them for not doing enough even when residents died:

> **Celia, nursing auxiliary:** Some people are always finding fault, some people are like that.
>
> **Hortense, nursing auxiliary:** Always finding fault, never satisfied.
>
> **Celia:** No matter the way we care.
>
> [pause]
>
> **Maria, nursing auxiliary:** Complaining at the end as if we are to be blamed.
>
> Extract from a Reflective Work Group

In this data extract, the care staff suggest they felt a lot of pressure to please and satisfy the residents' relatives. They suggest this was an impossible task because residents' relatives were bound up in their own feelings of guilt and grief about someone else caring for their loved one. The care staff seemed to find the weight of this responsibility both frustrating and burdensome.

WORKING WITH ANXIOUS RESIDENTS AND RELATIVES

The process of adapting to living in Willow Ward was part of the admission period, but for some residents and their relatives, the separation from each other continued to be a prevailing issue. Separation from the security of home often created a similar sense of loss. When people became distressed and anxious at the loss of security provided by the emotional attachment to a loved one or home, the staff found it stressful and became frustrated if the anxiety continued. For example, one resident's wife was very anxious about her husband who had advanced dementia and was dependent on the nursing staff for all care. His communication and comprehension was very limited. He and his wife had been married for more than 50 years and she did not like to be apart from him. She visited every day and had a strict routine related to the time she spent with him. When she went home in the evening she telephoned the ward twice before she went to bed, often worrying about whether the staff were taking proper care of her husband. The staff were frustrated by the relative's behaviour and her inability to take in any of their reassurances.

> **Susan, staff nurse:** Sometime I say, 'Oh what do you want?' 'Oh this and that.' 'OK we'll do it, don't worry, that's fine go home and rest and we'll do it for him, we'll put him to bed'. Not confronting her helps calm her. [said in a soothing tone]
>
> **Meena, nursing auxiliary:** Then, five past seven every night she calls... [said in an agitated tone]
>
> **Susan:** Every night she calls wanting to know about Cyril [resident], then again at ten past ten. You know at times she will ask if you've put him in the lounge and not to bed [laughter], I mean...
>
> **Patience, nursing auxiliary:** And you can't tell her anything, it just doesn't go in.
>
> Extract from a Reflective Work Group

Caring for residents and their families whilst they experienced the difficulties of separation presented the staff with practical and emotional problems. Residents were often confused by separation from familiar people and environments which added to the complexity of care needed. Witnessing people in such anxious states was often disturbing for carers and other residents present.

WORKING WITH RESIDENTS' DEGENERATING BODIES AND MINDS

All the residents who were admitted to Willow Ward were at the end stage of debilitating disease processes such as stroke and dementia. When residents were in the final stages of these degenerative conditions the boundary between them and their surroundings seemed less intact.

The type of care required frequently involved practices and interactions that crossed usual boundaries to human relationships such as cleaning someone after he or she had been incontinent or dealing with behaviour that broke the usual taboos such as racist remarks. This meant that relationships involved a complex sense of intimacy between care staff and residents.

Although the care staff realised that most people considered this type of work unpleasant or even offensive, they minimised its impact by using strategies such as humour and stressing the ordinariness of their situation.

Rita, nursing auxiliary: That's nothing, they call us all sorts: blackie, black bastards, paki, whores, monkey.

Gloria, nursing auxiliary: Even little Lucy [resident] called me blackie.

Cheryl, researcher: That made me feel terrible as you said that, the hairs on my arms stood up, it's so awful and hurtful.

Joyce, nursing auxiliary: Yes, it hurts.

Celia, nursing auxiliary: No, it's not hurtful, it's just one of those things. We have to go to work every day. So we get used to it and laugh about it.

Extract from a Reflective Work Group

In this example the care staff try to gloss over or deny the impact of the residents' hurtful remarks. The care staff rarely complained about the residents' behaviour or the difficulties of providing such intimate care. This served two purposes; first, it prevented them getting in touch with the residents' feelings of hatred and resentment, and second, it prevented them expressing their own anger about the residents. This was a fundamental aspect of the emotional demands of their work.

WORKING WITH DYING RESIDENTS

The majority of residents who lived on Willow Ward died there. Most residents lived on the ward for months or years and staff frequently experienced the death and dying process of residents with whom they had formed emotional attachments. The anticipation of death and actual deaths of residents often provoked a grief response in staff. When a resident died, the staff's most frequently expressed feelings of grief were shock, sadness and a sense of failure. When staff spoke about a resident's death, the mood was usually sombre and they clearly articulated feelings of sadness. A less frequent response was shock. This may be because residents often had a period of acute illness before they died, providing a degree of predictability. Staff frequently expressed a sense of failure when someone died. This stemmed from their attitude towards the aims of their care. Although the residents were elderly, at the end stage of disease processes and living dependent lives, the staff focused on providing care that was life-sustaining rather than palliative. This was despite the inevitability that residents would eventually die in their care.

> **Celia, nursing auxiliary:** I wish we could have tried a PEG feed with Biddy [resident]. Just to try.
>
> [Silence]
>
> **Cheryl, researcher:** How did Biddy's death make you feel?
>
> **Celia:** Sad, she was a nice lady, no trouble.
>
> **Theresa, nursing auxiliary:** She was a lovely lady.
>
> **Cheryl:** Do you think Biddy would have wanted a PEG feed?
>
> [Silence]
>
> **Celia:** She had given up because she was lonely and had nothing to live for.
>
> **Cheryl:** If you all were Biddy would you have wanted a PEG?
>
> **Gloria and Patience, nursing auxiliaries:** No.
>
> **Theresa:** I feel like we have failed.
>
> Extract from a Reflective Work Group

Although the staff featured in the data extract above were able to acknowledge that the resident had come to the end of her life and would not have wanted active treatment such as tube feeding, they still experienced a sense of failure when the resident died. Staff seemed to focus on their care as a means of sustaining life and on top of usual grief emotions, felt a sense of failure at this time.

Issues that lay below the surface

In the participant observation, the researcher was struck by issues related to loss and grief that seemed to be missing or were 'glossed over' in the regular discussions that were initiated by staff in the Reflective Work Groups. The researcher concluded that the care staff were aware of some aspects of the emotional demands of their work and had considerable insight into their feelings. It is suggested here that other aspects of the emotional demands were not spoken about because unconsciously, the care staff defended themselves against the pain and disturbance of the feelings they stirred up. This is consistent with Menzies Lyth's (1959/1988) seminal work. She suggested care work that involved close contact with pain, dependence and death would inevitably provoke deep anxieties in caregivers. It is not possible to elaborate on this theory in full in the space of this chapter, but the research suggests that some of the deeply disturbing aspects of working in continuing care include: contact with non-responsive people who live a life close to death while not actually being in the process of dying; coping with a sense that care delivery may not improve the quality of life of those being cared for; being on the receiving end of residents' anger and envy; and being isolated from the rest of the healthcare community.

In line with Menzies Lyth's (1959/1988) model that articulated social systems as a defence against anxiety in organisations, it was also possible to see how the care staff's avoidance of certain issues had become integrated into the systems of nursing. For example, there was a focus on more lively residents whereas less responsive residents tended to remain in their rooms and were rarely discussed by the staff. When planning improvements in practice, it was important to consider how these unconscious defence mechanisms might be challenged in a containing and supportive way for staff. In the next section some of the key activities from the practice development are discussed and linked to the research findings.

Using the research findings to inform the practice development of psychosocial care

The research helped identify areas of practice that could be developed. The following aspects of care delivery were considered a priority:

- helping residents and their families adjust to the continuing care
- improving all residents' opportunities for social interaction
- developing a more palliative approach to end-of-life care.

HELPING RESIDENTS AND THEIR FAMILIES ADJUST TO THE CONTINUING CARE

The lead clinician adopted strategies that would foster positive relationships between the residents, their families and the care staff. He introduced pre-admission assessments for all new residents. A series of meetings between the lead clinician, the resident and, if requested, the resident's family, aimed to give the resident information about the continuing care ward and find out about his or her wishes and expectations. This information was fed back to the care staff and documented in the care plan. The resident's expectations and wishes were then discussed as part of a care plan review. This process helped clarify for residents and their families what they could expect from the continuing care staff. Staff members were also clear about the plan of care and could use the Reflective Work Group to explore their feelings about it. A simple example involved a male resident whose wife wanted to visit every day and have private time with her husband with the door shut. In the Reflective Work Group the care staff discussed their feelings about the possibility of the couple having a sexual relationship. The staff were able to explore this possibility and try out new ways of thinking about it without actually intruding on the resident and his wife's privacy.

IMPROVING ALL RESIDENTS' OPPORTUNITIES FOR SOCIAL INTERACTION

Individual and organisational changes were instituted to promote more social interaction. One practical intervention was the assessment of individuals and provision of supportive armchairs. This meant the more dependent residents could be comfortable out of bed and access the communal sitting room. Sometimes the interventions were welcomed by the care staff. For example, many of the staff enjoyed taking part in, and facilitating organised social interaction such as art classes, quizzes and other forms of entertainment which promoted positive social experiences. Sometimes, however, the staff resisted the changes. For instance, when the lead clinician made changes to the infection control policy, reducing the need for residents to be isolated in their rooms, staff were concerned about the risk of becoming infected and risking the health of their families. These issues were brought up in the Reflective Work Group. The group discussed the implications of the change for infection control and safety issues. In the light of the research findings some of the staff's objections could be seen as a sign of unconscious anxieties. The process of acknowledging the care staff's feelings and exploring their meaning with them helped contain anxiety about certain individuals integrating with other residents. The care staff could then discuss their anxieties with the lead clinician and be more open to his explanations and rationale for the change.

DEVELOPING A MORE PALLIATIVE APPROACH TO END-OF-LIFE CARE

The research findings suggested that although care staff were able to empathise with some of the residents' difficulties when dying, some seemed to focus on their care as a means of sustaining life rather than adopting a palliative approach. In keeping with current policy and a belief that this was the best approach, the lead clinician aimed to change the delivery of care to reflect a more palliative philosophy. Key strategies were implemented to find out the wishes of individual residents, and where appropriate their families, in relation to treatment and care in the end stages of life. During the admission assessments residents were encouraged to speak about their thoughts and feelings in relation to dying. Their wishes were documented and discussed by care staff in the care plan reviews. When residents (or their families) requested a less active approach to treatment, for example not wanting life-sustaining medications or artificial nutrition, this could cause sadness and sometimes anger amongst the care staff. In these circumstances, the Reflective Work Groups were available to process such feelings. Some of the care staff's personal and cultural beliefs supported their desire to prolong life at all costs and these types of decisions could cause them a lot of anguish. The groups could not take away such feelings but they offered staff the opportunity to have their 'side of things' understood as separate from the residents' needs and wishes. This made it more tolerable to follow the residents' wishes, even if they were not the same as the care staff's. This is a good example of how attending to the care staff's feelings can directly enhance the quality of care they offer to the residents. This is in keeping with the philosophy of relationship-centred care promoted in *My Home Life* that emphasises the need to examine all aspects of the relationship dynamic in order to ensure quality of life for all those living, dying, visiting and working in care homes for older people (Owen and NCHRDF 2006).

Conclusion

We have described how research underpinned by psychoanalytic theory was used to illuminate care staff's experiences of loss and grief in Willow Ward. We suggest that aspects of the emotional demands of caring for older people in continuing care settings are likely to remain unconscious because the nature of the work involves close contact with conflicts and anxieties related to pain, dependence and death. Our points for consideration for others concerned with continuing care for older people stem from this understanding. We urge those who wish to promote change and quality of continuing care to acknowledge the complexity of the emotional demands that continuing care staff of all levels work with in their everyday lives. Our points for consideration are the need to:

- integrate containing structures into everyday work practices, e.g. regular care plan reviews

- develop specific containers of anxiety that have links with external supervision, e.g. Reflective Work Groups

- recognise that changes in systems may impact on care staff's ability to cope with the emotional demands of their work

- attend to the care staff's feelings separately from the residents' feelings so as to free up the care staff to attend to the residents' feelings.

In order for person-centered end-of-life care to impact upon the quality of life for residents in care homes it is important to develop the capacity of continuing care settings to work with and contain emotions. For this to be a reality it is vital that careful consideration is paid to the needs of care staff and the way an organisation responds to the anxiety provoked by the care work. A strategy that can deal with a full range of experience rather than avoiding unbearable feelings is more likely to produce a creative and sensitive response to emotional difficulties.

References

Cowles, K.V. and Rodgers, B.L. (1991) 'The concept of grief: A foundation for nursing research and practice.' *Research in Nursing and Health 14*, 119–127.

Davies, S. and Seymour, J. (2002) 'Historical and policy contexts.' In J. Hockley and D. Clark (eds) *Palliative Care for Older People in Care Homes.* Buckingham: Open University Press, pp.4–33.

Department of Health (DoH) (1999) *In Respect of Old Age – Royal Commission into the Funding of Long Term Care.* London: HMSO.

Department of Health (DoH) (2001) *The National Service Framework for Older People.* London: Department of Health.

Department of Health (DoH) (2006) *A New Ambition for Old Age. Next Steps in Implementing the National Service Framework for Older People.* London: Department of Health.

Fielding, N. (2001) 'Ethnography.' In N. Gilbert (ed.) *Researching Social Life* (2nd edn). London: Sage Publications, pp.154–171.

Hinshelwood, R.D. and Skogstad, W. (2000) *Observing Organisations. Anxiety, Defence and Culture in Health Care.* London: Routledge.

Holman, C. and Jackson, S. (2001) 'A team education project: An evaluation of a collaborative education and practice development project in a continuing care unit for older people.' *Nurse Education Today 21*, 2, 97–103.

Holman, C., Meyer, J. and Cotter, A. (2004) 'The complexity of loss in continuing care institutions for older people: A review of the literature.' *Illness, Crisis and Loss 12*, 1, 38–51.

Hunt, J.C. (1989) *Psychoanalytic Aspects of Fieldwork.* Newbury Park, CA: Sage Publications.

Klass, D. and Walter, T. (2001) 'Processes of grieving: How bonds are continued.' In M.S. Stroebe, W. Stroebe and R.O. Hanson (eds) *Handbook of Bereavement Research: Consequences, Coping and Care.* New York: American Psychological Association, pp.431–448.

Menzies Lyth, I. (1959/1988) 'The function of social systems as a defence against anxiety: A report on a study of the nursing service of a general hospital.' In I. Menzies Lyth, *Containing Anxiety in Institutions. Selected Essays. Vol 1.* London: Free Association Books.

Obholzer, A. and Roberts, V.Z. (eds) (1994) *The Unconscious at Work. Individual and Organizational Stress in the Human Services.* London: Routledge.

Owen, T. and NCHRDF (eds) (2006) *My Home Life: Quality of Life in Care Homes.* London: Help the Aged.

Parkes, C.M. (1998) 'Bereavement in adult life.' In C.M. Parkes and A. Markus (eds) *Coping with Loss.* London: BMJ Publishing Group.

Robinson, D.S. and McKenna, H.P. (1998) 'Loss: An analysis of a concept of particular interest to nursing.' *Journal of Advanced Nursing 27,* 4, 779–784.

Rustin, M. (2003) 'Learning about emotions: The Tavistock approach.' *European Journal of Psychotherapy, Counselling and Health 6,* 3, 187–208.

Thompson, N. (2002) *Loss and Grief. A Guide for Human Services Practitioners.* London: Palgrave.

Waddell, M. (2002) *Inside Lives. Psychoanalysis and the Growth of the Personality.* London: Karnac.

CHAPTER 9

Changing Cultures: Partnership Working through a Care Home Learning Network

Tina Fear

Introduction

This chapter describes the developmental process of initiating a Care Home Learning Network (CHLNetwork) in the south west of England. It presents the benefits, challenges and constraints to partnership working between care home organisations and individual care homes (residential and nursing), in the independent health and social care sector, and NHS Trusts across a wide geographical area. The Network was established by staff in a higher education institution who sought to meet the assumed learning needs of care homes. This approach reflected some of the key messages of the *My Home Life* programme about keeping the workforce fit for purpose, identifying the need for education and training and promoting care homes as learning environments (NCHRDF 2007). Over time, Network members have assumed leadership and ownership of the Network to ensure its future.

The chapter follows the journey of the development and evaluation of the CHLNetwork and demonstrates the willingness of its members to sustain the network to further enhance the care of their residents. Through the development of new initiatives a cultural shift from isolated ways of working to working in partnership with other care homes and organisations has evolved. The commitment by members four years later to instil and promote a shared culture of learning is enabling the Network to establish a self-regulating group. Through this group, the Network is continually expanding, with the goal of enhancing care for older people in the care home sector through new learning.

The specific objectives of this chapter are:

- to describe how the Care Home Learning Network was initiated and established

- to identify the benefits, challenges and constraints to partnership working between individual care homes in the independent health and social care sector and other health and social care providers

- to provide an understanding of how partnerships can be forged between care home organisations and NHS Trusts across a wide geographical area

- to describe how a cultural shift to new ways of partnership working evolved.

Background to the network

The care home sector has historically worked in relative isolation, with limited contact with other statutory and independent health and social care organisations. It has been excluded from mainstream care systems and training as a result of different employment conditions within the independent health and social care sector. Within the context of the current UK Government Agenda (DoH 2006) the independent sector is now seen as an essential component of health and social care provision for older people. An emphasis by policy-makers on interdependence, rather than independence, exists within service provision across the health and social care sectors. As such, a greater need for education and training in care homes through interagency working, in particular for diabetes, dementia care and other medical conditions, has been identified (Bartlett and Burnip 1999).

This backdrop of current policy agendas raises opportunities for new ways of cross-sector working, to address the needs of the independent sector care homes in their continuing care provision. Networking is one way of enabling cross-sector working and is often discussed within the social and working contexts of people's lives (Branfield et al. 2006). The benefits of networking can be seen through bringing people together to make new contacts to gather and share information (Branfield et al. 2006). The CHLNetwork stemmed in 2003 from these contexts with a strong commitment from the Chief Executive of the Bristol Primary Care Trust (PCT),[1] the University of the West of England and other local independent health and social care sector organisations. The CHLNetwork originated as a funded project supported by the PCT, TOPPS (now Skills for Care)[2] and the university to provide three programmes of learning for senior care home staff in Bristol. These were to be based on the Essence of Care Benchmarks[3] set by the DoH (2003). An interagency, interprofessional advisory group including a family carer representative has guided the Network development from the outset. The Network is facilitated by two senior university academics (facilitators) and members of the local NHS Trusts have been invited to contribute to the programmes of learning.

The original four aims of the CHLNetwork were set to meet policy and nursing agendas (see Box 9.1). However, it soon became clear that without the development of partnership working with other organisations these aims would be difficult to attain, therefore this became the fifth core aim. Partnership working within the context of health and social care is increasingly being used to encourage health and social care sectors to work together, as in the CHLNetwork. Developing partnerships is seen as one way to address fragmented service provision between the National Health Service and independent health and social care sector.

Box 9.1 Aims of the CHLNetwork

- to improve and enhance quality of care in care homes
- to develop all staff working in care homes
- to introduce research activities primarily through evidence-based practice
- to develop and support student placements (DoH and ENB 2001)
- to develop partnership working between care homes and other statutory and independent sectors

---

1   PCTs provide and commission health across England through direct budgets from the Department of Health.

2   Skills for Care is an independent organisation in England working with carers, employers and service users to ensure that qualifications and standards of care meet the needs of people who use care services.

3   Benchmarks are standards against which care can be measured or assessed. See Chapter 10 for a more detailed discussion of the Essence of Care.

Theoretical perspectives

The development of the Network is underpinned by two key concepts: organisational culture and partnership working. A brief introduction to these terms and their relevance for the Network is now described.

ORGANISATIONAL CULTURE

Many definitions of culture within organisations confirm that the phenomenon is socially constructed (Scott *et al.* 2003). The concept of culture is complex and in terms of care homes may evolve and be reinforced by the way care staff regularly behave through the use of language and customs that emanate over time (Trice and Beyer 1993). Culture within the context of this chapter is defined as the way in which an organisation promotes certain behaviours, and ways of doing activities and care practices. It is suggested that leaders, in this case care home managers, can be change agents, transforming cultures and improving practice in care homes (Forsythe 2005). Conversely, culture could be seen as another way of managers dominating the care home workforce (Willmott 1993).

PARTNERSHIP WORKING

Partnership working has many interpretations and the term is often used synonymously with collaboration and networking (Mandell and Steelman 2003; Tomlinson 2005). In the context of the project described within this chapter, partnership working involved developing supportive relationships between care homes, PCTs and the university in order to improve efficiency by disseminating services widely to enhance care provision (Glasby and Peck 2004). Vangen and Huxham (2003) indicate that the benefits of partnership working can be seen through sharing resources and expertise. Therefore, it appears that there are many beneficial outcomes to collaborating with others that would be unattainable by working alone (Huxham 1996).

Care for older people in the United Kingdom (UK) is often fragmented and in some areas poorly organised across all health and social care sectors (Help the Aged 2007). Partnership working could be a way to facilitate best practice and more flexible care for our increasingly ageing population. There is a need for professionals within all health and social care sectors to become more aware of each others' roles, to share information and training to enhance care for older people.

Glasby and Peck (2004) define successful partnerships as those founded on culture and organisational behaviour, rather than structural design, where working together in new ways results in real and sustainable partnerships. The CHLNetwork provides a forum that encourages dialogue for like-minded people through access to personal and professional development across similar organisational cultures. The success of the CHLNetwork could be ascribed to these attributes, where values and cultures are shared within like organisations.

The history of the Network

Initially, three programmes of learning were planned to initiate the CHLNetwork. Managers from 30 care homes in the Bristol area were identified from a local database and invited to join the first programme of learning. Although 28 members from nursing homes and two from residential care homes were approached, only 13 actually attended the first programme held in the city centre. These key individuals committed themselves to attending monthly meetings for six months. The initial Network members completed a learning contract to identify both personal and professional needs. Topics identified for the programmes of learning were selected from those defined in the Essence of Care benchmarks (DoH 2003). A range of learning techniques was used, such as action learning sets and reflective practice approaches to facilitate learning both at meetings and within practice. Each member was encouraged to reflect on his or her practice by writing an individual learning contract document and compiling a portfolio of learning. This provided a personalised and concrete record of their learning and the changes that resulted from their involvement in the Network.

To encourage the CHLNetwork members from all three programmes to meet, all participants were invited to attend sessions in the subsequent programmes to that which they attended. This provided opportunities for original members to share the benefits of the Network with new members. Members were also encouraged to delegate attendance to another member of staff from their care home in their absence. This gave flexibility to the Network and an ebb and flow of membership potentially involving other members of staff from each care home. The facilitators saw this as another benefit in helping to embed Network activities into care homes and avert the possibility of the CHLNetwork being seen as solely relevant to senior staff. By the end of the third programme of learning members from 35 care home organisations had been recruited to the Network and were committed to work together and support professional development in the care home sector.

Evaluation

An evaluation of programmes was undertaken in two distinct stages. The first stage involved a formative evaluation to assess effectiveness of the first programme of learning in terms of learning approaches and appropriateness. The second stage consisted of a formal evaluation to assess the outcomes of the Network development process and guide the way forward (Robson 2004).

Evaluation methods

The stage one formative evaluation involved CHLNetwork members from eight nursing homes and one residential care home. They were asked to complete a question-and-answer evaluation form at the end of each teaching and learning session of the first programme. This practical approach was utilised to access as many participants as possible without demanding more time from them outside of the programme (Robson 2004). The questions asked specifically about the teaching methods, relevance to practice and what they had learnt. These questionnaires were informally collated and comments extracted to guide the way the next programme was facilitated.

The second evaluation was undertaken at the end of the three programmes. This formal process involved gaining ethical approval from the University of the West of England. Following consent an audio-taped focus group was held at the end of three programmes of learning. Only three members attended the focus group, therefore ethical consent was gained to utilise the topic guide as a postal questionnaire. This was sent to all 36 CHLNetwork members at the end of the three programmes of learning. Twelve members returned a completed postal questionnaire. Results of these evaluative methods with a total of 15 participants provided useful data that assisted in guiding the CHLNetwork forward.

Findings

STAGE 1

The first programme of learning was seen as an opportunity to gain and share information with staff from other care homes and all members saw peer and facilitator support as invaluable to share information and ideas. However, all members found the topics selected did not always meet their specific needs and requested that they choose the topics and discussions for the remaining two programmes. They appreciated the action learning sets as a good way of learning but found applying the learning in their workplace very onerous and difficult to implement without support. The members requested that more discussion time should be built into the programme itself. These findings assisted the changes made for the second and third programmes and informal feedback at the end of the programmes demonstrated that the changes were successful.

STAGE 2

The audio-taped focus group and completed questionnaire data was transcribed and coded using Qualrus software. Themes were identified from both the focus group discussion and the completed postal questionnaires. The six themes were: views about the Network; working with other care home staff; building portfolios; individual reflection; benefits and constraints; and sustaining the Network, and these are summarised here.

Themes

1. VIEWS ABOUT THE NETWORK

There were no pre-conceived ideas of what the Network was going to be and how it would develop. One care home manager responding to the postal questionnaire described how her initial feelings of positivity that the 'university was interested in the care home sector' have remained over time. One member attending the focus group said she was 'still pleased to be part of it' and found it 'very useful to share information and ideas'. There were some mixed feelings about what a Network would mean to them in terms of committing themselves to attending Network meetings; however, all members reported that information sharing, peer and facilitator support were invaluable.

2. WORKING WITH OTHER CARE HOME STAFF

Initially there was a curiosity about how others coped with common issues such as funding systems. One member stated in the postal questionnaire that the Network was a 'golden opportunity to work with staff from other care homes and to explore what other homes are doing'. The focus group participants saw no competitive problems with different homes working together and new relationships have developed over time, with members making contact outside the Network. Opportunities were used to write and share protocols and policies such as the provision of clinical supervision, and a protocol for verifying death.

3. BUILDING PORTFOLIOS

The development of a portfolio from a learning contract was identified as the greatest benefit to care home staff and residents for members of the Network. The commitment the participants showed to the writing of this portfolio meant that they found time to meet their objectives to develop and change practice to enhance the care of their residents. For some, improved time management seemed to evolve from these practice developments. As one member stated in the questionnaire, 'I have achieved my objective which now leaves me time to supervise and spend quality time with overseas adaptation students and residents.'

4. INDIVIDUAL REFLECTION

This theme emerged from the impact the Network had on some individual members. Although individual Network members did not overtly recognise their expertise of reflection, it became obvious through their discussions: for example the Network 'inspired me to look at the ways in which we care for our residents' (postal questionnaire). Another member completing the postal questionnaire felt the increased confidence resulting from member-ship of the Network 'helped the staff in the care home stay positive and recognise the good we do instead of the negative aspects' of working in a care home.

5. BENEFITS AND CONSTRAINTS

A number of benefits and constraints were identified by the Network members. Through the development of policy and protocols as a consequence of Network meetings, such as risk assessment for falls, changes in practice were seen to enhance care for the residents.

Two members in the focus group discussed an 'increased confidence in knowledge of current standards and practices' which they felt would benefit all members of the Network. One postal questionnaire respondent said debates and discussions at Network meetings had 'helped me to find the best way forward'. The 'ability to share ideas with others and gain knowledge' was viewed by one focus group member as the most important function of the Network. 'Opportunities to discuss specific areas of care and problem-solving difficult issues with like-minded professionals' (postal questionnaire) were seen by one member as invaluable. Speakers from clinical practice were invited in where specialist knowledge was needed, such as person-centred care for people with dementia. This was much appreciated by members who responded to the questionnaire. They expressed a need to be able to improve their care for residents with dementia.

Initial constraints identified by CHLNetwork members have changed little over time. The major barriers concerned difficulties attending the meetings as a result of time, travel and workload constraints.

6. SUSTAINING THE NETWORK

Two members responding to the postal questionnaire reiterated their concern about how the Network could survive after the programmes were completed. Another postal questionnaire respondent saw the constraints of being released from day-to-day work and geographical distances as detrimental to the Network's survival. This equates with other studies of partnership working with care homes, where similar challenges have been shown to prohibit sustainability (Froggatt et al. 2006). Members saw the development of local groups held across the area as beneficial to recruitment, and to members' attendance at meetings, and perceived this as a potential way forward.

Members of the focus group discussed the need to seek innovative and leading-edge practice issues through the Network to enthuse new and existing members. One member responding to the postal questionnaire saw the return of student nurse placements as a positive development of the Network through valuing the work of care homes in caring for older people and providing opportunities for shared learning. One Network member in the focus group said they were striving for a voice in caring and felt the need to 'get the message out that we are first-rate nurses'. Another postal questionnaire respondent saw the future success of the Network lying in discussion of issues important for care homes, such as stress management, care plans and regulatory issues.

The next development stage

The evaluation provided valuable information for development and sustainability of the Network meetings and a core group of members agreed to meet regularly with facilitators to decide the future of the Network. These initial core meetings led to the beginnings of a shift in ownership of the Network from facilitators to members. Future decisions were beginning to be made by core group members with support from the university facilitators.

The learning programmes had brought care home staff together from different care home organisations on a regular basis and this helped to avoid potential barriers between competitive businesses through sharing knowledge and problem-solving. The Network was now a medium for successful working links between care homes. Members were beginning to work with each other across different organisations to share and develop new initiatives such as joint documentation for clinical supervision and a resuscitation policy. Here was an opportunity for care home staff to share their expertise, experiences, anxieties and successes with like-minded individuals. The success of this new partnership working between care homes was based on their shared cultures, ways of working and organisational behaviour (Glasby and Peck 2004).

Prior to the evaluation it seemed impossible to visualise the CHLNetwork beyond the three programmes of learning. The three learning programmes had been held in a training department at one care home. This venue had been arranged by the facilitators and the care home involved because of its assumed geographical centrality to the city and suburbs. However, it became very apparent from the programme evaluation that time and travelling constraints for care home staff in relation to being released from work to attend meetings was a major issue. Therefore, there was a realisation that a centrally held CHLNetwork meeting group would not advance activities, increase membership or promote partnership working. Through discussion with facilitators, CHLNetwork members decided that Network meetings had to reach out to care homes and be accessible to their workplaces in a given area if the CHLNetwork was to be a continued success and enabled to move forward.

Through discussions between members and facilitators a number of decisions were made regarding Local Groups, a Core Group and communication through a website.

Local Groups

Six Local Network Groups (LNG) have been set up across Bristol city, its suburbs and Bath. Each LNG became dependent on care home managers volunteering a space in their home as a base for regular meetings. As a result, these self-selecting care home managers have held regular meetings at their care homes and are gradually becoming the natural leaders of their LNG. In some groups two leaders have emerged and the LNG meetings rotate between care homes. Facilitators supported the members in the initial setting up of LNGs and they attended all meetings until each group was established.

Although most members drift towards the LNG nearest to their workplace some members attend the group near to where they live. This flexibility has been welcomed by members as it has allowed them to choose a group by geographical area, and by the topics to be discussed. Facilitators have encouraged each LNG to decide topics in advance and disseminate this information to all members, to allow any Network member to attend individual sessions. A list of topics and discussions is placed on their dedicated website (paper copies available where there is no internet access). Disseminating information in this way allows all members the opportunity to network with other members outside their geographical area between meetings and each group respects and values the ebb and flow of CHLNetwork members.

It is interesting to note that each LNG runs differently, providing a sense of individuality. One group has emerged from an existing managers' meeting and the LNG meeting follows the managers' meeting. Topics and discussions are identified, and specific dates set for the sessions with other care homes invited by the Local Group lead. This arrangement suits this location and up to 35 members attend each session. Another LNG prefers to meet six-weekly with dates and topics for the whole year decided in advance. All topics and discussions are publicised on the dedicated care home website to enable all members to access events.

Local Network Groups were established by university facilitators. However, leadership and recruitment in two of the Local Groups are increasingly undertaken by CHLNetwork members. These are mostly care home managers who are happy to lead and direct the group. These leaders have actively recruited not only new members but also more junior care home staff. This gradual Network leadership shift from university facilitator to Network member is almost complete in two of the LNGs. The university facilitators are still available for support, information and contacts for the established groups; however, this shift has enabled more time to expand the CHLNetwork through the setting up of new Local Groups regionally. An LNG has been requested in Bath for residential care homes to support this group of care homes during and following an End of Life learning programme provided by a local hospice. It is anticipated that this group will embrace the breadth of discussion of other LNGs.

The Core Group

Leads from the LNGs form the Core Group. They meet quarterly with the facilitators to discuss development and sustainability of the CHLNetwork and also to provide feedback from individual Local Groups. The Core Group assisted in the development and design of a CHLNetwork leaflet for recruitment purposes. This group also contributed to the compilation of a business plan for future development of the CHLNetwork. It is clear that these members are committed to increasing membership and sustaining the CHLNetwork. They are keen to further Network activities for the benefit of individuals, organisations and, most importantly, for older residents in their care. Two Core Group members attend the ongoing CHLNetwork Advisory Group that meets six-monthly.

A DEDICATED WEBSITE

The need for a communication strategy for members to contact and support each other outside meetings was identified. A website dedicated to CHLNetwork members was developed by the university facilitators, providing information from speakers, web links and a discussion area for members. There is a facility for members to e-mail each other and this has been quite popular with some members. However, even though IT training has been offered to promote the use of the website, it remains under-used by members, especially within the care home workplace. The reasons given by members are time constraints, lack of access to the web as a result of restricted licensing by the organisation, and loss of password. The website is, however, accessed by members on their home computers, suggesting that lack of time in the workplace is a constraint. Facilitators continue to encourage the use of the website, but are mindful of members without computer access.

CHLNetwork initiatives

A number of initiatives have been undertaken during the life of the Network. The initiatives (Figure 9.1) can be divided into: projects currently implemented and those arising from Network discussions; and current policy drivers such as implementing aspects of the Mental Capacity Act into care home practice.

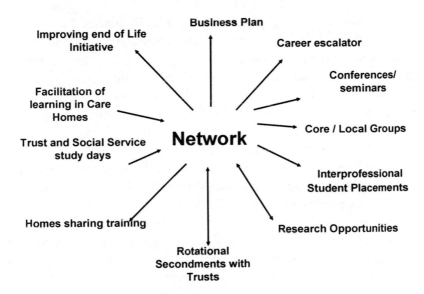

Figure 9.1 Activities of the CHLNetwork

CURRENT PROJECTS

A number of projects within the CHLNetwork are linked into other national service and educational initiatives. As a result of the national End of Life initiative (DoH 2007), 45 nursing homes in the south west of England have undertaken a local programme of learning to implement the Gold Standards Framework aimed at improving end-of-life experiences for their residents (DoH 2007). This project used the CHLNetwork as a route to access care homes and has supported the development of strong links between a local hospice and the CHLNetwork. Network facilitators are now involved in a joint initiative to introduce and evaluate this programme in residential care homes with a local hospice. It is apparent that these homes are requesting information on other topics outside the remit of end-of-life care. A new LNG is being developed to meet this need.

Support has been offered to individual care homes by university facilitators where implementation of change is desired. A local PCT offers NHS study day places for care homes in their geographical area and details are placed on the CHLNetwork website. Where geographically possible, a few care homes have been able to share training across homes as a reciprocal arrangement.

One initial aim of the CHLNetwork (Box 9.1) was the development of pre-registration nursing placements in nursing homes. Members of the CHLNetwork were committed to accommodating 12-week student placements in their nursing homes. A strategy was set up by a university facilitator to enable students to experience a sound educational placement. CHLNetwork members saw the value of two-way learning between students and staff in the nursing homes. They identified that nursing home staff had many skills to offer students in addition to knowledge of the roles of nursing homes in the provision of care for older people.

Nursing home staff volunteered for mentorship training and the university and the Regional Strategic Health Authority offered funded modules to sustain this placement strategy. Guidance was developed for mentors and students and 12-week placements for pre-registration nursing students commenced in May 2006. To date 45 diploma and degree students have undertaken placements in a nursing home. Student evaluations have demonstrated the benefits and several students have requested to return to nursing homes for their third-year management placements with a view to remaining as staff nurses. A formal evaluation of nursing home placements is currently in progress. The benefits of these placements lie in the nature of essential nursing care and the ability to care for older people from a whole-systems approach. Students take major responsibility for four residents under the supervision of registered nurse mentors.

These learning opportunities have enabled students to follow the resident's journey from pre-admission assessment in hospital and home to complex care management and end-of-life care. Opportunities to spend time with community pharmacists and funeral directors have provided students with contextual information invaluable to them in their future nursing career. Although it is expected that the students spend most placement time with qualified nurses, it is recommended that they also work with other members of staff in the nursing home, such as kitchen staff to gain knowledge of the nutritional needs of older people.

FUTURE INITIATIVES

As a result of CHLN discussions it is apparent that there is a lack of knowledge of nursing roles within both the independent and statutory health and social care sectors. In an attempt to address this, a secondment approach was developed to enable staff to work for a period of four weeks across the statutory and independent sectors. Care home staff are committed to take this opportunity to experience care of older people within the NHS and there is a strategy in place to discuss with NHS Trusts. The benefit of this activity is to develop meaningful links between the sectors and address barriers to working together through lack of knowledge of roles and new ways of working. A learning contract and action plan have been developed for this initiative to ensure that learning is applied to practice following secondment.

As some students have shown an interest in returning to a nursing home for employment in the sector after qualifying, it seems pertinent to encourage nursing homes to offer a career pathway for staff. A career escalator has been developed by a university facilitator to provoke thinking about recruitment and retention of staff amongst the CHLNetwork members, and to encourage future qualifying nursing students to visualise a career in caring for older people in nursing homes.

Reflections on the development of the Network

In summary, the CHLNetwork has provided a number of benefits that correspond to the five original aims of the CHLN (Box 9.1).

1. Improving and enhancing the quality of care in care homes

It is appreciated that not all the activities within the CHLNetwork can be seen as having an impact on individual members. However, membership and participation in the LNG meetings demonstrate the members' commitment to enhancing care for their residents. There is a great demand from care home staff to access current knowledge to improve care in spite of high workloads and minimal staffing levels.

Some successes of the CHLNetwork can be seen through changes in practice that subsequently improve quality of life for residents. For example, small environmental changes in one home have assisted residents with dementia experiencing difficulties in recognising toilet doors and subsequently suffering indignities. A CHLNetwork member painted the edge of the toilet door frame red and this resulted in a vast improvement in recognition for these residents.

As a direct result of a CHLNetwork programme learning session on dementia care a member has accessed a person-centred care training package and led her team through major changes in practice to interpret ways that people with dementia communicate their needs. For example, regular episodes of screaming from a resident were only fully understood through talking to the relatives and friends of the individual. This revealed that she had always had a cup of tea when getting out of bed. Screaming was her way of communicating this and when tea was provided the screaming stopped.

Developing, sharing and implementing new protocols and documentation for care homes has also provided professional development opportunities for CHLNetwork members and forged new networking practices. Members have developed processes and documentation for clinical supervision and a resuscitation policy. These success stories demonstrate some of the benefits of the CHLNetwork.

2. Developing the care home workforce

The CHLNetwork members, as care home sector workers, are required by their inspectorate to develop their workforce; however, there is a desire that goes beyond these statutory requirements. In addition to the internal training that organisations provide for their staff, they are taking up opportunities to undertake development courses offered by the university through professional development and mentor training. Financial constraints are similar to other sectors, but some care home organisations are investing in staff development. However, some registered nurses are motivated to fund their own professional development and see this as a way of progressing their career in addition to enhancing care for older people.

One Network member approached the CHLNetwork for assistance in updating staff in medication issues. A session was developed to address this and the care home staff regularly attend a Local Network Group. Some Network members have described how the CHLNetwork has challenged their traditional ways of working and enabled them to embrace change. This cultural shift, driven by Network activities, has enabled members to reflect on and discuss changes in practice needed to enhance the care for the older residents of their care homes.

3. Introducing research activities through evidence-based practice

Research activities are embryonic in care homes. The CHLNetwork encourages care homes to base care around evidence-based practice. The dedicated website provides accessible material enabling care homes to download relevant information. Two CHLNetwork members with support from a facilitator have submitted an article for publication.

There are currently three projects in progress involving care homes, as a direct result of the CHLNetwork. One project involves an evaluation of implementing the Mental Capacity Act into care home working. Another project explores student nurses' attitudes to nursing home placements and it is hoped the findings will assist in further placement developments. The third project is piloting and evaluating the implementation of an End of Life programme in residential care homes, with the potential to roll this out nationally through development of a guidance strategy.

4. Developing and supporting student placements

Nursing homes have found it beneficial to support student nurse placements as a two-way knowledge exchange. They see student placements as an additional opportunity to gain access to current knowledge and working. Pre-registration nurses now experience sound educational placements in nursing homes. Other allied professions need to recognise the benefits of working with older residents and invest in support for this.

5. Developing partnership working between care homes and other statutory and independent providers

This aim has been the most challenging aspect of the CHLNetwork. Meaningful partnership working between care homes has seemed less complex and challenging than initiating partnership working with NHS Trusts. Although Trust staff are committed to working with the independent sector and have contributed to programmes of learning for the Network, role definitions, workload constraints and dynamic changes within the NHS have hampered sustainable meaningful partnerships.

The most effective way to enable partnership working with NHS Trust personnel appears to be through the inclusion of care homes in ongoing and new initiatives with other health and social care sectors. To this end nursing homes have been included in the Department of Health-funded Improving End of Life initiative to improve care at the end of life for older residents. However, this has involved training completely separate from the training offered to NHS primary care staff and although this ensures that care home staff are included in the initiative, it does little to develop meaningful partnership relationships with NHS Trust colleagues.

Similarly, nurse specialists have an interim arrangement in some care homes where contact is made when necessary. This goes some way to reducing staff isolation in caring for residents with specific needs, such as stoma care and Parkinson's disease and also provides care home staff with continued support to care for residents. Facilitators are currently working with local health organisations to develop further links across the health and social care sectors and the CHLNetwork.

A developmental model

As the CHLNetwork has expanded, a developmental framework has evolved to demonstrate the processes that have led to its success. The framework denotes three stages to initiate, develop and sustain such a Network (Figure 9.2). The first stage involves bringing senior care home staff together to identify learning needs. It is important that the group can develop ways of working and learning together over a period of time. The second stage involves dividing the group into smaller Local Groups across different localities. This outward-reaching approach needs the support of a facilitator with capacity to invest time in these new Network members. Leads will emerge over time and, with support, will develop confidence to run a Local Group. In stage 3, once Local Groups are established it is important to develop sustainable partnership links with other local publicly funded health organisations. It is vital during the whole development process that the CHLNetwork is developed by its members and sustained by them to realise its full potential.

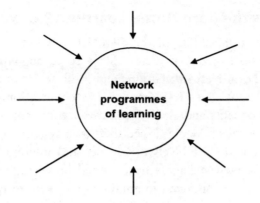

Stage 1 Bringing nursing/residential homes together

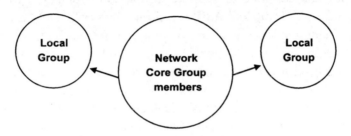

Stage 2 Outward reaching

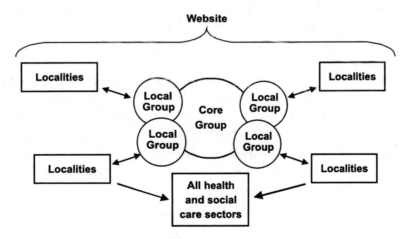

Stage 3 Developing partnerships across the sectors

Figure 9.2 A CHLNetwork developmental model

A future for the Care Home Learning Network

The future and sustainability of the CHLNetwork lies primarily with its members. It is envisaged that there will be some ongoing support from links between Local Network Groups and local Trusts in addition to the university facilitator. The CHLNetwork has come a long way since its inception, and benefits and challenges have become apparent. The Local Network Group leads have developed their own system for recruiting new members through the CHLNetwork leaflet and inviting them to Local Group meetings. New members have gained knowledge of future topic discussions and have continued to attend and actively recruit others. This snowballing effect has been the most successful recruitment strategy for the CHLNetwork.

Facilitators continue to support further development with existing LNGs, the Core Group and Advisory Group; however, new Local Groups are now being requested in areas where the nearest group is too far away. It needs to be accepted that where there is a need for an LNG, however small, it can survive if a Lead is able to accommodate meetings, collate topic discussions and contact experts. Where other meetings or types of groups are already meeting, an LNG can co-exist. It is not always necessary or possible to have a free-standing Local Group.

In less accessible geographical areas it is possible to join the CHLNetwork solely through the website. This would provide access to information and discussion online to support members who have no access to a Local Network Group. However, until the website is accessible to care home staff it will be dependent on members using the website outside work hours.

Opportunities to develop the CHLNetwork further are endless but are dependent on the needs expressed by members through their individual learning contracts or discussions at meetings. Further work is needed to develop more links with all of the PCTs local to the established LNGs, enabling them to contribute their expertise to the CHLNetwork. Currently only a few of the PCTs are involved with the CHLNetwork.

Conclusions

This chapter has explored the developmental process of initiating a Care Home Learning Network (CHLNetwork). The journey of change for both the CHLNetwork members and the university facilitators is worth noting in this chapter. As a result of new knowledge and understanding of current issues care home staff have embraced opportunities for introducing practice developments to enhance care for their residents.

Network members have challenged the concept of 'fixed ways of doing things' and have adopted a less isolated way of working, developing new opportunities to share information across organisations. This cultural shift has brought a new confidence to care home managers and their staff, which is evident in their 'hunger' for knowledge and change. They value the importance of the work they do and have a desire to make the care they provide more visible to other health and social care sectors. Small changes in practice to enhance care for older residents in individual care homes have been disseminated and celebrated across the Network. CHLNetwork members are committed to using this forum to invite other care home staff into the Network to further enhance quality of care for older people and reverse some of the negative stereotypes of working in the care home sector and being a resident. Their enthusiasm is commendable and has been very evident through the gradual shift to self-regulation of the CHLNetwork.

The university facilitators have learnt much from this journey of developing an appropriate, accessible, flexible and nurturing forum, where care home staff can be enabled to develop opportunities to improve practice and work with other health and social care sectors. With continued support from others in both the independent and statutory health and social care sectors this initiative has the potential to become an integral and important part of working within the care home sector.

The CHLNetwork values inclusiveness and equity for all care home staff in their professional and personal development. Members are leading the way in developing the Network and are striving for excellence in care for older residents. Care home staff and facilitators in other geographical areas considering setting up a CHLNetwork need to consider this framework and how it could be adapted, especially in rural areas where distance is a barrier to bringing care home staff together. Establishing a Network is easier than sustaining it beyond facilitator withdrawal. Therefore, it is suggested that a long-term sustainable strategy must be in place from the outset for a Network to survive.

Recent links with the *My Home Life* programme will enable the CHLNetwork to lead the care homes in the south west of England to further the Network and embrace the key principles of the national programme. There are also new links developing between the CHLNetwork and Care Learning, the regional Skills for Care agency, which will provide added knowledge and resources for the members. With the sustainability strategies in place to allow it to evolve and take shape, the future of the CHLNetwork is promising.

References

Bartlett, H. and Burnip, S. (1999) 'Improving care in nursing and residential homes.' *Generations Review: British Journal of Gerontology 9*, 1, 8–10.

Branfield, F., Beresford, P., Andrews, J., Chambers, P. *et al.* (2006) *Making User Involvement Work: Supporting Service User Networking and Knowledge.* York: Joseph Rowntree Foundation.

Department of Health (DoH) (2003) *The Essence of Care: Patient-focused Benchmarks for Clinical Governance.* London: Modernisation Agency.

Department of Health (DoH) (2006) *A New Ambition for Old Age.* London: Department of Health.

Department of Health (DoH) (2007) *Building on Firm Foundations: Improving End of Life Care in Care Homes.* London: Department of Health.

Department of Health (DoH) and English National Board (ENB) (2001) *Placements in Focus: Guidance for Education in Practice for Health Care Professionals.* London: Department of Health.

Forsythe, L. (2005) 'Using an organizational culture analysis to design interventions for change.' *AORN Journal 81*, 6, 1290.

Froggatt, K., Davies, S., Atkinson, L., Aveyard, B. *et al.* (2006) 'The joys and tribulations of partnership working in care homes for older people.' *Quality in Ageing 17*, 3, 26–32.

Glasby, J. and Peck, E. (2004) *Care Trusts: Partnership Working in Action.* Oxford: Radcliffe Medical Press Ltd.

Help the Aged (2007) *Care Homes.* London: Help the Aged.

Huxham, C. (1996) *Creating Collaborative Advantage.* London: Sage.

Mandell, M. and Steelman, T. (2003) 'Understanding what can be accomplished through inter-organisational innovations: The importance of typologies, context and management strategies.' *Public Management Review 5*, 2, 197–224.

NCHRDF (2007) *My Home Life: Quality of Life in Care Homes. Review of the Literature.* London: Help the Aged (also available from www.myhomelife.org.uk).

Robson, C. (2004) *Small-Scale Evaluations.* London: Sage.

Scott, T., Mannion, R., Marshall, M. and Davies, H. (2003) 'Does organisational culture influence health care performance?: A review of the evidence.' *Journal of Health Service Research and Policy 8*, 2, 105–117.

Tomlinson, F. (2005) 'Idealistic and pragmatic versions of the discourse of partnership.' *Organizational Studies 26*, 8, 1169–1188.

Trice, H.M. and Beyer, B.M. (1993) *The Cultures of Work Organizations.* Harlow: Prentice Hall.

Vangen, S. and Huxham, C. (2003) 'Enacting leadership for collaborative advantage: Dilemmas of ideology and pragmatism in the activities of partnership managers.' *British Journal of Management 14 (Supplement)*, Dec, 61–76.

Willmott, H. (1993) 'Strength is ignorance; slavery is freedom: Managing culture in modern organisations.' *Journal of Management Studies 30*, 4, 515–552.

PART 3

Beyond Care:
The Wider Perspective

Collaborating with Primary Care: Promoting Shared Working between District Nurses and Care Home Staff

Claire Goodman, Sue Davies, Chris Norton, Mandy Fader, Heather Gage, Stephen Leyshon, Mandy Wells and Jackie Morris

Introduction

The majority of older people living in a care home do so because they have been assessed as needing extra help to address their personal and social care needs and, for some, their nursing care needs. They will usually have entered a care home as a result of progressive chronic disease resulting in disability and loss of function, rather than for social needs or frailty alone (Bowman, Whistler and Ellerby 2004). The majority of care homes for older people in England and Wales do not provide on-site nursing care and rely on their local primary healthcare services for health needs assessment and care. Although older peoples' access to healthcare and related services should be equivalent to that of an older person who is living in his or her own home, studies consistently suggest that they have inequitable and erratic access to healthcare services (Glendinning *et al.* 2002; Goodman, Robb and Drennan 2003a; Goodman *et al.* 2005; Jacobs *et al.* 2001). Remarkably little research or development work with care homes has considered how care home staff can work with NHS healthcare staff. This chapter describes an intervention study that considers the response of community nursing services to working with and in care homes. It asked whether district nurses working with care home staff, using the quality improvement tool *Essence of Care* (DoH 2003), could improve the bowel-related care of older people, in a way that was fit for purpose, promoted a positive culture for ongoing quality improvement and reflected the needs of both older people and staff.

This chapter will provide a summary of previous research on how primary healthcare services work with, and for, older people in care homes, and the rationale for focusing on bowel care as an area of unmet need in care home populations. The quality improvement tool *Essence of Care* is described, together with the research approach and methods used to test its effectiveness within the participating care homes. The findings from the study are presented including how care home staff and district nurses were able to work together to agree priorities and improve practice. The implications of, and recommendations from, this study are specific to those care homes that do not have on-site nursing provision.

Background

Within the UK, government policy places an increasing emphasis on improving the quality of care through partnership working between health and social care services (DoH 2004). District nurses and general practitioners spend significant amounts of time providing care for older people resident in care homes (Audit Commission 1999; Kavanagh and Knapp 1998), and they are the gatekeepers to other primary and specialist healthcare services for older people. On average, district nursing teams spend four to six hours each week working in care homes, with some teams spending as much as 27 hours a week in these settings (Goodman *et al.* 2003a, 2005). Often what constitutes district/community nursing work in care homes is defined in terms of what care staff do *not* do rather than a clear understanding of how the two roles complement each other (Perry *et al.* 2003; Royal College of Physicians, Royal College of Nursing and British Geriatrics Society 2001). Issues of equity of access to healthcare services for this population are also complex. There is the known (horizontal) inequity of access to services when compared to older people in their own homes (Jacobs *et al.* 2001) but possibly of more significance is the (vertical) inequity where healthcare services are not sufficiently or appropriately differentiated to address the particular needs of older people in care homes who are more frail and more dependent, and have more complex needs than their community-dwelling counterparts (Dixon-Woods *et al.* 2005).

It would be inaccurate to suggest that healthcare services are not concerned about the quality of healthcare and support that older people in care homes receive. A study in five primary care organisations reviewed past healthcare led initiatives for care homes and revealed a 30-year history of specially created schemes, forums, new roles and teams all designed to support older people in care homes (Goodman, Woolley and Knight 2003b). What they all held in common was a history of short-term funding: there were demonstrable achievements, but no evidence of a coherent approach that addressed issues of equity, coverage, access and sustainability. The study reported within this chapter aimed to develop new ways of working within existing structures and patterns of NHS community nursing service provision to care homes. It focused on continence care (bowel care), because, for older people resident in care homes, this is a good example of where the responsibilities of health and social care staff overlap. Meeting the bowel care needs of older people is defined as personal care and is routinely provided by care home staff. It can, however, easily become a healthcare issue, and many frail older people tread a fine dividing line between constipation and incontinence (Potter, Norton and Cottenden 2002). Bowel-related problems can cause discomfort and distress, and lead to increased demands on primary care services and ultimately admission to acute hospital care (Petticrew, Watt and Sheldon 1997).

Research on bowel care in care home settings

Seventeen per cent of people over 65 years and as many as 80 per cent of people in care homes are believed to suffer with constipation (Brocklehurst, Dickinson and Windsor 1999; Potter and Wagg 2005). Studies strongly support the need for a more structured approach to continence care and for NHS services to work more closely with care home staff and residents (Mangnall et al. 2006; Wagg et al. 2005).

Although it is known to be a healthcare need for many older people that is responsive to targeted interventions, there are relatively few studies in care homes on improving bowel-related continence care. We were only able to identify two intervention studies to improve bowel care for older people living in care home settings. Both focused on the treatment of faecal incontinence using laxatives and enemas and did not involve the care home staff or the patients in the treatment choices and decisions that were intended to improve the older people's experience of care (Chassagne et al. 2000; Tobin and Brocklehurst 1986). Studies on the use of care pathways, guidelines and protocols in care homes suggest that they are largely ineffective in raising standards of continence care for older people who are frail, have cognitive impairment and may reside in care homes (Button *et al.* 1998; Wells 2001).

The study

The research questions were:

- Can the clinical benchmarking process be incorporated into care homes for older people with the support of NHS primary care nursing staff?

- Does the introduction of clinical benchmarking in bowel care contribute to increased collaborative working between primary healthcare and care home staff?

- What are the costs of implementing benchmarking and how will any improvements that it might generate impact on the costs of care delivery?

- Will older people in care homes suffering from chronic constipation and/or faecal incontinence have improved bowel habits and bowel-related life quality in care homes where clinical benchmarking that involves care staff, residents and NHS primary care nursing staff has been introduced?

This chapter considers what the findings revealed about shared working and focuses on the findings that relate to the first three questions. More detailed findings about the impact of the study on bowel-related outcomes for the individual residents are reported elsewhere (Goodman *et al.* 2007).

Method

This feasibility study used a quasi-experimental design to test the effectiveness of the *Essence of Care* benchmarking intervention to improve bowel care in care home settings. A mixed-method approach was used to capture the context and process of district nursing teams working with care home staff and the quantifiable resident, service and organisational outcomes of the benchmarking intervention.

Ethical review

The proposal was reviewed and supported by the appropriate NHS research ethics committee and research governance approval was obtained from the three Primary Care Trusts[1] involved. At the time the study began the research governance framework for social care had not been implemented. The study included people with cognitive impairment and in addition to the provision of information booklets and leaflets and formal consenting procedures, the research team saw consent as an ongoing, context specific, process (Dewing 2002).

Recruitment

The recruitment of the care homes and their partner district nursing teams was reliant on the participants' expressed willingness to engage with the study. It was therefore important to recruit care homes and teams that were perceived to be already providing good-quality care by their colleagues, managers and peers (and in the case of the care homes, by the regulatory body, the Commission for Social Care Inspection (CSCI)). Any known deficits of practice prior to starting the study would be likely to influence the findings but be unrelated to the intervention. Meetings were held across London with interested care homes, involving the care home management, senior care staff and the homes' residents' forums. Meetings were held in nine care homes and of the seven care homes that had agreed to participate, one became the pilot site to refine the data collection methods. There were three phases to the study which ran from June 2004 to September 2006:

- phase 1: baseline assessment to establish characteristics of participants, existing patterns of working and collaboration

- phase 2: intervention with district nurses and care home staff from three care homes using the *Essence of Care* benchmarking approach for six months, and three care homes and their linked district nursing teams working together as usual

- phase 3: repeat of baseline measures.

---

1   In the UK, Primary Care Trusts are the NHS organisations responsible for planning and commissioning health services and improving the health of their local population.

Phase 1: Baseline assessment

The baseline assessment involving the six care homes and their partner district nursing teams established the characteristics of each care home's population, the prevalence of bowel care-related problems, and the health of older people and their daily routine. It also reviewed the assessment and management strategies for bowel care in each care home, care home staff and district nurses' training, knowledge and attitudes on continence care, and the resources, district nursing time and access to healthcare services available to residents in the participating care homes.

Data collected for the older people in the study included a review of their care plans and notes, standardised measures of health and dependency and a prospective bowel diary. Semi-structured interviews were also conducted with residents about how they felt about their health, diet and ease in going to the toilet. District nurses completed a diary summarising their work in the care homes. The findings from phase one were fed back to all the participants and were also the basis for the information provided to the care homes that were testing partnership working using *Essence of Care*. Staff were encouraged to use the baseline information to inform the first two stages of the benchmarking process. The non-intervention homes and their linked district nursing teams received the same information and could use it to review their practice and act on the information as they wanted.

All care home staff received certificates of participation and statements outlining their involvement in the study for inclusion in individual staff NVQ portfolios and when there were inspection visits. If care home staff attended for interview in their own time they received a gift voucher.

Phase 2: Intervention phase

The six participating care homes were matched as closely as possible into three paired groups to reflect their approach to care, physical environment and numbers of residents and staff. The care homes were then randomly allocated to one of two groups: one that introduced partnership working using *Essence of Care* tools (n = 3) and the other (n = 3) that worked as before with their district nursing teams.

ESSENCE OF CARE

Essence of Care is a clinical benchmarking tool that aims to support continuous improvement in the quality of nine fundamental aspects of healthcare, of which continence (bladder and bowel care) is one (DoH 2003). It encourages a structured and iterative approach to sharing and comparing practice enabling nurses and others to identify and sustain best practice and to develop action plans together to remedy poor practice. For each aspect of care there are factors or components of care that should be considered in order to achieve overall patient-focused outcomes (11 for continence care). These are broken down into indicators for best practice and activities that support its attainment. The *Essence of Care* tool kit also provides guidance on how to use the benchmarks and supporting documentation. Ellis (2006) argues that the key to success in using the *Essence of Care* benchmarking approach is the level of reciprocity and exchange of information achieved between patients and professionals, its ability to motivate practitioners, and the level of involvement and ownership achieved by participants in agreeing the benchmarks that will mark improvements in patient care. The emphasis, therefore, is on collaboration and not primarily on the measurability of specific outcomes.

The care home staff and the district nursing teams that were using the *Essence of Care* approach both received the *Essence of Care* folder that contained information about the approach, the suggested indicators and supporting paperwork to document change, and agreed implementation strategies and evaluations. Both care home and district nursing staff were encouraged to arrange regular meetings to discuss how they were going to use the quality framework. Who took the lead on arranging meetings was left to their discretion: it was not assumed that this would necessarily be the responsibility of the district nurses. A member of the research team attended each meeting and discussions were audio recorded. All changes arising from the meetings and using the benchmarking approach were documented. Within the context of the study, the three care homes using the *Essence of Care* approach had six months to work together, although in two care homes they continued with planned initiatives and meetings after this phase of the study was complete.

Phase 3: Follow-up and repeat of baseline measures

After the six-month period, the data collection methods used at the beginning of the study were repeated across the six participating care homes. This allowed a before-and-after comparison of how the individual care homes and their partner district nursing teams had interpreted and acted on the information about the health and bowel-related care needs of the older people in their care. It also allowed a comparison of outcomes between the care homes that had introduced the *Essence of Care* benchmarking approach and those that had not.

Findings

It is not possible within one chapter to provide an account of all the findings from the study. The main focus of the findings and subsequent discussion presented here will consider how care home staff and district nurses were able to work together, a brief summary of how effective the intervention was in improving the bowel-related care of older people, and what supported or inhibited their collaboration.

Care home staff and district nurse participants

At the beginning of the study 148 care home staff, 151 older people and 12 district nurses participated. All six district nursing teams were GP attached[2] and visited other care homes regularly in addition to the study care homes. At the beginning of the study, time spent in the care homes ranged from ten minutes to nine hours 30 minutes per week per team, although it was clear that the nurses underestimated the time they spent in the study care homes. Planned care reported by the nurses involved routine tasks such as dressings, flu vaccinations, continence care and insulin injections. Ten out of the 12 district nurses who participated had completed training courses in bowel care, but only one had taken an accredited course. Two district nurses had given training to care home staff on bowel care, while six had given occasional advice.

The majority of care home staff involved in the study worked full-time and were experienced in working with older people: 93 per cent (n = 138)

2   GP attachment occurs when the patients that the district nurse (home nurse) visits and admits to her caseload are identified by being registered with a named GP practice.

had worked in the care home for a significant amount of time (median three years, range one month to 28 years). The care home staff had a range of qualifications but only 27 per cent (n = 13) of those interviewed had completed a care qualification (NVQ at level two or above). Less than a third of the care home staff interviewed reported having received any specific training on continence care.

The majority of staff had English as their second language. According to the King's Fund (2005), around 60 per cent of care workers in London are from minority ethnic groups. Over the study period and despite evidence of long service in some staff members, 20 per cent (n = 30) of the staff had left. This was in part attributable to a sense of increased job uncertainty as the owner organisations of three of the care homes were planning to reduce involvement in the care home sector.

Prior to the introduction of the *Essence of Care* benchmarking process, only 60 per cent (n = 31) of care home staff interviewed had worked with the district nurses. Care home staff contacts with the district nurses were limited by their differing shift patterns.

Unexpectedly, over the study period there was also considerable change and staff turnover in the district nurse teams. Fifty per cent of the district nurses involved had left by the end of the intervention. This challenged assumptions about the continuity and stability of the primary care nursing workforce visiting care homes.

Older people

The demographic and health-related data obtained portrayed an older, dependent population of residents with complex health needs, including a large number of residents with dementia. A total of 151 residents had their care home notes reviewed at the beginning of the study, although some only consented to a partial review. Hence the sample numbers vary according to how much information was available. The residents were predominantly white and female; out of 119 residents 80 per cent were women. Their ages ranged from 64 to 100 years with a mean age of 85 years (n = 119, std dev 7.77, median 86.0). The national average age for female residents is 85.6 years compared to 83.2 for men (Office of Fair Trading 2005).

The number of residents with medical conditions was based on the information that was recorded in their care home notes and is likely to be an underestimate. Data were available for 113 residents, 39 per cent (n = 44) of whom had three or more co-morbidities. The range of health need was not dissimilar in each of the participating care homes. The five most commonly recorded medical conditions in the residents' notes across the six care homes are shown in Table 10.1. They are likely to be an underestimate, and reflect the paucity of information in the care home notes.

The number of medications prescribed for residents ranged from zero to

Table 10.1 Five most common medical diagnoses among residents at start of study

Diagnosis	Number of residents (%) *Time 1 n = 113*
Dementia	48 (n = 54)
Depression	24 (n = 27)
Hypertension	23 (n = 26)
Diabetes (type 1 and 2)	16 (n = 18)
Osteoarthritis	10 (n = 11)

13 with a mean of 5.27 (std dev 2.31, median 5.0). Four or more medications were taken by 77.2 per cent (n = 88) of the residents with more than a third having been prescribed seven or more drugs. Laxatives were the most commonly prescribed medication and were included in the scripts of 56 per cent (n = 65) of residents (Table 10.2). This suggests that constipation was a problem for a large number of residents. The most commonly prescribed laxatives were senna and lactulose, which respectively have poor and moderate evidence bases for their use (Potter *et al.* 2002). Polypharmacy is an independent predictor of constipation. In addition, 74 per cent (n = 86) residents were taking medication associated with constipation, most commonly some diuretics and calcium supplements.

Table 10.2 Most commonly prescribed medication for residents at start of study

Medication	Number of residents prescribed (%) *Time 1 n = 117*
Laxatives	56 (n = 65)
Mineral/vitamin supplements	56 (n = 65)
Analgesia (84% non-constipating e.g. paracetamol, 16% constipating)	46 (n = 54)
CVA prophylaxis e.g. aspirin	35 (n = 41)
Diuretics	32 (n = 38)
Antidepressants	28 (n = 33)
Antipsychotics	21 (n = 25)
Peptic ulcer healing drugs	20 (n = 23)
Antihypertensives	19 (n = 22)

It was striking how rapidly the population of the care homes changed. There were 37 resident deaths over the study period: ten in the care homes, nine following admission to hospital and three following transfer to a nursing home.

Interviews with the older people highlighted the impact of bowel-related problems on their day-to-day lives, including how unwell it made them feel and the humiliation attached. Many of the experiences they described were characterised by needing help to go to the toilet but not wanting to be perceived as a burden and so not always getting their elimination and related needs met.

Out of the 77 bowel charts that were completed for a week at Time 1, 33 per cent (n = 25) of residents had at least one episode of faecal incontinence, and only 6 per cent (n = 5) had what could be defined as a normal bowel pattern. It was difficult to interpret the charts as it was not possible to confirm whether gaps were due to the absence of bowel-related activity or incomplete data.

In contrast to the amount of bowel-related problems experienced by residents and discussed by care home staff, diaries indicated that the amount of bowel care that the district nurses carried out was limited.

The impact of using *Essence of Care* on partnership working between care home and district nursing staff

Introducing *Essence of Care* benchmarking into the three care homes challenged and altered how the care home and district nursing staff identified priorities for care and worked together. Benchmarking and *Essence of Care* were developed for use in NHS settings, and introduction into a care home environment required the hierarchies, teams and organisation of two different systems of working to realign themselves to arrange meetings and agree actions.

The care homes that participated either had staff working 12-hour shifts (and therefore were only in the home for three days a week) or staff working set days and shifts, often to fit with other family or job requirements. District nursing teams were also having to fit in meetings around the (sometimes unpredictable) demands of their caseload. Consequently, benchmarking meetings and action plans had to be carefully coordinated to ensure that the key people were present. Previously there had been a heavy reliance on oral communication and written notes in message books; there had been no tradition of forward planning of how to communicate shared information to support change and innovation or engage older people in that communication process. In the care home that was most engaged with the benchmarking process and managed to complete a full cycle of implementation, senior personnel were able to commit to meetings in both the district nursing team and the care home workforce and agree actions and meetings well in advance.

All the participants working in, and with, the intervention care homes were positive about their involvement in the benchmarking process. However, the six months that had been allowed to introduce and implement *Essence of Care* was too short a period. For two of the three care homes, support from the research team was needed to help district nurses and care home staff to begin to work together.

The discipline of meeting to discuss general issues of care created new opportunities for a wide range of care and management issues to be discussed in all the participating care homes. It increased the nurses' awareness of how care for the older people was organised, and demonstrated the level of expertise and insight of many of the care home staff. The structured approach of the *Essence of Care* tool was key in helping to re-order and challenge previous patterns of working. This was the first time that both sets of practitioners had sat down together to discuss their work in a way that did not focus on an individual older person or a single issue. The baseline data and the review of care identified older people previously unknown to the district nursing team who were at risk and had complex health problems. This encouraged a proactive approach for this smaller group of older people. Their care was reviewed and the nurses initiated visits to see them and discuss their needs in more detail with care home staff outside of the *Essence of Care* meetings. The use of the tool also exposed issues around how care home staff and residents accessed NHS services and the range of support they might need to achieve better health outcomes.

It had been an assumption in the rationale and design of the study that the continuity of the district nursing team in the care home had the potential to develop and sustain practice development. This was not supported in our findings. The only constant during the study period was the benchmarking tool. *Essence of Care* allowed care home staff and district nurses who became involved intermittently or in the last stages of the study to participate and contribute in reviewing the action plan and implementation strategies. However, the level of organisational and personnel turbulence in both NHS and care home settings were significant in slowing the benchmarking process overall.

The benchmarking process gave the care home staff the opportunity to discuss some of the complexities and challenges of care they faced often, and exposed how little professional support they received. There were multiple examples where helping older people to the toilet, trying to improve fluid intake, change diet or persuade residents to consider taking or, conversely, stop taking laxatives were problematic because of reasons completely unrelated to bowel care. The cognitive problems older people had, or the complex interplay of having more than one long-term condition, countered the assumption that helping people with their toileting and changing diet and medication was 'simple'. The benchmarking process challenged the nurses' knowledge and willingness to liaise with other services on the older people's behalf. It also made their accountability more explicit and helped the care home staff and NHS staff debate how their roles overlapped.

Many of the care home staff were aware of the shortcomings of their knowledge, and discussions about bowel-related care led to questions about how to assess pain and discomfort, interpret different symptoms and know when and how to involve the GP. It was evident that care home staff relied on their everyday knowledge of the older person to decide whether he or she needed help. An increasing reliance on agency staff threatened this kind of continuity and knowledge of the residents. It could also mean that care home staff were drawing on a narrow range of explanations for residents' behaviour that if not discussed could mean other problems such as anaemia, depression or possible malignancy were not considered. One district nurse team leader used these discussions to offer support and alternative reasons and solutions for the problems that the older people were reported as experiencing.

Changes that were implemented across the intervention care homes as a direct result of using the quality improvement tool included a review of menus and diets with the catering staff, more systematic documentation of continence-related problems and care, teaching on how to help older people go to the toilet as part of the staff induction programme, increased availability of drinks in the living areas and more staff training and support by nurses and specialist advisors on continence care.

Using *Essence of Care* also exposed ongoing deficits in care and where opportunities to offer support from NHS staff were not acted upon. A striking finding about the older people in the study was the high level of polypharmacy, and the amount of medication being taken that had the potential to cause bowel problems. The study exposed the lack of clarity around prescribing and the apparent absence of discussion between district nurses and GPs about the care of older residents. This prompted a lot of discussion, but we were unable to demonstrate any changes in prescribing approach or the introduction of systematic approaches to medication review. All the district nurse team leaders were qualified to prescribe laxatives and could review medication. There was no evidence of nurses assuming prescribing responsibilities in the care homes and care home staff appeared to be unaware that the district nurse could prescribe. In this aspect of care it is likely that the partnership working and review of care would have benefited from the involvement of the GPs who were visiting the care homes on a regular basis.

District nurses were suggesting and introducing change largely by proxy, mediated by the care home staff. In some settings there was a question as to whether the benchmarking intervention was medicalising the situation and increasing a level of monitoring that might not be welcomed by residents. Implementing change that might improve physical care had the potential to reduce resident choice and increase surveillance to possibly unacceptable levels. Without this explicit commitment to inclusion and the active involvement of residents and/or their representatives, it was a finding of the study that the benchmarking process, by focusing on largely physical outcomes, had the potential to initiate change in residents' lives that possibly did not address the particular needs of living in a care home.

Bowel-related problems and medications following the introduction of *Essence of Care* into three care homes

Following the introduction of the *Essence of Care*-based intervention in the three intervention homes, a repeat assessment was made of older people's bowel-related problems and medication. Overall, we found that residents in the intervention care homes showed an increase in normal bowel patterns and decreasing laxative-induced diarrhoea post-intervention. However, most of the changes in bowel pattern could be accounted for by the one care home that showed the highest level of engagement with the benchmarking intervention. Laxatives remained the most commonly prescribed medications and after introducing *Essence of Care* there was an increase in the number used. Also, bowel-related care-planning did not appear to be markedly improved. Given the small numbers involved and the changes in the resident population, any changes must be treated with caution. It was not possible to demonstrate significant improved outcomes for the older people as a direct result of the intervention.

The costs of partnership working and introducing *Essence of Care*

To achieve partnership working required a commitment of resources by both health and care home organisations. Time spent by care home staff members in the implementation of benchmarking was recorded and costed according to post held and grade using published sources (Curtis and Netten 2005). One intervention care home put resources into meetings and training sessions for care staff. The other intervention care homes allocated relatively few resources to the benchmarking intervention over the 22 week period. As a result, the total direct costs incurred in implementing the intervention varied amongst the experimental homes (£552.50 vs £276.90 vs £203.00). The associated expenditures per resident were £16.74, £8.93 and £7.25 respectively.

We found no evidence that participation in the benchmarking intervention affected the overall workload of the district nurse (DN) teams. Pre – post analysis of the whole sample of homes showed that the mean number of visits to care homes per week, and the mean number of residents seen by DNs, remained constant. However, the mean time spent by the DNs in care homes, and with individual residents, fell (by 52 and 2 minutes per week respectively) between Time 1 and Time 2. District nurses across the three intervention homes reported spending more time and seeing more residents than was reported by DNs in control homes at both the baseline and post intervention. Differences in activity between the intervention and control homes were less at follow-up than baseline, but variation within groups was substantial at both observation points, so no effect of the benchmarking intervention on DN work could be identified. District nurses reported delivering very little bowel- specific care to individual residents in any home throughout the study, and no changes were apparent following the introduction of benchmarking in the intervention homes.

Implications

The benchmarking process was an acceptable approach for care home settings that did not have on-site nursing provision. In the three settings it was clear that the participants were at different stages of readiness to participate and there was a continuum of engagement that affected the extent to which they were able to complete the process. A high level of external facilitation and encouragement was crucial in keeping two of the three study sites involved. Nevertheless, there were three key achievements: improved interdisciplinary collaboration and reduction of care home isolation, increased understanding of care home staff preoccupations and need for clinical support, and the identification and support of older people who were possibly at risk and in need of extra, proactive care.

The study found that in the short term and with support, district nurses could work with care home staff to use clinical benchmarking to begin to review and address the quality of care for older people. This study was able to involve practitioners who had an ongoing involvement in the care home. There were many benefits. The use of the comparison group and data from the other homes helped staff to make judgements about how good their care was in relation to best evidence and other care homes, and helped to counter their isolation. It provided a robust structure that both care home staff and district nurses could work with and it encouraged discussion and shared problem-solving activities. This challenged, and, for the period of the intervention, modified the task-focused orientation of NHS staff (Froggatt, Poole and Hoult 2002; Goodman *et al.* 2003b, 2005). A number of infrastructure and hierarchy issues arose because the two groups involved had different employment structures, patterns and care priorities. Nevertheless, by encouraging practitioners to discuss, plan and jointly review changes in care, benchmarking helped to dismantle the traditional divisions of health and social care working and demonstrated the potential of joint working and review (Glendinning 2003).

In the time allowed to introduce *Essence of Care* we were unable to demonstrate that clinical benchmarking led to measurable improved outcomes of bowel-related care for older people or that a proactive supportive approach was sustained by NHS staff. The reasons for this are many. Issues specific to benchmarking such as the amount of external facilitation required, the time it takes to complete the cycle of change for each indicator, the minimal involvement of the older person in the process, and the complete lack of medical involvement are echoed in the accounts of practitioners and researchers who have implemented *Essence of Care* in NHS settings (e.g. Bowers, Tooth and Nolan 2005; Cotton 2004; Matykiewicz and Ashton 2005). This reinforces the importance of allowing sufficient time to incorporate the cycle of problem identification, implementation and review for improvements to be achieved.

Most quality improvement models (including benchmarking) rely on expert opinion as opposed to the views and experiences of older people themselves (Bowling *et al.* 2002; Gabriel and Bowling 2004). The biomedical (and with it an assumption of recovery) and health service orientation of the benchmarking indicators of *Essence of Care* did obscure many underlying issues that informed why and how continence problems occurred for this population. There was also a risk of medicalising an environment that was primarily the older person's home. The indicators needed to be amended to incorporate an understanding of how good continence care (and what it means to the older person) is achieved for this population and in a long-term care environment where access to healthcare is mediated through others.

This study was relatively inexpensive to implement, introduced with minimal external involvement and within existing resources. However, the findings clearly showed that attaining a symmetrical and equal relationship involving senior staff from both groups requires them to be equally keen to find new ways of reviewing and improving care. The potential for benchmarking to generate higher resource use was apparent. The study reinforced how few extra health resources were readily available to older people resident in care homes and the lack of transparency and accountability in how nurses and others acted on their behalf to secure extra support and specialist review.

Contrary to expectations the district nurses' involvement in benchmarking did not increase their documented work with older people on bowel-related care. Unlike social stereotypes of people who work in care homes, the data showed high levels of commitment and job satisfaction around working with older people. It was care home staff who led on changes to care.

By the end of the study all the participants who had been directly involved believed they had gained through taking part. This supports the work of other practice-based interventions and collaborative approaches that identify the isolated nature of much of primary care/community-based working and the receptivity of care home staff to working with healthcare staff (Goodman *et al.* 2005; Meehan, Meyer and Winter 2002).

Clinical benchmarking provided clarity of purpose, encouraged commitment, helped to develop trust and built-in methods for monitoring, reviewing and shared learning, all of which are key requirements to enable cross-agency working (Wildridge *et al.* 2004). The benchmarking approach was a resource for continuity. It also changed and supplemented a largely oral tradition of communication and reactive working to one that planned documented decisions and evaluated the impact of the changes.

Limitations of the study

The main limitation of the study was the minimal involvement of the older people in the benchmarking process and its evaluation. There was a gap between the aspirations for the involvement of older people that was explicit in both the *Essence of Care* tool and the study design, and the reality of its implementation. Attempts to involve older people were only successful at the beginning of the study and with those who were interviewed. The lack of active involvement reflected the everyday experience of many older people in care homes (Abbott, Fisk and Forward 2000). The study underestimated the sensitivities of asking people about their bowel function over a sustained period of time. The absence of the GP view and contribution is a further limitation of the study and it is likely that had there been medical, therapist and community pharmacist involvement in the benchmarking process more could have been achieved.

This was a small study and this limits the generalisability of the findings. Nevertheless, the numbers of older people involved and the information obtained compare favourably with other studies in this area (Tobin and Brocklehurst 1986; Wagg *et al.* 2005). The key findings and themes around working in care home settings show what can be achieved within a relatively short space of time within a constantly changing environment.

Conclusions

This study demonstrated that it was possible to introduce the *Essence of Care* quality improvement tool in a non-NHS setting, and that it enabled district nurses and care home staff to work together to improve care for older people. The following summary points are based on the findings of the study.

- The *Essence of Care* tool was a context-sensitive innovation that could encourage shared learning to improve care for older people.

- It supported motivated practitioners to review, discuss, improve and develop practice together.

- It highlighted areas where older people had inequitable access to healthcare services and health needs not previously known or addressed by NHS practitioners.

- The *Essence of Care* benchmarking tool provided continuity in environments that are constantly changing and a structured approach to the resolution of complex care problems.

- It enabled practitioners to make explicit their roles and responsibilities and held them to account for their practice.

- The focus on a single aspect of care was not restrictive and triggered wider discussions about wider health and personal care support needs of the older people in the care home.

- There is a need to develop indicators of good practice that can account for the complexity and range of health and care needs of older people in care homes.

The study was funded by the Department of Health Nursing Quality Research Initiative and the views expressed in this chapter are those of the authors and not necessarily those of the Department of Health.

References

Abbott, S., Fisk, M. and Forward, L. (2000) 'Social and democratic participation in residential settings for older people: Realities and aspirations.' *Ageing and Society 20*, 327–340.

Audit Commission (1999) *First Assessment: A Review of District Nursing Services in England and Wales.* Abingdon: Audit Commission Publications.

Bowers, S., Tooth, S. and Nolan, P. (2005) 'An evaluation of the implementation of the Essence of Care in South Staffordshire Healthcare NHS Trust.' Unpublished report. Stafford: University of Staffordshire.

Bowling, A., Banister, D., Sutton, S., Evans, O. and Windsor, J. (2002) 'A multidimensional model of the quality of life in older age.' *Ageing and Mental Health 6*, 355–371.

Bowman, C., Whistler, J. and Ellerby, M. (2004) 'A national census of care home residents.' *Age and Ageing 33*, 6, 561–566.

Brocklehurst, J., Dickinson, E. and Windsor, J. (1999) 'Laxatives and faecal incontinence in long-term care.' *Nursing Standard 13*, 52, 32–36.

Button, D., Roe, B., Webb, C., Frith, T. *et al.* (1998) 'Consensus guidelines for the promotion and management of continence by primary health care teams: Development, implementation and evaluation. NHS Executive Nursing Directorate.' *Journal of Advanced Nursing 27*, 1, 91–99.

Chassagne, P., Landrin, I., Neveu, C., Czernichow, P. *et al.* (2000) 'Faecal incontinence in the institutionalized elderly: Incidence, risk factors, and prognosis.' *American Journal of Medicine 106*, 2, 185–190.

Cotton, J.A. (2004) 'Essence of Care: Implementing continence bench marks in primary care.' *British Journal of Community Nursing 9*, 6, 251–256.

Curtis, L. and Netten, A. (2005) *Unit Costs of Health and Social Care.* Kent: Personal Social Services Research Unit, University of Kent at Canterbury.

Department of Health (DoH) (2003) *Essence of Care: Patient Focused Benchmarks for Clinical Governance.* London: NHS Modernisation Agency.

Department of Health (DoH) (2004) *National Standards, Local Action: Health and Social Care Standards and Planning Framework 2005/06–2007/08.* London: Department of Health.

Dewing, J. (2002) 'From ritual to relationship: A person-centred approach to consent in qualitative research with older people who have dementia.' *Dementia 1*, 157–171.

Dixon-Woods, M., Kirk, D., Agarwal, S., Annandale, E. *et al.* (2005) *Vulnerable Groups and Access to Health Care: A Critical Interpretive Review.* London: National Coordinating Centre for Service Delivery and Organisation.

Ellis, J. (2006) 'All inclusive benchmarking.' *Journal of Nursing Management 14*, 377–383.

Field, D. and Froggatt, K. (2003) 'Factors affecting provision of palliative care.' In J.S. Katz and S. Peace (eds) *End of Life in Care Homes.* Oxford: Oxford University Press, pp.175–194.

Froggatt, K., Poole, K. and Hoult, L. (2002) 'The provision of palliative care in nursing homes and residential care homes: A survey of clinical nurse specialist work.' *Palliative Medicine 16*, 6, 481–487.

Gabriel, Z. and Bowling, A. (2004) 'Quality of Life from the perspectives of older people.' *Ageing and Society 24*, 675–691.

Glendinning, C. (2003) 'Breaking down barriers: Integrating health and care services for older people in England.' *Health Policy 65*, 2, 139–151.

Glendinning, C., Jacobs, S., Iborz, A. and Hann, M. (2002) 'A survey of access to medical services in nursing and residential homes in England.' *British Journal of General Practice 52*, 480, 545–549.

Goodman, C., Davies, S., Norton, C., Leyshon, S. *et al.* (2007) 'Can clinical bench marking improve bowel care in care homes for older people?' Unpublished research report. Hatfield: Centre for Research in Primary and Community Care, University of Hertfordshire.

Goodman, C., Robb, N. and Drennan, V. (2003a) 'Training and development needs of care staff, nurses and therapists working in care homes.' Unpublished report. London: North Central London Workforce Confederation.

Goodman, C., Robb, N., Drennnan, V. and Woolley, R. (2005) 'Partnership working by default: district nurses and care home staff providing care for older people.' *Health and Social Care in the Community 13*, 6, 553–562.

Goodman, C., Woolley, R. and Knight, D. (2003b) 'District nurses' experiences of providing care in residential care home settings.' *Journal of Clinical Nursing 12*, 67–76.

Jacobs, S., Alborz, A., Glendinning, C. and Hann, M. (2001) *Health Services for Homes. A Survey of Access to NHS Services in Nursing and Residential Homes for Older People in England.* Manchester: NPCRDC, University of Manchester.

Kavanagh, S. and Knapp, M. (1998) 'The impact on general practitioners of the changing balance of care for elderly people living in institutions.' *British Medical Journal 317*, 322–327.

King's Fund (2005) *The Business of Caring: King's Fund Inquiry into Care Services for Older People in London.* London: King's Fund.

Mangnall, J., Taylor, P., Thomas, S. and Watterson, L. (2006) 'Continence problems in care homes: Auditing assessment and treatment.' *Nursing Older People 18*, 2, 20–22.

Matykiewicz, L. and Ashton, D. (2005) 'Essence of Care benchmarking: Putting it into practice.' *Benchmarking: An International Journal 12*, 5, 467–481.

Meehan, L., Meyer, J. and Winter, J. (2002) 'Partnership with care homes: A new approach to collaborative working.' *Journal of Research in Nursing 7*, 348–359.

Office of Fair Trading (2005) *Care Homes for Older People: A Market Study.* London: Office of Fair Trading.

Perry, M., Carpenter, I., Challis, D. and Hope, K. (2003) 'Understanding the roles of registered general nurses and care assistants in care homes.' *Journal of Advanced Nursing 42*, 5, 497–505.

Petticrew, M., Watt, I. and Sheldon, T. (1997) 'Systematic review of effectiveness of laxative use in the elderly.' *Health Technology Assessment 1*, 13.

Potter, J., Norton, C. and Cottenden, A. (2002) *Bowel Care in Older People.* London: Royal College of Physicians.

Potter, J. and Wagg, A. (2005) 'Management of bowel problems in older people: An update.' *Clinical Medicine 5*, 289–295.

Royal College of Physicians, Royal College of Nursing and British Geriatrics Society (2001) *The Health and Care of Older People in Care Homes – A Comprehensive Interdisciplinary Approach.* London: Royal College of Physicians.

Tobin, G.W. and Brocklehurst, J. (1986) 'Faecal incontinence in residential care homes for the elderly: Prevalence, aetiology and management.' *Age and Ageing 15*, 41–46.

Wagg, A., Mian, S., Lowe, D. and Potter, J. (2005) *National Audit of Continence Care of Older People.* London: Clinical Effectiveness and Evaluation Unit, Royal College of Physicians.

Wells, M. (2001) 'An audit of care pathways use by district nursing teams.' Unpublished MSc dissertation. London: Middlesex University.

Wildridge, V., Childs, S., Cawthra, L. and Madge, B. (2004) 'How to create successful partnerships – a review of the literature.' *Health Information and Libraries Journal 21*, 1, 3–19.

CHAPTER 11

Making It Work: A Model for Research and Development in Care Homes

Jan Dewing

Introduction

This chapter came about as a result of both my varied practice development experience in care facilities in the Republic of Ireland and planning my own research in a UK care home. In preparing for my own research, I undertook several activities (Dewing 2007a). First a focused literature review of other researchers' experiences of conducting research in care homes was carried out. Second, I reflected on my values and beliefs about care homes. Third, as an outcome of several structured written reflections, I developed a framework to enable me to be self-facilitating in relation to working through ethical situations I might encounter. In preparing for any systematic practice development work Garbett and McCormack (2002) and Dewing *et al.* (2007) suggest developing a detailed appreciation of the existing workplace culture and its historic factors. Drawing on this previous experience, I present here a model to facilitate researchers undertaking research and development in care homes. This comprises two main elements: first, awareness about the cultural setting where the research is to be conducted and second, specific issues faced by researchers that need to be addressed.

The chapter begins with an exploration of culture within care homes. The *My Home Life* review (NCHRDF 2007) suggests that the culture of a home directly affects the quality of life of those who live and work there. I propose that researchers and practice developers (and educationalists providing a range of link roles) need to have salient preparation for working in a care home. Central to this is having an understanding of, and working with, the culture of the care home. Knowing what the culture is (its enabling factors, attributes and consequences) can prepare the researcher for the way things are done in the home, how the team functions and the degree to which care is person-centered. Reflecting in a systematic way on the concept of workplace culture in the context of care homes can be invaluable to entering the home, knowing what to expect, and what will be seen and heard. Researchers are not detached observers of culture in a care home. As soon as they enter the home, they are contributing to, and shaping the culture in some way, even if it is simply passive acceptance of what they see. The model for understanding culture, as presented here, can be used for research and practice development. The chapter builds on previous contributions to summarise some of the key literature pertaining to carrying out gerontological research in a care home. Five key themes are discussed. I also describe and illustrate the use of a particular model for critical reflection that can be useful when trying to process intellectually and emotionally some of the experiences that may be encountered in care homes.

As it is clumsy to continually use the terms 'research and practice development' and 'researcher and practice developer' throughout the chapter, the terms 'research' and 'researcher' will be used. Since systematic practice development is a form of practitioner research, much of what is said in this chapter can equally apply to practice development as to research.

Workplace culture and context

Definitions of culture are many and varied. Martin and Bonder (2003) take a pragmatic approach and suggest that culture can best be thought of as dynamic processes acquired by individuals throughout life from a variety of sources. It has been suggested that culture is the 'glue' that holds an organisation together (Siehl and Martin 1984). The glue, according to Gibson and Barsade (2003), is the shared patterns of meaning, values and beliefs, and expectations held by members of the organisation. Manley (2004), drawing on Drennan (1992), states that culture is fundamentally 'how things are done around here' (Drennan 1992, pp.3–4). Manley specifically focuses on values and beliefs as expressed, and as lived out and experienced by others. Values and beliefs shape (1) the rites, rituals and ceremonies of the care home; (2) communications, stories and myths; (3) many physical forms within the home (such as design and decor, uniforms, notices and furniture); and (4) everyday language and the way people and things are talked about in the home.

Organisations comprise multiple cultures that, in the practice development literature, are thought of as workplace cultures. In a workplace there needs to be one central culture that is shared (recreated and experienced) by all workers. However, where leadership or values are not strong sub-cultures can form and gain influence. Care homes can be vulnerable to this as many may be both isolated and insulated workplaces, and may sometimes have difficulties in recruiting or retaining effective leaders and experienced staff (Foner 1994). Ruckdeschel and Van Haisma (1997), writing about workplace culture in American care homes, suggest that some cultural practices and rituals make life bearable for staff, especially for support or care workers, yet they can create problems for residents. One example offered is the attribute of the workplace culture where socialising and joking can mean that jokes are made about residents.

The culture of a care home workplace has multiple consequences for all staff and residents. The culture impacts on the sense of purpose of the home, consistency between dominant values, how and whether these are put into action, or the degree of adaptability and flexibility in the home and the sorts of systems and processes in the home for supporting practice and meeting residents' needs. Thus, Manley (2001) argues effective cultures, through adaptability and learning, have empowered staff, allowing practice to develop that enables a constant fit between the environment and the culture to be maintained. The importance of a creative learning culture for both staff and residents in this respect has also been identified elsewhere (NCHRDF 2007).

Manley (2004) sets out a framework for an effective culture which she terms a transformational culture. This has three components:

- practice development with a focus on person-centred and evidence-based care

- staff empowerment

- a set of workplace characteristics that include:

    o shared values and practices

    o a common mission

    o consistency and involvement

    o adaptability, internally and externally reflected by a learning culture

    o services that match the needs of users

- ○ valuing all stakeholders
- ○ valuing leadership and the development of leadership potential at all levels (not just in the named leader or manager).

Being attentive to the attributes of the workplace culture, and to how effective the culture is, can be very helpful in enabling researchers to know what to expect from staff (and residents) and to know how things are done in the home. According to Powers (2003), the attributes of culture can be heard, seen and felt everywhere in a home; for example, in how the staff talk with each other and with residents and families, in the way memos and notices are written and in the way that care is organised and delivered on a day-to-day basis (Tuckett 2007). Knowing as much as possible about the culture can help researchers in several ways: in knowing how staff are likely to act and respond in certain situations and in thinking through what they as a researcher might feel or do in a situation where they observe or witness certain things, such as something that they regard as unacceptable practice.

Sometimes observed practice may seem unacceptable to a researcher; yet this does not necessarily mean it is poor or unsafe practice. It may be that the researcher's values and beliefs are being challenged by witnessing something that fits in with the care home culture, but not with the values and beliefs of the researcher. Appreciating the power and influence culture has on individuals can enable researchers to feel more empathetic towards individuals and recognise why they do things the way they do. This can aid understanding of how staff and residents become encultured, replicating and sustaining the dominant culture. In these situations, people with different values and beliefs to the majority find it hard to put these into action in consistent ways, as the dominant workplace culture undermines attempts to do so.

Issues for researchers in care homes

Prior to beginning work in a care home, researchers can prepare on a number of levels. Where researchers are going into a clinical or practice setting that is vastly different from ones they have known, careful preparation is essential in order to have a sense of what to expect. In addition, self-preparation is a central element of particular research approaches such as action research, forms of ethnography and hermeneutic phenomenology. Emancipatory and transformational approaches to practice development also emphasise the need to attend to self-awareness and cultural factors within the research context.

To complement what is already known more generally about workplace cultures, I undertook a literature search to learn more about other researchers' experiences of entering care homes. The purpose of the focused literature review was to identify concerns and issues which other researchers had encountered in the course of conducting gerontological research in a care home and to establish how they addressed them, in order that this might assist my own preparations for entering and working in a similar setting (Dewing 2007a).

Literature review method

The literature search was undertaken in three databases widely available in the UK (Table 11.1). The review was not exhaustive and could be expanded upon. Papers with content on personal experience of, or reflections on, conducting gerontological nursing research in care homes were included in the review.

Table 11.1 Scope of the literature review

Databases searched	BNI; Cinahl; RCN
Key words	Gerontology; older people; elderly; ethics; care home; nursing home; research experience
Abstracts reviewed	57
Papers retrieved	15

Five tentative themes were identified, which were:

1. experience, skills and readiness of researchers
2. resources of researchers to cope with culture in the care home
3. researchers' contemplation of their own ageing
4. research reflexivity and supervision in order to know when it was timely to intervene and how to intervene, with either care delivery or the routine in the home
5. access and consent.

The themes could be further condensed into three themes: (1) about the researcher (for example previous experience, own ageing), (2) contextual challenges (access, culture and consent) and (3) ways to support researchers (resources, reflexivity and supervision). However, as there was not a great amount of literature within some of the original five themes I was cautious about condensing any further.

The literature varied between researchers who offered descriptions of their experiences of a single research project or of carrying out research in a single care home and those who described a collection of experiences over time. The five themes will now each be discussed in more detail and strategies for improving a researcher's work in each of the areas are proposed.

EXPERIENCE, SKILLS AND PREPAREDNESS OF RESEARCHERS

Apart from a paper by Mentes and Tripp-Reimer (2002), there is a notable omission of reflections on the researcher's experiences and skills, and how this influences their preparedness. This seems unusual given that generally the research literature is full of accounts of the researcher's influence on the research, such as on the collection of data (see for example Finlay 2002; Leslie and McAllister 2002). Fay (1996) adds to this, stressing that social science researchers need to be aware of who and what they are, and what they bring to any social analysis. I also noted that the accounts of carrying out research in nursing homes are all written by researchers, with no accounts by care staff or residents. Further, researcher-based accounts rarely consider or represent the care staff's perspective in any detail. In contrast, Fay (1996) states that researchers need to be reflexive regarding how they are seen by others. This highlights the need for self-awareness and for reflection on the perspectives care staff and residents may have about research, both generally and specifically. Silverman (2000), amongst others, suggests that researchers should keep reflective or personal notes as part of a research diary. However, if done as a private activity this will not necessarily lead to, or enhance, self-awareness and indeed it may only serve to reinforce already established perceptions, values and beliefs held by the researcher.

Mentes and Tripp-Reimer (2002) suggest that the most significant factors influencing the skill and preparedness of researchers working in care homes are twofold: (1) the researcher's compatibility with the care home setting and staff, and (2) the communication they have with staff. They also observe that the presence of an effective leader in the home is a key contextual factor. The most notable feature in the literature reviewed pertaining to this theme is that reflective accounts by researchers tend to focus on the degree to which the researchers felt they had previous experience of either working in a care home or working with frail older persons in any capacity at all, and not necessarily as a researcher. Descriptions tend to be dominated by resident characteristics (usually framed in terms of medical diagnosis and functional dependency) and attributes of the home. There was no sense that personal and biographical knowledge about the residents as individuals was valuable. Some accounts were factual (e.g. size of home, its location and the resident profile) and several contained descriptions about the rites, rituals and communications within the home. In other words they were describing the researcher's initial assumptions about the culture. For example, Allan (2001), reporting an intervention study in UK care homes, describes 'challenging' factors pertaining to the presence of people with dementia, as well as contextual factors, for example the physical form of the home, the staff and the way the organisation worked. However, in the context of a care home all these factors may be viewed as being very much the norm and thus to be expected.

Maas *et al.*'s (2002) account focuses more on the residents and concludes that the issues and challenges in carrying out ethically acceptable and rigorous research in a home are strongly influenced by resident dependency and the effects of institutionalisation. It could be argued that institutionalisation is largely a consequence of the culture that staff create. From their experience, Maas *et al.* suggest there is a need to explore and describe the internal and external context of the home so that researchers can design better studies. Care homes are dynamic, not static, communities with their own cultures, where there is a way of life for residents, staff and families/visitors (Stafford 2003). Roles and relationships are continually being negotiated and renegotiated, sometimes minute-by-minute, between staff and residents and between residents themselves (see Brown Wilson, Cook and Forte, Chapter 4 of this volume). I concluded from the literature that knowing about medical diagnoses and dependency was not sufficient preparation for being in a communal care facility where many older persons were living. These factors offered little appreciation of what it might be like for the older people living there or for the researcher emotionally encountering this community.

In another account, Beattie and Algase (2002), carrying out research on older people with dementia, suggest that researchers need to be experienced and prepared enough to cope with three factors. First, cognitively impaired residents are extremely sensitive to environmental changes. Second, there are problems in carrying out undetected observation of the resident and the nurse–resident dyad, without the resident being aware. Clearly both these issues are relevant only to certain research methodologies and methods. For some researchers this issue may also raise ethical concerns about whether residents, no matter whether they have dementia or not, should be observed without their knowledge, a subject discussed by Bland (2002). Third, the complexity of the layout in the care home environment makes it hard for researchers to collect data. By this, I assume they mean that in comparison with a hospital setting, observation is not easy for the researcher as the layout may be complex. This may reveal the researcher's expectations that a care home should make observation easy and should be more like a hospital setting. However, this highlights the necessity of clarifying values and beliefs about what a care home is, and planning to get to know both the layout of the home and the relationship between different spaces. Researchers also need to learn about how space is used in the home and what sort of things go on in different areas (Andrews *et al.* 2005; Wiles 2005). Similarly, it is important to understand which spaces certain residents prefer over others. Sometimes this can be straightforward. However, in many areas, as well as the obvious functions or activities going on, rooms or spaces can have more than one purpose or function. For example, in the home in which I carried out my research, the space referred to by staff as the 'small dining room' was also used as the music group room and the exercise group room. It was used for small birthday parties and as a more private space for visitors. Having a diagram of the home layout or making a sketch can help to understand the layout.

Based upon her experiences undertaking a phenomenological study in a US nursing home, Higgins (1998) developed 20 themes for other nurse researchers to consider as part of their preparations. Several of the themes overlap and can be condensed. Three themes are particularly useful here, because they relate to central concerns associated with researching in care homes: (1) potential difficulties with gaining access to residents because of the day-to-day routine or activities going on in the home, (2) the time-consuming nature of working with residents and (3) creating closure at the end of research. In the account by Higgins (1998), the routine of the home, the staff and to a certain point the demands of older people are described as obstacles to be overcome in order to get to the data. Although residents are clearly visible or even appear unoccupied, this does not mean they are doing nothing according to Wadensten (2007). It also does not mean they are easy to access or recruit into a research project. Being with frail older persons at a pace they can deal with takes time, and sometimes this time can feel prolonged. Additionally, being in a social community with many residents can also mean becoming involved in interactions with residents not involved in the research. I argue this is something that it is necessary to expect and prepare for.

RESOURCES FOR COPING

Carrying out research in any setting can be demanding, requiring personal commitment and stamina. The care home is no exception. For example, getting to and from the care home, being there for long periods of time, focusing on demonstrating expertise in relationship and communication skills, as well as utilising or embodying the principles of the chosen research approach and methods, can all stretch the researcher's personal resources and coping abilities. In addition, many novice researchers may be undertaking 'part-time' data collection as part of an academic research programme while also working full or part time. The ability to cope with delays and diversions in the research has been described in terms of the varied frustrations researchers encounter along the way, for example in recruiting residents (Rapp, Topps-Uriri and Beck 1994), and adapting to the physical dependency of residents and their frequency of care needs (Mentes 2001; Mentes and Tripp-Reimer 2002).

The key point arising from researchers' accounts relating to this theme was the effect on the researcher of observing how some frail older people were living and being cared for, and the more intense experience of what I interpreted as bearing witness (i.e. being present and attentive to the truth of the older person's experience) (Naef 2006). I noted in my own reflections the complex feelings I sometimes had about how some of the residents were living and the level of distress I saw and felt being expressed by residents. Reflections similar to those by Higgins (1998) could deter many researchers from conducting research in care homes or at least fill them with foreboding about entering a nursing home as a researcher. As with an account by Miller and Evans (1991), Higgins identified emotional and ethical difficulties associated with being present and seeing what was going on in the day-to-day life of residents, and through what was revealed by residents in interviews. The accounts, in places, are sympathetic. Whilst being able to sympathise is an important attribute, it is vital to move beyond sympathy and to be aware of possible projection and transference issues when working with older people, and to separate out the older person's issues of ageing from one's own.

Observing and reporting as honestly as possible legitimates one's own and others' lived experiences and offers a way of moving beyond sympathy. However, observing can be a detached state and does not necessarily enable researchers to work through feelings associated with what they are seeing (Hubbard, Backett-Milburn and Kemmer 2001) or even offer anything to support or hold feelings the resident may have. The notion of witnessing as a form of attentive valuing, seeing, understanding and telling what goes on for another has a place in some approaches to gerontological research and also in coping with being a researcher in care homes, regardless of the approach being taken. In my research one of the participants repeatedly shared with me how she wanted to 'lose all connection with this place', and another did not feel she was at home or even understood what the place was for. I would ask the research participants what they wanted me to tell others about their experience. This appeared to help them and also helped me too.

Witnessing has diverse origins ranging from moral, faith or religious perspectives to legal ones. In addition, some psychoanalytical therapies utilise witnessing as a curative element in treatment (Ullman 2006). It is this latter perspective that is of interest here. Ullman suggests that bearing witness as a social process can expose often unspoken realities of suffering and serves as a distinct function of the therapist in psychoanalytical therapies. In this instance, witnessing is founded on the researchers' ability to recognise 'otherness' in the residents. Witnessing can enable the recognition of a denied or dissociated reality of suffering and offer researchers a framework for working with aspects of ageing in others which they may find troubling. Fundamentally, witnessing legitimises the older person's right to be or do as he or she is. Attending, in emotional and intellectual modes, to lived experience and its meanings, is critical. Deeper levels of critical reflection will enable connection with older individuals and also an increased recognition of the researcher's 'self' as a distinct person, rather than a blurring or merging of identities. This connection can be validating for the older person as well as assist relationship-building and data-gathering for research purposes. However, the researcher's personal resources and coping are fundamentally influenced by his or her own values and beliefs about ageing.

RESEARCHERS' CONTEMPLATION OF THEIR OWN AGEING

As already mentioned, accounts of the challenges of care homes research could deter many researchers from conducting research in these settings, or at least create serious apprehension. In Higgins' (1998) account, it seems that her values and beliefs about ageing, especially her own ageing, were tested. Thus, as well as researchers recognising and witnessing the consequences of ageing processes for others, they also need to be prepared to reflect on the ageing process with regard to their own family and self. Carrying out research in nursing homes where many residents are extremely frail and often approaching the end of their life can have a profound effect. For those who are new to the care home context there may be a shock effect of simply seeing so many older frail persons together in one place. Such an effect can feel exacerbated if the physical form of the home and/or the culture of care is less than optimal. Being in a care home and attending at a deeper level to what is going on brings the researcher closer to the lived experience of the older persons who live there. It reveals aspects of the experience of ageing that are not usually seen by others and can have the effect of presenting researchers with a possible view into the future of someone they know and love and even their own future. The first visits to a care home can potentially be challenging as a result of the unfamiliarity of the environment, as well as the staff and residents, and the routines of the home.

Hubbard *et al.* (2001) reflect the traditional view that researchers can and should screen out their emotions in the processes of research fieldwork, analysis and reporting, in order somehow to protect themselves from involvement, and primarily in order to protect the objectivity of data. The researcher's 'self' is clearly of secondary concern in this perspective. I would argue that any proposition that researchers can and should react in a way devoid of emotions is not reasonable or sustainable when in the midst of a dynamic community of people. Nor is it consistent with being a registered nurse or practitioner, or with certain methodologies, such as interpretive phenomenology. Emotions alert researchers to issues that need attending to (Fay 1996; Mezirow and Associates 1990). Having a heightened rather than a dulled sense of what is going on and how things are done can bring to the fore numerous ethical issues for the researcher's attention which, once addressed, add to the rigour of the study and to the well-being of the researcher. In addition, working through issues so that the overall experience of conducting research in a care home can be looked back on as something positive is helpful when encouraging and supervising future researchers to carry out research in similar settings. Thus, it seems advantageous, both to the researcher and for gerontological research, to use a process that promotes reflexivity, ethically appropriate decision-making and action within the home. This will be discussed in more detail in the next section.

RESEARCH REFLEXIVITY AND SUPERVISION

There is a mass of literature concerning reflexivity in research (see Holliday 2002) and research supervision is generally said to be both necessary and helpful for both the researcher and the research. Three key concepts emerged from the literature review in relation to reflexivity: (1) dissonance and how this was managed by a registered practitioner working as a researcher, (2) attending to emotions and (3) reflexivity and supervision. Several papers discuss how researchers were unsure how to deal with either observing or witnessing practice that might not be evidence-based or person-centred while being in the home as a researcher and not a caregiver. Although not explicit, there was a sense in some of the literature that novice researchers felt isolated when they were engaged in data collection in care homes.

A tool derived from work by Wuest (1998) to promote and structure critical reflection can enable researchers to respond in a person-centred way to situations where there is a sense of dissonance; where the researcher is either not sure what to do or in what capacity he or she would respond. Wuest's work is underpinned by feminist grounded theory and explored the strategies women use to respond to competing and changing demands of caring. This work appeals because it is consistent with the principle of 'an ethic of care' (Gilligan 1982, 1987) and working in a way that supports connected relations (McCormack 2003). Wuest uses a specific strategy of setting boundaries, a process that, whilst defining the limits of caring, illuminates the place of reciprocity, commitment, love and obligation in the caring process (Wuest 1998). Setting boundaries is the process of identifying which caring demands should be accepted and which should be excluded, and making judgements about the conditions under which help may need to be sought from others. Wuest recognises that emotion plays a major role in decisions about caring and thus for women, caring is conceived of as having competing and changing demands. This, or a similar reflection tool, can also lessen the need to take concerns or issues to supervision as they can often be satisfactorily worked through. The tool (Table 11.2) enables emotionally intelligent decisions to be made about interventions in specific situations within the home. Thus, the researcher is attending to his or her own voice and the voice of the resident or staff member; responding to competing demands as a nurse/practitioner and a researcher; and responding to changing demands from the resident as a research participant and a resident in need of care.

Table 11.2 Tool to promote reflexivity in setting boundaries

Themes	Sub-themes	Ethical action
Attending to one's own voice (attending to the emotional relational material and motivational processes)	Knowing personal limits and strengths	Using knowledge and strengths
		Being self-aware of fatigue
	Trusting judgements	Learning from successes and mistakes
		Achieving consistency
	Developing a philosophy	Having principles to base decision-making on
		Clarifying motivational forces
Determining legitimacy (making judgements about whether caring demands are tenable)	Nature of the demand	Discounting non-legitimate demands
		Nature of legitimate demands:
		• source of demand and degree of dependency
		• degree of obligation felt by me as nurse
		• potential harm to the other
		• expectations of others
	Attributes of the caring interaction	Distance or closeness in the relationship
	Weight of counterbalancing conditions	Weighing up other demands, skills and 'having something to give'

The literature showed that the majority of researchers working in care homes tended to be novices. This would indicate that research supervision would be both required by the organisation leading on the research, as well as necessary for the researcher to develop competence and to ensure safe and ethical research practice in the field. Research supervision is beneficial to research for several reasons. For example, according to Sinclair (2004), supervision that is more structured and occurs regularly tends to be associated with faster rates of research completion and more completions, especially at PhD level. Supervision that is less frequent and has a more 'hands off' approach, except in a minority of cases where researchers already have research expertise, tends to be associated with slower progress with research and higher rates of non-completion. Supervision can also contribute towards reflexivity as decisions can be made about actions to be taken (Maas *et al.* 2002). McCormack (2003) argues for five necessary conditions in order to have person-centred research: informed flexibility, sympathetic presence, negotiation, mutuality and transparency. Whilst the extent to which these conditions are the totality of conditions necessary for person-centred research can be questioned, they offer a loose framework for promoting reflexivity and could be used to frame research supervision.

ACCESS AND CONSENT

Issues of access and consent were an important theme within the literature. However, differences can be seen in this area between the North American and UK papers. That the US and Canadian literature focuses more on consent, whilst the UK literature focuses more on access, can be explained in several ways. In the US, research in nursing homes is generally more prolific than in the UK, and consequently nurses working in homes are more familiar with research. In the US there tends to be more of an expectation that citizens will participate in research for the benefit of others. In the UK, researchers may be undertaking research in homes where the organisation and the staff have previously had little experience of research taking place. They may adopt more protective roles with regard to older persons with dementia being exposed to research or in relation to being exposed to research themselves. A set of sub-themes was noted in the US and Canadian nursing research literature. These concerned perceived problems with informed consent, cognition, memory changes and proxy consent (Slaughter *et al.* 2007). In the UK literature, the issue of access was identified as an area of concern. The literature tends to deal with access and consent in a linear and uncomplicated way. However, experience has shown me that the notion of access is more complex and is related to being acceptable to key caregivers. This whole process is often referred to as gatekeeping in the UK literature (for example Bartlett and Martin 2002) and this in itself is a two-way social process and, therefore, is not always overtly negotiated.

Bartlett and Martin (2002) identify health professionals as one set of gatekeepers and claim that access to participants is influenced to a great extent by the gatekeepers' views about involving older people with dementia in research, and individual gatekeepers' personal preferences. Bartlett and Martin appear to have a negative experience of health professionals in their gatekeeper function. This may have been because in their research, the gatekeepers held views about the residents (persons with dementia) as needing to be protected from others, which were regarded as being non-person-centred. Thus researchers should prepare for gatekeeping as a process that may take some time, particularly where residents are frail or deemed to be vulnerable by staff. Dewing (2007b) suggests that researchers should expect gatekeeping to occur, as clinical staff have professional responsibilities to ensure the welfare and safety of their patients or clients. This is one of the areas where the presence of effective leadership and team working, to be referred to by Maas et al. (2002) and Mentes and Tripp-Reimer (2002), can act to ensure more appropriate access within the care home for the researcher.

Establishing and maintaining evidence of informed consent from older persons living in care homes can be ethically challenging. Miller and Evans (1991) suggest that research in a nursing home can impact on most, if not all, of the residents, and consent should, therefore, be periodically reviewed. When it comes to older persons with mental illness and dementia, the area of consent becomes increasingly more challenging (Dunn et al. 2001). This might be one reason why the UK dementia care field has concentrated on persons who may be said to be in the earlier part of dementia (see, for example, Clarke and Keady 2002; Dewing 2002). It may be easier to work with this group than with persons who have more advanced dementia, in terms of developing consent and appraising how meaningful participation is for them.

Although progress is being made across the UK regarding inclusion of persons with dementia, there are still many uncertainties about persons with more advanced dementia participating in research. Indeed, there is still a debate about whether older persons with dementia, especially when advanced, can participate in research. Williams and Tappen (1999), for example, ask if it is possible to create therapeutic relationships with nursing home residents in the later stages of Alzheimer's disease. They conclude the literature provides ample evidence that older persons with Alzheimer's are not good candidates for therapeutic relationships. This argument of seeing overwhelming deficits in the person as being a good enough reason for exclusion from research needs to be reframed as it hinders researchers from seriously examining what attributes and skills they need to carry out research with these residents. As Hubbard *et al.* (2001) observe, there is little serious discussion in the literature about the attributes and skills needed by researchers to achieve consent with older persons who have dementia and live in a care home. Researchers need to find ways to make it possible for older people with dementia and other frailties to have therapeutic relationships within a qualitative research context, rather than accepting it as somehow inevitable that they do not make good research participants (Dewing 2002, 2007b).

A central tenet of capacity legislation, such as the Scottish incapacity legislation (Office of Public Sector Information 2000) and capacity legislation in England and Wales (UK Parliament 2005) states that persons lacking capacity are required to be given every opportunity by those around them to demonstrate consent, before they are assessed as lacking capacity. These acts legally enable substitute decision-making on behalf of persons with dementia who lack capacity for informed consent. Achieving substitute decision-making is a quicker process than working to achieve consent with some people with dementia. The result may compound exclusion of persons with dementia and further limit creative and developmental approaches to consent, necessary to enhance participation by persons with dementia.

Research Governance Frameworks across the UK for health and social care research have both helped and hindered the agenda. The frameworks have helped by supporting national principles of good research governance (DoH 2005; Scottish Executive Health Department 2006). However, the processes researchers are expected to undertake in research submissions, particularly in relation to ethics, may limit the creativity that I would argue is necessary for developing alternative consent methods where persons with dementia are excluded from informed consent (Dewing 2007a).

Key action points

On the basis of the literature review reported in this chapter, the following key action points were identified for researchers working in care homes:

- Develop an appreciation of the culture and context.
- Become familiar with the layout of the home and relationships between spaces in the home and how residents and staff use them.

- Be open to when residents can and want to be available.

- Recognise that residents may need more time than you initially feel is needed.

- Consider the use of witnessing, which may be a therapeutic way for both residents and researchers to cope with some aspects of life in a care home and ageing.

- Develop skills in critical reflection and reflexivity to deal with tensions or dissonance between competing responsibilities of being a professional and a researcher.

- Engage actively with research supervision.

- Pace yourself and research time-planning carefully to accommodate gaining access and working through consent issues.

Conclusion

Entering a care home in a state of readiness takes systematic preparation and a good deal of time. This preparation is vital as there is no fixed protocol to deal with all possibilities and challenges that face researchers and practice developers preparing to carry out research and development in care homes. Preparation can help to avoid some of the common pitfalls experienced by other researchers when conducting research within the nursing home context. I have suggested that preparation for conducting research and development in a home includes gaining an understanding of the context and culture of the home and attending to five key issues: attending to their experience and skills, their resources, their own ageing, to reflexive and supervision processes and issues of access and consent. In this way, the demands put upon a researcher, with or without a background of working in practice within a care home, can be appropriately addressed. Researchers can then be supported in their engagement with care homes as organisations and the people who live, work and visit in such settings.

References

Allan, K. (2001) *Communication and Consultation: Exploring Ways for Staff to Involve Persons with Dementia in Developing Services.* Bristol: Joseph Rowntree Foundation.

Andrews, G.J., Holmes, D., Poland, B., Lehoux, P. *et al.* (2005) '"Airplanes are flying nursing homes": Geographies in the concepts and locales of gerontological nursing practice.' *International Journal of Older Persons Nursing 14*, 8b, 109–120.

Bartlett, H. and Martin, W. (2002) 'Ethical issues in dementia care research.' In H. Wilkinson (ed.) *The Perspectives of Persons with Dementia: Research Methods and Motivations.* London: Jessica Kingsley Publishers.

Beattie, E. and Algase, D.L. (2002) 'Improving table-sitting behaviour of wanderers via theoretical substruction: Designing an intervention.' *Journal of Gerontological Nursing 28,* 10, 6–11.

Bland, M. (2002) 'Patient observation in nursing home research: Who was that masked woman?' *Contemporary Nurse 12,* 42–48.

Clarke, C.L. and Keady, J. (2002) 'Getting down to brass tacks: A discussion of data collection with persons with dementia.' In H. Wilkinson (ed.) *The Perspectives of Persons with Dementia: Research Methods and Motivations.* London: Jessica Kingsley Publishers.

Department of Health (DoH) (2005) *Research Governance Frameworks for England, Wales, Northern Ireland and Scotland.* London: Department of Health.

Dewing, J. (2002) 'From ritual to relationship: A person-centred approach to consent in qualitative research with older persons who have a dementia.' *Dementia: The International Journal of Social Research and Practice 1,* 2, 156–171.

Dewing, J. (2007a) 'An exploration of wandering in older persons with a dementia through radical reflection and participation.' Unpublished doctorate in philosophy thesis. Manchester RCNI/The University of Manchester.

Dewing, J. (2007b) 'Participatory research: A method for process consent with persons who have dementia.' *Dementia: The International Journal of Social Research and Practice 6,* 1, 11–25.

Dewing, J., McCormack, B., Manning, M., McGuinness, M., McCormack, G. and Devlin, R. (2007) *The development of person-centred practice in nursing across two continuing care/rehabilitation settings for older people. Final programme report.* Unpublished Report. Leinster and Dublin: University of Ulster and Health Service Executive Nursing and Midwifery Planning Unit.

Drennan, D. (1992) *Transforming Company Culture.* London: McGraw Hill Publishers.

Dunn, L.B., Lindamer, L.A., Palmer, B.W., Lawrence, J., Schneiderman, L.J. and Jeste, D.V. (2001) 'Enhancing comprehension of consent for research in older patients with psychosis: A randomized study of a novel consent procedure.' *American Journal of Psychiatry 158,* 1911–1913.

Fay, B. (1996) *Contemporary Philosophy of Social Science: A Multicultural Approach.* Oxford: Blackwell Publishers.

Finlay, L. (2002) 'Outing the researcher: The provenance, process, and practice of reflexivity.' *Qualitative Health Research 12,* 4, 531–545.

Foner, N. (1994) *The Caregiving Dilemma.* Berkeley, CA: University of California Press.

Garbett, R. and McCormack, B. (2002) 'A concept analysis of practice development.' *NT Research 7,* 2, 87–100.

Gibson, D.E. and Barsade, S.G. (2003) 'Managing organisational culture change: The case of long term care.' In A.S. Weiner and J.L. Ronch (eds) *Culture Change in Long Term Care.* New York: Haworth Social Work Practice Press, pp.11–34.

Gilligan, C. (1982) *In A Different Voice: Psychological Theory and Women's Development.* Cambridge, MA: Harvard University Press.

Gilligan, C. (1987) 'Moral orientation and moral development.' In E. Kittay and D. Meyers (eds) *Women and Moral Theory.* Cambridge, MA: Rowman and Littlefield.

Higgins, I. (1998) 'Reflections on conducting qualitative research with elderly persons.' *Qualitative Health Research 8,* 6, 858–866.

Holliday, A. (2002) *Doing and Writing Qualitative Research.* London: Sage.

Hubbard, G., Backett-Milburn, K. and Kemmer, D. (2001) 'Working with emotions: Issues for the researcher in fieldwork and teamwork.' *International Journal of Research Methodology 4*, 2, 119–137.

Leslie, H. and McAllister, M. (2002) 'The benefits of being a nurse in critical social research practice.' *Qualitative Health Research 12*, 5, 700–712.

Maas, M.L., Kelley, L.S., Park, M. and Specht, J.P. (2002) 'Issues in conducting research in nursing homes.' *Western Journal of Nursing Research 24*, 4, 373–389.

Manley, K. (2001) 'Consultant nurse: Concept, processes, outcome.' Unpublished PhD thesis. Manchester: University of Manchester Faculty of Nursing, Midwifery and Health Visiting.

Manley, K. (2004) 'Transformational culture.' In B. McCormack, K. Manley and R. Garbett (eds) *Practice Development in Nursing.* Oxford: Blackwells Publishing.

Martin, L. and Bonder, B.R. (2003) 'Achieving organisational change within the context of cultural competence.' In A.S. Weiner and J.L. Ronch (eds) *Culture Change in Long-term Care.* London: Haworth Social Practice Press, pp.81–94.

McCormack, B. (2003) 'Researching nursing practice: Does person-centeredness matter?' *Nursing Philosophy 4*, 179–188.

Mentes, J.C. (2001) 'Hydration management: A long term care nursing intervention to prevent acute confusion and other hydration-linked events.' Unpublished doctoral thesis. *Dissertation Abstracts International 61*, 4079.

Mentes, J.C. and Tripp-Reimer, T. (2002) 'Barriers and facilitators in nursing home intervention research.' *Western Journal of Nursing Research 24*, 8, 918–936.

Mezirow, J. and Associates (1990) *Fostering Critical Reflection in Adulthood.* San Francisco, CA: Jossey-Bass.

Miller, J. and Evans, T. (1991) 'Some reflections on ethical dilemmas in nursing home research.' *Western Journal of Nursing Research 13*, 3, 375–381.

Naef, R. (2006) 'Bearing witness: A moral way of engaging in the nurse–person relationship.' *Nursing Philosophy 7*, 146–156.

NCHRDF (2007) *My Home Life: Quality of Life in Care Homes. Review of the Literature.* London: Help the Aged (also available from www.myhomelife.org.uk).

Office of Public Sector Information (2000) *Adults with Incapacity (Scotland) Act.* Edinburgh: Office of Public Sector Information.

Powers, B.A. (2003) *Nursing Home Ethics.* New York: Springer.

Rapp, C.G., Topps-Uriri, J. and Beck, C. (1994) 'Obtaining and maintaining a research sample with cognitively impaired nursing home residents.' *Geriatric Nursing 15*, 193–196.

Ruckdeschel, K. and Van Haisma, K. (1997) 'Research with nursing home staff: Challenges and solutions.' *Journal of Mental Health and Ageing 3*, 2, 209–219.

Scottish Executive Health Department (2006) *Research Governance Framework for Health and Community Care* 2nd edition. Available at www.scotland.gov.uk/Topics/Research/by-topic/health-community-care/chief-scientific-office/6864/6933, accessed 5 November 2008.

Siehl, C. and Martin, J. (1984) 'The role of symbolic management: How can managers effectively transmit organisational culture?' In J. Hunt and D. Hosking (eds) *Leaders and Managers: International Perspectives on Managerial Behaviour and Leadership.* New York: Pergamon, pp.227–239.

Silverman, D. (2000) *Doing Qualitative Research: A Practical Handbook.* London: Sage.

Sinclair, M. (2004) *The Pedagogy of Good PhD Supervision.* Queensland: Central Queensland University.

Slaughter, S., Cole, D., Jennings, E. and Reimer, M. (2007) 'Consent and assent to participate in research from people with dementia.' *Nursing Ethics 14*, 1, 28–40.

Stafford, P.B. (2003) 'The nursing home as cultural code.' In P.B. Stafford (ed.) *Gray Areas: Ethnographic Encounters with Nursing Home Culture.* Santa Fe, CA: School of American Research Press, pp.3–22.

Tuckett, A. (2007) 'The meaning of nursing-home: "Waiting to go up to St Peter, OK! Waiting house, sad but true" – An Australian perspective.' *Journal of Ageing Studies 21*, 2, 119–133.

UK Parliament (2005) *Mental Capacity Bill.* Available at www.publications.parliament.uk/pa/cm200304/cmbills/120/04120.i-vi.html, accessed 25 June 2005.

Ullman, C. (2006) 'Bearing witness: Across the barriers in society and in the clinic.' *Psychoanalytical Dialogue 16*, 181–198.

Wadensten, B. (2007) 'Life situation and daily life in a nursing home as described by nursing home residents in Sweden.' *International Journal of Older People Nursing 2*, 180–188.

Wiles, J. (2005) 'Conceptualising place in the care of older persons: The contribution of geographical gerontology.' *International Journal of Older People Nursing 14*, 8b, 100–108.

Williams, C.L. and Tappen, R.M. (1999) 'Can we create a therapeutic relationship with nursing home residents in the later stages of Alzheimer's disease?' *Journal of Psychosocial Nursing 37*, 3, 28–34.

Wuest, J. (1998) 'Setting boundaries: A strategy for precarious ordering of women's caring demands.' *Research in Nursing and Health 21*, 39–49.

CHAPTER 12

Reflections on the Way Forward

Sue Davies, Katherine Froggatt and Julienne Meyer

Introduction

The purpose of this final chapter is to draw together the threads that have emerged in the contributions to this book, with a view to identifying lessons that might inform future research and development initiatives within care homes. By drawing on these threads we hope that older people, their families and staff within care homes can be assisted to work together to improve the community of the care home for all concerned. Previous chapters have considered research and development projects within care homes at a number of different levels. Part 1 explored developments that primarily impact at the level of individual residents and their families. Part 2 includes projects with a broader organisational remit, whereas the initiatives described in Part 3 adopted a wider community focus. In spite of these varying foci, a number of consistent messages emerge across the contributions and these are the focus of this chapter.

The first part of the chapter demonstrates how the research described in the book is consistent with a relationship-centred, evidence-based vision for best practice that is widely supported by the care home sector across the UK (*My Home Life* programme: www.myhomelife.org.uk). The vision is based on the extensive literature review undertaken by the National Care Homes Research and Development Forum and outlined in Chapter 1. The second section summarises the lessons learned from the contributors' experiences of attempting to undertake research and development work in care homes. We conclude with some reflections on what needs to be considered when addressing change at different levels: individual, organisational and the wider community.

My Home Life: Strengthening the knowledge base for work within care homes

In Chapter 1, we outlined the key themes that emerged from an extensive review of the literature on quality of life in care homes commissioned by the charity Help the Aged as part of *My Home Life*, a collaborative initiative aimed at improving quality of life for those who are living, dying, working and visiting in care homes. Contributors to this text were identified prior to publication of the *My Home Life* review and, at the outset, it was not our intention to reflect explicitly the themes emerging from the review. However, as the text came together, we realised that the contributions provided further evidence of the significance of these themes. Anecdotal information is suggesting that the *My Home Life* campaign is providing a framework by means of which staff in care homes are able to articulate what they do and is putting care homes 'in the spotlight' in a positive way. The first section of this chapter is therefore devoted to a consideration of the ways in which the various contributions to this text further illuminate the *My Home Life* themes.

Managing transitions

Moving to a care home is a major, often final, transition in life and may involve considerable losses (NCHRDF 2007). However, research reviewed for *My Home Life* suggests that, if properly planned and managed, the move can bring benefits and a better quality of life. Having access to all the relevant information and making decisions jointly and without pressure have been associated with positive experiences of admission to a home. Involving family members, both in the move and in the life of the home, can aid the transition and reduce the guilt and loss associated with entry to a care home.

The idea that care homes are places of multiple transitions finds strong support within the contributions to this volume. As several chapter authors point out, older people, their families and staff who come to work with them are all adjusting to new roles, routines and relationships. Furthermore, the rapid turnover among both staff and residents revealed in several of the contributions provides an additional challenge to continuity and results in an almost constant state of change and transition.

Brown Wilson, Cook and Forte, in Chapter 4, vividly capture the hard work that residents and their families put into reconstructing their lives following the move to a care home. The challenge of sensory and cognitive impairment in working with frail older residents to sustain and develop relationships is also clearly revealed within this chapter. Similarly, David Stanley, writing in Chapter 3, highlights the challenge of integrating residents with dementia for all concerned.

One aspect of ensuring that the transition to a care home can be viewed as a positive option depends on transforming the negative perception of care homes, and in fact this is the *raison d'être* of this book. All of the contributions highlight the very positive and creative work that is taking place in care homes to improve the quality of life of residents, their families and staff. Many of the transformative initiatives described within this volume are concerned with protecting the personhood of residents and it is to this idea that we now turn.

Maintaining identity

The move to a care home can undermine an older person's sense of identity in a number of ways. Declining health and loss of independence can threaten self-esteem and for some individuals a care home may offer few links to their personal or cultural past. In this context the relevance of care that is truly person-centred becomes clear, and understanding what matters to an individual, including his or her values and wishes, is crucial.

In Chapters 2, 3, 4, 5 and 6 of this volume, the value of narrative and biography in getting to know what is important to residents and their families is clearly demonstrated. In Chapter 2, Charlotte Wilkinson and colleagues describe how they encouraged care staff to develop life story booklets based on interviews with residents, and involving families where appropriate. Life stories were then discussed with staff in weekly supervision sessions. The authors conclude that the collection and sharing of biographical information changed relationships and attitudes within the care home. David Stanley in Chapter 3 describes how life stories formed part of intensive data collection with residents with dementia as one approach to promoting person-centred care-planning. Care staff found this activity very rewarding and residents benefited from having the undivided attention of a staff member.

David Stanley also highlights the importance of recognising emotional and social needs as well as physical needs in achieving person-centred care. He reveals how spending time engaging people with dementia in conversation can be therapeutic as it provides necessary social interaction.

This remedies the often short task-orientated exchanges between residents and caregivers which is unfortunately too common in many care settings. Meaningful conversation with a person provides them with opportunities for self-expression. Furthermore, the caregiver becomes aware of the self-identity roles of the person which the caregiving process and activity interventions can then be designed to support.

The value of meaningful conversations is also highlighted in Garuth Chalfont's chapter, in which he describes how connection to nature can provide a tool for self-expression and reinforcing identity. Christine Brown Wilson and colleagues also provide numerous examples of how engaging residents in story-telling can help staff to find out what is important to them, providing a basis for planning care and the development of relationships

Creating community

Developing a sense of community within a care home is dependent upon relationships and as emphasised within many of the contributions to this volume, relationships are developed through interaction. For residents of care homes, this is most likely to be with care staff, with other residents and with members of their own family. In Chapter 4, Christine Brown Wilson and her co-authors point out that the social interaction between people living and working in a care home is qualitatively different to engagement between family and friends, with the latter being grounded in shared history, common bonds, mutual understanding and reciprocity. In contrast, those living and working in care homes are in relationship as the result of the need to receive and give care. As a result, interaction tends to focus on functional aspects of life and there is a need for staff to be creative in engaging residents and their families in a wider range of conversations. As the people who spend most time with residents, care assistants have the greatest potential to influence experiences of care home life and it is essential that these relationships are given centre stage in development initiatives.

Creating community within a care home also involves fostering relationships between residents and this can present its own challenges. For example, David Stanley highlights the 'peace-keeping' role that staff may have to perform in assisting residents with very different care needs to live together in harmony. Facilitating opportunities for residents to assist each other can be helpful in this respect and again, narratives can play a role in identifying shared interests that might provide the basis for mutually supportive relationships.

Also in Chapter 3, David Stanley demonstrates how involvement of family members can help to achieve project goals. Family involvement is crucial to a sense of community and creative approaches are needed to ensure that visiting the home is a pleasurable and meaningful activity. The value of 'friends' groups in providing a forum for family members to make a contribution has been highlighted in several chapters here, together with the importance of maintaining links to individuals and organisations outside the home. In addition to extending the network of relationships beyond the boundaries of the care home, this can also increase the resources available to residents and staff. Furthermore, collaboration with outside agencies can help staff to see the value of the work they do, strengthening their sense of significance (see Chapters 7 and 9).

Garuth Chalfont (Chapter 6) makes the point that a care home involves residents, their families, staff, the building and the outside world, and argues persuasively that successful improvements need to involve both 'people' and 'place'. He proposes that connections with nature can enhance the community within a care home through prompting social interaction, providing topics of conversation, improving caregiver interaction and enhancing family visits. Garuth also highlights the therapeutic role of normal domestic activities in creating a sense of community. Another important component of community is shared responsibility for decision-making and this theme is considered next.

Sharing decision-making

Participation, choice and involvement are emphasised throughout this volume. However, the various chapters suggest that there may be a need to empower people to feel that they can make a contribution. It is important to establish mechanisms that will enable participation to happen, rather than assuming that people will automatically get involved. In particular, several chapters suggest a need to create more opportunities for sharing views and information, for example the clinical supervision sessions described by Charlotte Wilkinson and colleagues in Chapter 2, and the friends of care homes groups described in Chapters 2 and 7. Sheila Furness and Bren Torry (Chapter 7) highlight the importance of seeking views of relatives and residents, particularly in the context of a reduced number of inspection visits by regulators (CSCI 2004), and homes need to seek creative ways to engage residents and family members in decision-making. There is often a mis-match of perception between staff and family members about how much family members want to be involved and staff should take the initiative in exploring this with relatives at the time of admission and at regular intervals. Relatives and friends can also play an important role in supporting and advocating for others who have no visitors to look after their interests.

Several contributions highlight the importance of wide consultation before planning changes. However, Claire Goodman and colleagues in Chapter 10 identify the challenge of involving older people in development initiatives and sustaining involvement over time. Others have described the practical difficulties of involving residents with advanced physical and cognitive frailty in decision-making processes (see, for example, Aveyard and Davies 2006; Reed, Cook and Stanley 1999) and it is clear that further work is needed to identify the most appropriate ways to achieve this.

Improving health and healthcare

As highlighted in Chapter 1, the diversity of care home provision across the UK has resulted in a fragmented and inequitable system of arrangements for providing health services to meet the needs of residents. Several contributions to this volume confirm that older people living in care homes have unequal access to healthcare services (see in particular Chapters 2, 4, 9 and 10). These studies point to short-term funding and lack of a coherent programme to develop health services for people living in care homes. Furthermore, strategies often involve the introduction of specialist workers rather than generic workers who could build support into their everyday work pattern. The study described by Claire Goodman and colleagues in Chapter 10 demonstrates how few extra health resources are readily available to older people resident in care homes and the lack of transparency and accountability in how nurses and others act on their behalf to secure extra support and specialist review. In Chapter 5, Robert Jenkins also highlights how older people with learning disabilities who live in a care home miss out on health promotion activities. Although not explicitly mentioned in other chapters, the absence of goal-setting highlighted in a number of contributions to this book suggest that health promotion is not seen as a priority in many care homes.

In spite of the current situation in many homes, there is enormous potential for developing new ways of working in order to offer a range of multi-professional healthcare services to care homes (Owen and NCHRDF 2006). Building development initiatives on the back of government policy, such as the *Essence of Care* benchmarking initiative described in Chapter 10, provides one way of engaging with homes in the private sector and developing links between NHS Trusts and homes.

Supporting good end of life

One of the key findings of the *My Home Life* report was the need to develop a culture within care homes that gives value to a person's dying as well as his or her living (NCHRDF 2007). The literature suggests a need for more openness and awareness about end-of-life care and more support for the dying person, his or her family, other residents and staff members at this time. These arguments find support within several contributions to this volume. In Chapter 4 for example, Christine Brown Wilson and colleagues describe how the use of story-telling reveals the impact of deteriorating health for residents and the potential for grief and sadness when relationships are interrupted by illness and death. Several contributions highlight the need to move away from a task-based system in order to allow the development of emotional care (see Chapters 2, 3, 5 and 8). The need to provide support for staff and family members is also repeatedly mentioned.

Keeping the workforce fit for purpose

Not surprisingly, the need to support and develop the care home workforce emerged as a strong theme within the *My Home Life* review. Until quite recently, education and training for staff working in care homes received little attention in the literature, and there is still an urgent need to identify what works in preparing care home staff for their roles. A further challenge, highlighted within several chapters here, is the difficulty for care home staff of knowing what exactly is 'best practice'. For example, David Stanley in Chapter 3 describes how care assistants lack skills and knowledge in the care of people with dementia and this limits their ability to provide person-centred care. There is a need for research-based information in an accessible format that provides guidelines and pointers for practice, specific to the needs of older people living in care homes.

In spite of the lack of a systematic body of evidence to demonstrate the impact of education on health and social care practice, nonetheless, the contributions to this book suggest the value of education and training in supporting staff working in care homes to deliver person-centred care. For example, several chapters highlight the importance of personal growth, self-reflection and development in overcoming difficulties of motivation and enhancing job satisfaction. Charlotte Wilkinson and colleagues (Chapter 2) and David Stanley (Chapter 3) both highlight the value of clinical supervision in staff development, particularly time spent with other staff reviewing and discussing the needs of residents.

However, keeping the care home workforce fit for purpose involves more than ensuring that staff have access to training and development opportunities. As several contributions reveal, it also involves recognising the personhood of staff and providing support to work in an emotionally charged environment. Care staff also need a clear sense of direction and purpose if they are to experience their work as meaningful. This is vividly expressed by Cheryl Holman and Keith Crowhurst in Chapter 8 as follows:

> contact with non-responsive people who live a life close to death whilst not actually being in the process of dying; coping with a sense that care delivery may not improve the quality of life of those being cared for; being on the receiving end of residents' anger and envy; and being isolated from the rest of the healthcare community. (p.168)

This quote captures the importance of establishing a clear therapeutic intention for residents and attending to the support needs of staff if they are to be enabled to meet the needs of residents and their families.

Several authors develop the theme of care homes as learning environments and this should apply to residents and families, as well as students and staff. Unfortunately, learning opportunities for residents are as yet underdeveloped in most care homes and, in particular, the contribution of information technology in this respect has yet to be fully exploited. Nonetheless, student placements in care homes are becoming more widespread and there is growing recognition of the need to develop a career structure for qualified and unqualified staff (see Fear, Chapter 9). The potential for generic roles combining a range of skills, including therapy and nursing skills, is also becoming apparent and would benefit from systematic evaluation.

Collaboration and partnership between homes and with external agencies emerge as key themes within several chapters. For example, the Care Home Learning Network described in Chapter 9 provides opportunities for staff to share experiences and learn from each other as well as the possibility of secondment to explore roles in different care environments. Strategies that involve shared learning and collaboration between care homes seem to be particularly helpful in reducing the isolation experienced by staff and making the best use of limited resources. Such initiatives can help to develop a positive culture within care homes, and this is our next theme.

Promoting a positive culture

It is increasingly recognised that care homes develop a distinctive culture, which determines the degree to which individual expectations are met (NCHRDF 2007). This culture also influences how people act. As a consequence, the dominant model of care within a nursing home, whether implicit or explicit, has important consequences for the experiences of residents and their close relatives, as well as for the experiences of staff (Davies 2003). In earlier work, Davies identified three broad types of culture operating within care homes: the controlled community, the cosmetic community and the complete community, and suggests that such cultures result from a complex interplay of factors, including values and objectives of the organisation, the nature of relationships within the home and leadership.

The chapters within this text provide substantial support for the existence of different cultures within care homes and elements of the three types of culture described by Davies are apparent within descriptions of individual homes (for example the home described by Charlotte Wilkinson and colleagues in Chapter 2 demonstrated many characteristics of the controlled community at the outset of the project). The complexity of the care home environment is also revealed within previous contributions. Garuth Chalfont, for example (Chapter 6), illustrates how residents, staff, visitors, the environment and the world outside all interact to create a distinctive culture. David Stanley refers to care homes as 'powerful and fragile environments' (p.65), intimating both the impact and instability of cultures within these care settings.

Closely associated with the idea of culture in care homes is the notion of culture change, and here the contribution of effective leadership becomes particularly apparent. Several contributors confirm the importance of commitment from the home manager in achieving change (Wilkinson and colleagues, Stanley, Furness and Torry, Fear, Goodman and colleagues) with the importance of staff being supported by managers to make time to engage in project-related activities as one example. The role of 'change agent' within any initiative is also identified as crucial.

David Stanley (Chapter 3) identifies a comprehensive list of the factors influencing the process of culture change in care homes. These include structural factors (such as type and size of home, and ownership); staffing issues including shift patterns, roles and responsibilities, stability and staff development; management culture – for example service models, values and philosophies; and external relationships (with inspectors, external health services, care managers). In summary, culture change in care homes is likely to require:

- a motivation to change practice through a cultural shift

- a commitment by care home staff to work with others both within and outside their organisation

- a commitment by care home staff to sustain this new way of working.

In the next section of this chapter we turn to some of the key messages emerging from preceding chapters in relation to undertaking research and development work, and achieving change, within care homes.

What can we learn from research and development initiatives in care homes?

Some important lessons emerge from the various contributions to this text in relation to undertaking research and development work in care homes. These have been organised in relation to the following themes:

- understanding the context and culture

- being explicit about values and principles

- having a clear theoretical perspective or framework

- having shared goals that include something for everyone

- using methods and strategies that are inclusive and authentic

- anticipating and dealing with barriers to change

- celebrating success.

Key points in relation to each of these themes will now be considered.

Understanding the context and culture

An important aspect of the rationale for this book was the recognition that care homes for older people represent a specific type of care environment and each have a unique 'culture'. It is therefore essential that anyone who wishes to engage with care homes with a view to improving quality of care and quality of life should have a thorough understanding of the context and needs to spend time getting to know the culture within each home. This is complex and time-consuming and it can be difficult to know where to focus to make the best use of the resources available to a project. The *My Home Life* themes previously described and the extent to which the culture within a care home is consistent with achieving these seem to us to be particularly crucial to an understanding of experiences of care home life. These may provide a useful starting point.

A recurrent idea within the contributions to this volume is the constant challenge for those involved with care homes to counteract negative perceptions of long-term care for older people. The richness of the accounts presented here reveals the complexity of care homes and the commitment and enthusiasm of many staff who work within them. This is in sharp contrast to the negative images of care homes often painted by the media, images that appear to be remarkably persistent, in spite of widespread regulation to improve standards, and examples of innovation and creativity. In reality, the picture is likely to be one of wide variability between care homes.

The negative image of care homes has understandably resulted in a certain amount of suspicion of outsiders on the part of staff, and this can be difficult for researchers to penetrate. Similarly, care homes are both public and private places and researchers are often wary of intruding into the private spaces of residents. This can limit the extent to which outsiders can develop a true understanding of the culture within a home. Previous chapters suggest that relationships are crucial here and that the time invested in getting to know individuals at a personal level can ensure that people both feel comfortable to participate in projects and are willing to share their time and energy, contributing to a successful outcome (see Chapter 11 in particular).

Being explicit about values, principles and frameworks

Fahey (2003) has proposed that one of the main problems of the current system of long-term care is that it is lacking in clear, coherent, conceptual underpinnings. The consistency of the values demonstrated within the contributions to this text is therefore encouraging and perhaps presents a common foundation that might inform and influence future projects. Fahey himself identifies a number of cultural values that are desirable within the context of care homes and these are replicated in Box 12.1 as they are highly consistent with the values identified within the contributions to this volume.

Box 12.1 Desirable cultural values within the context of care homes

- an atmosphere emphasising the identity of all who are part of the community
- alternatives and participation in decision-making
- a sense of mutual responsibility on the part of all community members
- personal relationships
- community and the promotion of the common good
- reciprocal interactions with the broader community
- a supportive environment
- ethical decision-making
- an atmosphere of caring
- good clinical interventions
- pleasant physical environment
- the opportunity for social, recreational and spiritual engagement. (Fahey 2003, p.42)[1]

We will return to the notion of a 'vision' for care homes later in this chapter.

Several contributors identify the value of different theoretical perspectives and traditions in helping them to identify a set of concepts to inform development work. For example, systems theory, psychodynamic theory and complexity theory are mentioned as providing useful insights to inform and provide structure for projects. Such theories assume acceptance of a specific set of values and principles underpinning initiatives. For example, the philosophies of humanism and person-centred/relationship-centred care

---

1   Copyright © 2003 from 'Creating community: The basis for caring partnerships in nursing homes.' by Fahey, C.J. in Weiner, A.S. and Ronch, J.L. (eds) *Culture Change in Long-term Care*. Reproduced by permission of Taylor and Francis Group, LLC, a division of informa plc.

that inform and influence many of the projects described here are consistent with the principle of equity within relationships. Humanism is a philosophy that attaches importance to humankind and human value (Stewart 2005). The philosophy not only provides pointers to how service users should be treated, but also reflects how practitioners respond to each other and the values of the organisation in which health and social care takes place. Importance is attached to self-awareness within caring relationships in addition to 'knowing the person' to whom care is being provided. The values of engagement, partnership and mutual learning are also highly consistent with these approaches and these figure frequently throughout this volume.

A humanistic perspective emphasises the emotional as well as the physical needs and experiences of participants within a culture. Recognising the emotion work that takes place within care homes is therefore an essential component of successful development projects and this is ably described by Cheryl Holman and Keith Crowhurst in Chapter 8. Several contributions acknowledge the relevance of 'relationship-centred care' as a framework to support the needs of staff and family members, as well as residents. Proponents of relationship-centred care (for example, the *My Home Life* programme) argue that relationships are a critical component of working effectively with older people and their supporters and that the needs of all parties must be taken into account. Although relationships are a prerequisite to effective care and teaching, there has been little formal acknowledgement of their importance, and few efforts to help students and practitioners learn to develop effective relationships in healthcare. Nolan *et al.* (2006) suggest that interactions are at the heart of relationship-centred care and are the 'foundations' of any therapeutic or healing activity. Again, this model is highly consistent with the approach described within many of the contributions here.

An important value not mentioned in the introduction, but clearly emerging within the various contributions to this book, is that of partnership – the notion that working collectively with common goals has the potential to achieve much more than individuals working in isolation. These values and principles are implicit to the caring work that occurs in care homes, but are also applicable to research and development initiatives.

Having shared goals that include something for everyone

While the contributions within this text are diverse in terms of the goals of the specific initiatives described, nonetheless a number of more general goals are implicit within the projects. These are:

- creating enriched care environments that are sustainable

- enhancing the profile of care homes by re-evaluating caring work in ways that recognise the skills, competencies and therapeutic relationships involved

- ensuring care that is evidence-based by identifying best practice and seeking to implement it.

These goals raise a number of questions, some of which are likely to require ongoing research and reflection. For example, what do enriched care environments look like? What are the skills, competencies and conditions needed to create therapeutic relationships? What kinds of evidence will enable us to identify best practice? These are the kinds of questions that can be used within development projects to enable the community within a care home to identify their own values and vision.

Given the many constraints on time and resources that are common-place within care homes, building development projects on the back of policy initiatives provides a valuable way of getting staff on board. For example, the establishment of 'Friends of Care Home' groups described in Chapter 7 provides a mechanism for achieving standards relating to the involvement of residents and relatives in decision-making that is consistent with government policy. Increasing age and dependency (frailty) means that those in care homes require more healthcare input and the workforce needs additional training to meet these needs. Health and social care services need to work more effectively together and this is where additional resources for development work might be forthcoming.

We now turn to a consideration of the methods for working in partnership with care homes described within the contributions to this volume.

Using methods and strategies that are inclusive and authentic

Individuals attempting to carry out research and development work in care homes face a number of challenges in identifying appropriate methods and strategies. In particular, it is essential that methods used for gathering and disseminating information do not intimidate or disempower older people, their families and staff working with them. Even when strategies are chosen that explicitly aim to be inclusive and to develop partnerships between stakeholders (such as action research) problems may still arise. For example, how do we create the conditions in which people feel comfortable to participate? How do we make sure that we use appropriate language that is accessible to everyone involved? How do we access the views of older people with cognitive frailty? How can we avoid undermining care staff who may not feel comfortable with writing or participating in formal meetings? Even the language of 'practice development', with its origins in professional agendas, can be alienating for users of services.

The contributors to this text have been inventive and creative in their approaches to these challenges and some of the most successful strategies are summarised in Box 12.2 below. What is demonstrated quite powerfully within this volume is that participation in research within care homes can be a creative and empowering experience for all concerned.

Box 12.2 Useful strategies and methods in care homes research and development

- participant observation – spending time getting to know participants and the context in which they live and work, and providing opportunities for them to get to know you
- action research/action cycles – especially where participants are involved in identifying the areas for development
- action learning sets – providing opportunities for staff to meet with peers with a constructive focus
- engaging with biography (residents, families and staff) and using this to create a sense of significance for participants
- using theoretical, conceptual and practice frameworks to provide a structure for a development or intervention and its evaluation
- supervision/reflection, particularly for staff
- looking for evidence of achievement
- staff nomination/allocating specific roles within an initiative or development
- developing partnerships with outside agencies (e.g. a lecturer in a school of nursing, a community practitioner)
- independent advocacy to empower residents, particularly those without any external support
- witnessing (attentive valuing, seeing, understanding and telling what goes on for another)
- rapid feedback of findings to avoid disillusionment with the process

Strategies that blur the boundaries between education, practice and research seem particularly promising and can ensure that ongoing reflection and development become part of the culture within a care home.

Other important facilitators are being inclusive (i.e. making sure that everyone has the opportunity to participate in developments) and adequate preparation. Consultation with all stakeholders before planning any changes can ensure that developments are informed by a range of voices. There are strong messages from the projects described here that every care home should have an established mechanism through which residents, relatives and staff have opportunities to be involved in decision-making. This could take the form of the 'Friends of the Nursing Home' group described by Charlotte Wilkinson and colleagues, or the 'Friends of Care Homes' groups described by Sheila Furness and Bren Torry. Ongoing evaluative research is also needed to identify the most appropriate ways for such groups to be established and enabled to feed into decision-making processes. Having dialogue with regulators prior to implementing systematic change is also an essential part of making facility staff feel secure about altering care practices (Rader and Semradek 2003).

The contributions to this book provide strong evidence that leaders of culture change in long-term care should have a clear plan to guide the entire process while at the same time allowing room for flexibility and responsiveness to new and emerging ideas. Linked to the notion of having a plan to guide innovation and development is the use of a framework to provide structure. Several of the initiatives described here made use of a specific framework to guide developments; for example the *Essence of Care* benchmarks. As previously mentioned, a number of contributions mention the use of relationship-centred care as a guiding philosophy.

For example, a number of studies have found the Senses Framework helpful in supporting change and development within care homes (Aveyard and Davies 2006; Faulkner, Davies and Nolan 2006). The Senses Framework provides an underpinning structure for the *My Home Life* initiative (Owen and NCHRDF 2006), described in the introduction to this text.

Anticipating and dealing with barriers to change

Some of the key challenges encountered within the projects and innovations described in previous chapters derive from the personal experience of being a researcher in this setting; for example:

- the intensity of data collection required for complete understanding and the demands this makes on the researcher

- the challenge of managing research relationships so that people are not left feeling exploited

- the need to manage differences in values and beliefs between various stakeholders.

The contributions to this volume show how these challenges can be successfully overcome if they are anticipated, and strategies put in place to manage them effectively.

Motivating people to change, and overcoming anxiety and defensiveness are mentioned repeatedly in accounts of attempts to develop care in care homes. Similarly, the sheer hard work and determination involved in keeping people 'on board' is vividly described in accounts within this volume. In Chapter 2 for example, Charlotte Wilkinson and colleagues describe the emotional challenges of attempting to work with an initially hostile staff group to achieve practice change and the role of personal support and supervision in achieving this. Relationships in care homes are often challenging and can be painful, particularly when loss and bereavement are involved. Added to this, the physical environment frequently limits opportunities for engagement and can be a significant barrier to the development of relationships and a sense of community. Providing regular opportunities for residents, staff and family members to come together, such as a brief daily meeting time, has been shown to be successful in achieving change through enabling the sharing of perspectives (David Stanley in this volume; see also Barkan 2003).

Although families and healthcare professionals have similar goals for the health and well-being of a patient or client, they approach care, especially long-term care, with different assumptions, values, attitudes and behaviours (Levine 2003). The challenge can often be to find a shared language and common ground, and this is where frameworks, such as the Senses Framework mentioned in the previous section, can be helpful.

We have already mentioned the high turnover of staff and the frequent changes in the resident population that can hinder a sense of continuity in care homes. In such a context the use of a tool or framework to guide developments can be helpful in providing a constant that all participants can relate to. Again, use of the *Essence of Care* benchmarking tool to improve continence care as described in Chapter 10 is a good example. 'Friends' groups such as those described in Chapters 2 and 7 can also be a mechanism for introducing new members of the care home community to ongoing initiatives, providing some continuity.

A further challenge to research in care homes lies within the ambiguity and lack of clarity surrounding research governance and ethical systems in relation to research in independent sector care homes. This has resulted in confusion and may even act as a barrier to research in these environments (Reed, Cook and Cook 2004). In particular, the appropriateness of seeking written consent for interviews and observational methods has been highlighted, raising questions about whether it is appropriate to seek consent by proxy for people with cognitive frailty. Jan Dewing addresses these issues in some detail in her chapter and advocates the use of creative approaches to developing alternatives to signed consent. These include the notion of 'witnessing', which involves asking residents what they would like the researcher to tell others about their experiences.

Insufficient resources, in terms of staffing levels, knowledge and skills, and expertise, were identified repeatedly by these authors as limiting the extent of change achieved. While it is almost a 'given' in care environments that staff will seek more resources than they have available, the complexity of care homes suggests that the potential for ensuring optimal quality of life for residents will not be achieved until staff are valued and rewarded in a way that recognises the complexity and skill involved in their work. There is accumulating evidence for this: for example, in a recent study of care-providers', residents' and family members' perceptions of relationships within care homes, all groups spoke about the need for connectedness, but mentioned inadequate staffing and workload as barriers to meaningful one-to-one relationships (McGilton and Boscart 2007). These challenges are likely to require a whole-systems approach to the funding of long-term care if significant and sustainable change is to be realised. However, in the short term, staff teams can be encouraged to review priorities to ensure that resources are being used most effectively. The use of community volunteers within care homes is also limited in the UK, when compared to the USA for example. Volunteers can provide a significant resource to care homes and can also provide a link to local communities (Davies and Brown Wilson 2007). There is a need for more research to explore how volunteers can most effectively be involved in supporting care homes within the UK context.

Celebrating success

As previously mentioned, an important aspect of research and development projects within care homes is the need to challenge continually the negative images and perceptions of these environments. In this context, celebrating and publicising achievements is vital. Even the process of self-reflection and examination can encourage participants to recognise what they do well instead of always focusing on negative areas. The contributions to this volume provide evidence that development projects can help staff to recognise the value of the work they do.

Providing evidence of change (even small changes) and celebrating these also appear to be characteristic of successful change initiatives. Ronch (2003) suggests that short-term wins might include activities such as a 'values in action' award ceremony that recognises special instances of staff behaviour that personify the mission and values in caring for residents, or 'mission moments', an award to celebrate the spontaneous little things that make residents feel special. Such events and activities are important in helping people to see that they can make a difference.

A number of contributions highlight the role of development projects in gathering information and evidence, which is then instrumental in achieving further change. For example, Charlotte Wilkinson and colleagues describe in Chapter 2 how the results of a Dementia Care Mapping exercise in one care home provided the impetus to seek funding to support occupational therapy input. Innovation and change have in themselves the potential to raise the profile of long-term care and improve the image of care homes (Aveyard and Davies 2006).

A vision for the future?

Within this book we have attempted to provide an up-to-date description of the context in which culture change in care homes is taking place, together with examples of initiatives that have enhanced experiences for residents, their families and staff. We have identified a set of key values that have been found to underpin successful development initiatives in care homes, as well as methods, frameworks and strategies that have been found to be acceptable to stakeholders and effective in achieving change. However, there are some important gaps in the information gathered here. In particular, an important challenge that features only minimally within the contributions to this text is the need to recognise the cultural diversity that exists within care homes and to develop methods that are fully inclusive of all cultural groups.

Similarly, Jan Dewing makes the important point that published accounts of the challenges of carrying out research and development work in care homes are predominantly written from the perspective of the researcher, with much less attention to experiences of residents and staff. There is obviously a need to continue to gather accounts of the experiences of all stakeholders in order to make sure that all views and opinions are represented. Nonetheless, we feel that there is sufficient evidence about 'what works' in attempting research and development in care homes to make a number of tentative recommendations for undertaking work in this field.

Within this volume, we have brought together exemplars of good practice in care homes which place particular emphasis on informing and supporting practice development through partnership working. As this text confirms, an increasing volume of such research and development work is being undertaken within care homes, and yet the public perception of these facilities remains predominantly negative. Examples of positive work and excellence in practice are largely absent from both the academic literature and the wider media, and this text represents one attempt to present a more balanced view. Nonetheless, ongoing research suggests wide variability in the standards achieved by individual homes and there is some way to go before all care homes across the UK achieve the quality of experience described within some of the initiatives considered here. While increased regulation and monitoring has had an important impact, there is a danger that such standards become the goal, rather than representing the minimum that is acceptable.

Vladeck (2003) argues that the problem for care homes is one of identity and that significant improvements in the quality of life and quality of care in care homes will only be achieved once we have a clearer consensus on the roles we want them to play in the healthcare and long-term care systems, and a vision for the kind of care we want to see. In recent years the position and role of care homes within the context of health and social care has been in a constant state of flux as a result of changing demographics and political preferences (see Chapter 1 for examples). As highlighted in Chapter 1, residents of care homes are now supported within a fragmented, mixed economy of care, with regular reconfiguration of services resulting in fears about the future, both for those connected with individual care homes and for long-term care services more generally. Furthermore, many care homes and the staff and residents within them have become isolated from wider care and practice communities. As commentators have pointed out, care homes suffer from a reluctance on the part of many individuals and communities to recognise any responsibility for what goes on within them (Stanley and Reed 1999). This may in part result from the image that many care homes themselves try to create. For example, it has been argued that the goal of re-creating 'home', with the emphasis on independence and privacy, is misguided and misses the potential for care homes to provide an alternative based upon notions of community and interdependence (Davies and Brown Wilson 2007; Peace and Holland 2001). In reality, care homes and those associated with them need to contribute to ongoing debates about their proper role and function, and there is a need for more collaborative research and development work, of the kind described within this volume, to enable this to happen. Through such initiatives we will be able to develop a vision for that future that will result in care homes being seen as a positive choice, one of a range of options for continuing care, by older people, their families and staff working with them.

References

Aveyard, B. and Davies, S. (2006) 'Moving forward together: Evaluation of an Action Group involving staff and relatives within a nursing home for older people with dementia.' *International Journal of Older People Nursing 1*, 95–104.

Barkan, B. (2003) 'The Live Oak Regenerative Community: Championing a culture of hope and meaning?' In A.S. Weiner and J.L. Ronch (eds) *Culture Change in Long-term Care*. New York: Haworth Social Work Practice Press. pp.197–222.

CSCI (2004) *When I Get Older: What People Want from Social Care Services and Inspections as They Get Older*. London: Commission for Social Care Inspection.

Davies, S. (2003) 'Creating community: The basis for caring partnerships in nursing homes.' In M. Nolan, G. Grant, J. Keady and U. Lundh (eds) *Partnerships in Family Care*. Maidenhead: Open University Press, pp.218–237.

Davies, S. and Brown Wilson, C. (2007) 'Creating a sense of community.' In NCHRDF *My Home Life: Quality of Life in Care Homes. Review of the Literature*. London: Help the Aged. pp.59–78.

Fahey, C.J. (2003) 'Culture change in long-term care facilities: Changing the facility of changing the system?' In A.S. Weiner and J.L. Ronch (eds) *Culture Change in Long-term Care*. New York: Haworth Social Work Practice Press. pp.35–52.

Faulkner, M., Davies, S. and Nolan, M.R. (2006) 'Development of the Combined Assessment of Residential Environments (CARE) Profiles.' *Journal of Advanced Nursing 55 (6)*: pp.664–77.

Levine, C. (2003) 'Family caregivers, health care professionals and policy makers: The diverse cultures of long-term care?' In A.S. Weiner and J.L. Ronch (eds) *Culture Change in Long-term Care*. New York: Haworth Social Work Practice Press. pp.111–124.

McGilton, K.S. and Boscart, V.M. (2007) 'Close care-provider/resident relationships in long-term care environments.' *Journal of Clinical Nursing 16*, 2149–2157.

NCHRDF (2007) *My Home Life: Quality of Life in Care Homes – Review of the Literature.* London: Help the Aged (also available at ww.myhomelife.org.uk).

Nolan, M., Brown, J., Davies, S., Nolan, J. and Keady, J. (2006) *The Senses Framework: Improving Care for Older People through a Relationship-centred Approach. Getting Research Into Practice Series.* Sheffield: University of Sheffield.

Owen, T and NCHRDF (2006) *My Home Life: Quality of Life in Care Homes.* London: Help the Aged (also available from www.myhomelife.org.uk).

Peace, S. and Holland, C. (2001) 'Homely residential care: A contradiction in terms?' *Journal of Social Policy 30*, 3, 393–410.

Rader, J. and Semradek, J. (2003) 'Organisational culture and bathing practice: Ending the battle in one facility.' In A.S. Weiner and J.L. Ronch (eds) *Culture Change in Long-term Care.* New York: Haworth Social Work Practice Press. pp.269 284.

Reed, J., Cook, G. and Cook, M. (2004) 'Research governance issues in the care home sector.' *Nursing Times Research 9*, 6, 430–439.

Reed, J., Cook, G. and Stanley, D. (1999) 'Promoting partnership with older people through quality assurance systems: Issues arising in care homes.' *NT Research 4*, 5, 257–267.

Ronch, J.L. (2003) 'Leading culture change in long-term care: A map for the road ahead.' In A.S. Weiner and J.L. Ronch (eds) *Culture Change in Long-term Care.* New York: Haworth Social Work Practice Press. pp.65–80.

Stanley, D. and Reed, J. (1999) *Opening Up Care: Achieving Principled Practice in Health and Social Care Institutions.* London: Arnold.

Stewart, W. (2005) *An A–Z of Counselling Theory and Practice.* Cheltenham: Nelson Thornes.

Vladeck, B.C. (2003) 'Unloving care revisited: The persistence of culture.' In A.S. Weiner and J.L. Ronch (eds) *Culture Change in Long-term Care.* New York: Haworth Social Work Practice Press. pp.1–10.

Subject Index

Author Index